Research Issues in Child Development

EDITORS

Chris Pratt
The University of Western Australia

Alison F. Garton
Murdoch University

William E. Tunmer
The University of Western Australia

Andrew R. Nesdale
The University of Western Australia

ALLEN & UNWIN
Sydney   London   Boston

First published in 1986
Allen & Unwin Australia Pty Ltd
8 Napier Street, North Sydney, NSW 2060 Australia

Allen & Unwin New Zealand Limited
60 Cambridge Terrace, Wellington, New Zealand

George Allen & Unwin (Publishers) Ltd
18 Park Lane, Hemel Hempstead, Herts HP2 4TE England

Allen & Unwin Inc.
9 Winchester Terrace, Winchester, Mass 01890 USA

National Library of Australia
Cataloguing-in-Publication

Research issues in child development.

  Bibliography.
  Includes index.
  ISBN 0 86861 414 9.

  1. Child psychology—Addresses, essays, lectures.
  2. Child development—Addresses, essays, lectures.
  I. Pratt, Chris.   II. National Child Development
  Conference (3rd: 1984: Perth, WA).

155.4

Library of Congress Catalog Card Number: 86-070001

Set in 10/12 point Bembo by Asco Trade Typesetting Ltd, Hong Kong
Printed by Koon Wah Printing Pte Ltd, Singapore

Contents

Contributors

Judith A. Bowey, Victoria College
Pia Broderick, The University of Western Australia
Yvonne Burns, University of Queensland
Mark S. Cescato, South Australian College of Advanced Education
Lorna K. S. Chan, The University of Western Australia
Peter G. Cole, The University of Western Australia
Sally M. Collett, La Trobe University
Agnes Dodds, Murdoch University
Carolyn Field, University of Auckland
Jeff Field, University of Auckland
Karen M. Fitzgerald, Flinders University of South Australia
Alison F. Garton, Murdoch University
Ron Gold, Deakin University
Lorraine Grimwood, University of Melbourne
David A. Hay, La Trobe University
Ian Hopkins, University of Melbourne
Carol Johnston, La Trobe University
Maggie Kirkman, University of Melbourne
Rosemary A. Knight, Australian Capital Territory Health Authority
Judith I. Laszlo, The University of Western Australia
Jeanette Lawrence, Murdoch University
David Luke, University of Queensland
Mary A. Luszcz, Flinders University of South Australia
Peter G. Mertin, Child, Adolescent and Family Health Service, South
   Australia
Heather Mohay, University of Queensland
Andrew R. Nesdale, The University of Western Australia
Pauline J. O'Brien, La Trobe University
Michael O'Callaghan, Mater Misericordiae Hospitals, Queensland
James Pearson, The University of Western Australia
Chris Pratt, The University of Western Australia
Margot Prior, La Trobe University
Peter D. Renshaw, Murdoch University
Elizabeth Rutherford, University of Melbourne
Michael Siegal, University of Queensland

Gordon Stanley, University of Melbourne
Lesley E. Tan, Melbourne College of Advanced Education—Institute
of Early Childhood Development
Dorothy Toussaint, Murdoch University
David Tudehope, Mater Misericordiae Hospitals, Queensland
William E. Tunmer, The University of Western Australia
Simone Volet, Murdoch University
Greg C. R. Yates, South Australian College of Advanced Education
Shirley M. Yates, South Australian College of Advanced Education

Preface

The studies reported in the chapters of this book are a selection from the papers originally presented at the Third National Child Development Conference in 1984 in Perth, Western Australia. The high standard of research based papers that were presented is a clear indication that there is a strong commitment in Australia to the study of developmental processes in children.

The book is divided into four sections, covering cognitive issues in development, language and reading development, perceptual motor development and social aspects of development. The research described in these papers reflects current developments both in Australia and overseas. Each section includes chapters that are concerned with basic and applied research issues and cover topics in developmental psychology from early infancy into adulthood. Editorial introductions have been included at the beginning of each section.

We would like to thank:

The Inger Rice Foundation
The Ian Potter Foundation
W. J. Moncrieff Pty Ltd
Department of Education, The University of Western Australia
Department of Psychology, The University of Western Australia
Arnott-Mills & Ware Pty Ltd
Bushells Pty Ltd
The British Broadcasting Corporation
Allen & Unwin Pty Ltd
Harper & Row
McGraw-Hill Book Company Australia Pty Ltd
Nestle Australia Ltd
Oxford University Press Australia
Prentice-Hall of Australia Pty Ltd
Town & Country Building Society
Trans-Australia Airlines
Westpac Banking Corporation

for financial assistance both for the conference and in the publication of this volume.

CHRIS PRATT
ALISON F. GARTON
WILLIAM TUNMER
ANDREW R. NESDALE

SECTION 1
COGNITIVE ISSUES IN
DEVELOPMENT

Cognitive development refers to the child's acquisition of intellectual skills, including remembering, thinking and problem solving. The eight chapters comprising this section are representative of the range of current research activity into aspects of cognitive development. The full age range from infancy to adolescence is encompassed in this selection of research papers, and a variety of theoretical orientations is expressed. The chapters are arranged developmentally.

The research on infancy contained in this section reflects two separate contemporary concerns. Firstly, one area of research is concerned with the long term effects of various conditions which are often regarded as handicapping later cognitive development. Mohay and her colleagues compare both prenatal and postnatal twin environments and their effects on later cognitive development, taking measures at various ages up to 4 years. They find that while the rate of development of twins may be delayed in the first two years of life, the disadvantages seem largely to disappear thereafter. The prenatal environment *per se* is not responsible, rather it predisposes the infants to complications which themselves may have adverse repercussions.

Cescato and Mertin explore the effects that a very low birth weight can have on later cognitive functioning, in comparison to a group of appropriate birth weight infants. The results show that although infants with very low birth weights do score lower than the controls on tests of cognitive functioning, they are still achieving scores within the normal ranges. Indeed, when allowances are made for prematurity, the scores of the groups are comparable.

1

The second area of infant research is represented by the study by Field and Field, who report an experiment on the cognitive capabilities of one-year-olds. Specifically, they investigate the use infants can and do make of auditory spatial information (a loud noise) in searching manually for an object. However, both hidden sounding objects and hidden silent objects are searched for successfully, causing methodological issues to be raised by the authors. Such research provides us with valuable clues regarding the infant's ability to integrate and use various types of sensory information.

Research on cognitive development is often guided by Piaget's theory of the growth of knowledge and many papers included in this selection have followed this tradition. The chapter by Gold seeks to establish the reasons for young children's failure on the standard Piagetian class inclusion and number conservation tasks by considering and evaluating two different interpretations, the 'misinterpretation' position and the conceptual deficit position. After reporting a series of experiments, Gold claims that both positions are tenable depending on the particular phenomenon being studied.

The influence of Piaget's theory is noted in the chapter by Renshaw and Garton, where the processes by which pairs of children solve goal directed problems are examined. However, a different theoretical explanation, namely that of Vygotsky's is invoked to account for the patterns of dyadic interaction that emerge. The provision of a social context allows the children to make explicit their strategies for solving problems, enabling the children to work together more collaboratively.

The influence of context is further examined in the chapter by Pratt and Pearson, where the memory skills of young children are examined. Drawing on the distinction between embedded and disembedded contexts, they report that children's memory performance is influenced not by the meaningfulness of the task but by specific factors contained in the particular contexts used in their experiments.

The Australian adolescent has been the focus of much research over the past 20 years, and the two papers using adolescent subjects continue this trend while also making contributions to research in cognitive development. Tan and Hay's chapter examines the scholastic ability of left handed adolescents. It thus continues to explore the theme of examining the determinants of later cognitive ability, exemplified in the earlier infancy studies. They propose that an interaction between genetic and environmental factors is responsible for the apparent lower ability of left handers in numeracy and reading.

Volet, Lawrence and Dodds' chapter considers how and why adolescents are less efficient and poorer in planning and cognitive organisation. Experimentally, adolescents' planning activities show none of the efficiency and adaptability shown by adults. Improvements in the adolescents' planning behaviour are noted when spontaneous monitoring and self evaluation occur in subsequent planning tasks. Self regulation, derived from an awareness of the need to plan and monitor one's behaviour, is deemed to be important for efficient cognitive organisation. This research, along with that of Renshaw and Garton, and Pratt and Pearson, represents aspects of a contemporary trend to examine 'everyday', practical cognition, or, in other words, the study of cognitive abilities in relevant contexts. Research efforts along these lines, where the practical uses and application of cognitive abilities are being examined and measured can only deepen our understanding of how we learn to deal with our world from infancy to adolescence.

ALISON F. GARTON

1

The Effects of Prenatal and Postnatal Twin Environments on Development

Heather Mohay, Yvonne Burns, David Luke
University of Queensland, Brisbane, Qld
David Tudehope and Michael O'Callaghan
Mater Misericordiae Hospitals, Brisbane, Qld

Introduction

It has been widely reported that the mean IQ of twins is somewhat lower than that of singleton children (Churchill & Henderson, 1974; Drillien, 1964; Record, McKeown & Edwards, 1970). The reasons for this difference are, however, by no means clear. Prenatal, perinatal and postnatal environmental factors have all been implicated by different authors.

The prenatal environment of twins is undoubtedly more hazardous than that of singletons and Churchill (1965) suggested that adverse factors during this period were primarily responsible for the subsequent delayed development observed in twins. This suggestion was strongly challenged by Record et al. (1970). Their monumental study of the verbal reasoning abilities of children taking the 11+ examination in Birmingham, England, confirmed previous findings that the scores of twins were significantly lower than those of singletons. In addition, however, they were able to demonstrate that the scores of single survivors of twin pregnancies were not significantly inferior to those of singleton children. On the basis of this evidence they concluded that the postnatal twin environment had a much stronger impact on development than the prenatal environment. It is important to note that the Record et al. data came exclusively from tests of verbal reasoning and there is considerable evidence that twins frequently display delayed language development (Davis, 1937; Day, 1932; Mittler, 1970; Savić, 1980).

5

Poor language skills are likely to have an adverse effect on performance in most intelligence tests but especially on the type of tests used by Record et al. Lytton and Conway (1977) provided evidence that the linguistic environment of twins was impoverished compared with that of singletons and suggested that this rather than prenatal or perinatal factors was responsible for their language delay. These findings support the conclusions of Record et al. However, further investigation is required to determine whether the scores obtained by twins in other areas of development are also depressed or whether their lower IQ scores are entirely attributable to problems related to the acquisition and use of language.

The possible influence of perinatal factors in subsequent development cannot be ignored. Twins are more likely than singletons to be born prematurely and to suffer injuries during birth. Thus their perinatal environment would appear to be fraught with more dangers which might have adverse effects on later development (Drillien, 1964). Advances in medical knowledge and technology have led to an increase in the survival rate of very low birth weight infants and a reduction in the incidence of handicapping conditions. A recent study (Tudehope, Rogers, Burns, Mohay & O'Callaghan, 1984) reported only a very small, non-significant, positive correlation between birth weight and developmental outcome at 2 years of age.

In contrast to all the previously discussed studies on twins, Wilson (1974) reported that, although twins were relatively delayed in their development at 18 months of age, by 6 years of age there was no significant difference between their development and that of singleton children. The early delay in development may have been due to the effects of adverse prenatal or perinatal events or to environmental factors related to the fact that parents are kept very busy caring for two young children and are therefore likely to have less time to devote to twins than they would to single children. Whatever the causes, they appeared to have been overcome by the time the twins entered school. Hence the twin environment did not appear to have any long term deleterious effects.

The Study

The majority of the studies reviewed failed to control for either prenatal or perinatal environmental factors. This study attempts to overcome this by:
1. Investigating the differential effects of prenatal and postnatal twin environments on development, and

2. Examining the pattern of development of twins and singletons from the age of one month to 4 years of age.

Method

Subjects
All the subjects were selected from a larger population study of infants cared for in the Intensive Care Nursery at the Mater Mothers' Hospital, Brisbane, between July 1977 and January 1982, who had birth weights < 1500 g or required prolonged mechanical ventilation in the neonatal period.

Group A comprised all the surviving sets of twins in the above population. A total of 24 pairs of twins was located, nine sets of male twins, 12 sets of female twins and three sets of opposite sex twins. This distribution suggests that there was a higher proportion of monozygotic twins in the sample than is found in the general population, possibly because monozygotic twins are more likely than dizygotic twins to be born prematurely or to suffer complications in the perinatal period (Bryan, 1983). In most cases no accurate determination of zygosity was available.

Group B comprised all the single survivors of twin pregnancies in the above population. There was a total of 13 such children, six male and seven female.

Group C comprised 37 singletons (18 male and 19 female) selected on the basis of being the next infant accepted into the population study after a twin.

Groups A and B were therefore matched for prenatal twin environment, and Groups B and C were matched for postnatal environment. As the three groups were selected from the same population, perinatal environmental factors were to some extent controlled (see Table 1.1).
There were no significant differences between the mean birth weights and gestational ages of the three groups. However, the single surviving twins and singletons were more likely than the twins to have had low Apgar scores and/or to have required mechanical ventilation. This suggests that they experienced a somewhat more hazardous neonatal period than the twins.

Procedure
All subjects were assessed on the Griffiths Scale of Mental Development at 1, 4, 8, 12 and 24 months after expected date of delivery

Table 1.1   Gestational age, birth weight and perinatal data for twins, single survivors and singletons

	Twins	Single survivors	Singletons
Number	48	13	37
Mean gestational age (weeks)	31	30	31
Mean birth weight (grams)	1476	1291	1523
Number requiring prolonged mechanical ventilation	22	10	24
Apgar < 5 at 1 minute	14	4	13

(Corrected Age) and on the McCarthy Scale of Children's Abilities at 4 years of age. The tests were administered by one of the authors or by one of several trained research assistants. As far as possible the testers had no knowledge of previous test results at the time of administering the test.

RESULTS

A General Quotient (GQ) and five subscale scores (locomotor, personal/social, hearing/speech, eye/hand and performance) were obtained from the Griffiths Scale of Mental Development at each assessment up to 24 months. At 4 years of age a General Cognitive Index (GCI) and four subscale scores (verbal, perceptual/performance, quantitative and memory) were obtained from the McCarthy Scale of Children's Abilities. The motor subscale was not administered, as an independent neuro-sensory-motor assessment was conducted. The results from the 4-year-olds must, however, be treated with caution as, at present, data are only available from a little over half of the subjects.

Figure 1.1 shows the mean GQs for the three groups up to 24 months corrected age (test mean = 100; standard deviation = 12) and GCIs at 48 months (test mean = 100; standard deviation = 16). The mean scores for all three groups remained within the average range at all ages. Therefore, the adverse perinatal environments experienced by all the infants did not appear to have had any detrimental effects on overall developmental outcome.

The mean GQ of the singletons was higher than that of the twins at

Fig. 1.1 Mean General Quotients of singletons, single surviving twins and twins

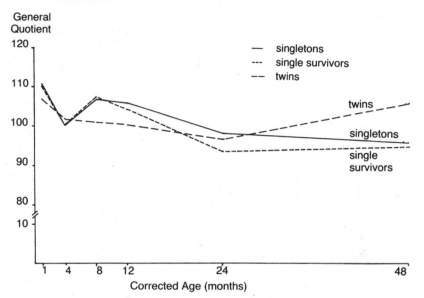

all ages except 4 months corrected age. These differences, however, only attained levels of statistical significance at 8 and 12 months corrected age, $t = 2.35$, $p = < 0.02$ and $t = 2.76$, $p < 0.01$ respectively. The GQs of the single surviving twins remained very close to those of the singleton children until 2 years of age when a marked drop in score was observed. No statistically significant differences were found between the scores of the single survivors and those of either the singletons or the twins at any age. At 4 years of age the mean GCI of the twins was significantly higher than that of the singletons, $t = 2.45$, $p < 0.01$. The mean GCI of the single surviving twins was very similar to that of the singletons. However, the difference between it and the mean GCI of the twins failed to reach statistical significance because of the small number of subjects.

It is important to consider the factors which contributed to the depressed scores of the twins up to 2 years of age; i.e., were the low scores primarily due to delayed language development or did the twins show delays in other areas of development as well?

The mean quotients were compared for the three groups on each of the subscales of the Griffiths Test up to 24 months corrected age. On each subscale the mean scores of the twins tended to be lower than

Fig. 1.2 Standard Scores of singletons, single survivors and twins on the subscales of the McCarthy Test at 4 years of age

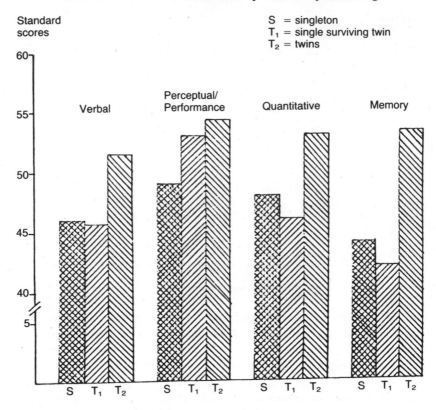

those of the singletons. However, the difference only reached statistical significance on the locomotor scale at 8 months and 12 months corrected age, $t = 2.97$, $p < 0.01$; $t = 2.24$, $p < 0.05$, on the hearing and speech subscale at 12 months corrected age, $t = 2.12$, $p < 0.05$ and on the performance subscale at 1 and 12 months corrected age, $t = 2.19$, $p < 0.05$; $t = 2.32$, $p < 0.05$. At 4 years of age the mean scores of the twins were superior to those of the singletons on all the subscales of the McCarthy Test (see Figure 1.2). However, the differences only reached acceptable levels of statistical significance on the verbal and memory subscales, $t = 1.96$, $p < 0.05$; $t = 3.23$, $p < 0.01$.

DISCUSSION

No evidence was found to support the notion that the hazards associated with a prenatal twin environment adversely affected subsequent development, as the development of the single survivors of twin pregnancies mirrored that of the singleton children.

The results of the present study supported the findings of Wilson (1974) which were previously discussed. It appeared that the rate of development of twins may be delayed in the first two years, possibly because the parents would be too busy taking care of the physical needs of the children to be able to provide the stimulation which they would provide for a single child. As the twins became more self sufficient these disadvantages would seem to disappear and they would be able to catch up with their singleton age mates.

Examination of the data from the subscale scores suggested that the delayed development observed in the twins was not primarily due to delayed language development but to the cumulative effects of mild delays in all areas of development. The significant difference between the language development of twins and singletons at 12 months corrected age might reflect the frequently reported observation that twins start talking later than singletons (Day, 1934; Mittler, 1970). Any inferiority in the language development of the twins seemed, however, to have all but disappeared by 2 years of age and by 4 years the twins were superior to the singletons in verbal skills.

The twins were also significantly slower than the singletons in motor development at 8 and 12 months corrected age. This may have been at least partly due to the somewhat precocious development of the singletons. In addition, three children in the twin group had physical handicaps which delayed their motor development and depressed the mean score of the group. As these children got older their physical handicaps interfered less with their performance on the test items. An increased incidence of cerebral palsy in twins has been reported by Eastman, Kohl, Maisel and Kavaler (1967) and Griffiths (1967).

In this study the incidence of handicapping conditions was higher in both the twins and single surviving twins than in the singleton group. Those found were: in the twin group one was blind in one eye and three had mild cerebral palsy; in the single survivors one had mild mental retardation and was blind in one eye. There was no significant condition in the singleton group. This suggested that the prenatal and perinatal environment of twins predisposes them to more handicapping conditions which may have long term effects on intellectual development.

In conclusion, the results of the present study suggest that the prenatal twin environment does not have an adverse effect on subsequent intellectual development. It does, however, predispose the infants to complications in the perinatal period which may have long term sequelae. The postnatal twin environment appeared to be related to mild delays in all areas of development in the first year or two of life. However, as the children got older these effects disappeared.

References

Bryan, E. (1983). *The nature and nurture of twins*. London: Bailliere Tindall.

Churchill, J. A. (1965). The relationship between intelligence and birth weight in twins. *Neurology*, 15, 341.

Churchill, J. A. & Henderson, W. (1974). Perinatal factors affecting fetal development. In K. S. Moghissi (Ed.), *Birth defects and fetal development* (pp. 69–76). Springfield, Ill.: Charles C. Thomas.

Davis, E. A. (1937). Linguistic skill in twins, singletons and siblings, and only children from five to ten years. *University of Minnesota Institute of Child Welfare Monographs Series no. 14*.

Day, E. (1932). The development of language in twins. 1. A comparison of twins and single children. *Child Development*, 3, 179–199.

Drillien, C. (1964). *The growth and development of the prematurely born infant*. Baltimore, Md: William & Wilkins Co.

Eastman, N. J., Kohl, S. G., Maisel, J. E. & Kavaler, F. (1962). The obstetrical background of 753 cases of cerebral palsy. *Obstetrics and Gynecology Survey*, 17, 459–497.

Griffiths, M. (1967). Cerebral palsy in multiple pregnancy. *Developmental Medicine and Child Neurology*, 9, 713–731.

Lytton, H. & Conway, D. (1977). The impact of twinship on parent-child interaction. *Journal of Personality and Social Psychology*, 35, 97–107.

Mittler, P. (1970). Biological and social aspects of language development in twins. *Developmental Medicine and Child Neurology*, 12, 741–757.

Record, R. G., McKeown, T. & Edwards, J. H. (1970). An investigation of the differences in measured intelligence between twins and single births. *Annals of Human Genetics*, 34, 11–20.

Savić, S. (1980). *How twins learn to talk*. London: Academic Press, 1980.

Tudehope, D., Rogers, Y., Burns, Y., Mohay, H. & O'Callaghan, M. (1984). *Recurrent apnoea in very low birth weight (VLBW) infants: outcome at two years corrected age*. Paper presented at the Australian College of Paediatrics Conference, Adelaide.

Wilson, R. S. (1974). Twins: mental development in the preschool years. *Developmental Psychology*, 10, 580–588.

2

Cognitive Functioning of Children Born With Very Low Birth Weight

Mark S. Cescato
South Australian College of Advanced Education
Peter G. Mertin
Child, Adolescent and Family Health Service, Adelaide

Obstetricians, pediatricians and other medical practitioners have for some time noted that newborn low birth weight and preterm infants appear different in certain respects from newborn full-term infants of appropriate weight, and they, as well as parents, have been confronted with the question of whether or not such children will be different later on in life. This question has become even more poignant as the survival rate of those infants born with birthweights below 1,500 grams has greatly improved in recent years (Sameroff, 1981).

One of the earliest follow-up studies in this field was a retrospective survey conducted by Alm (1953) on 1,000 premature (less than 2,500 grams birth weight) infants born in Sweden between the years 1900 and 1920. He compared his findings on these subjects with approximately 1,000 control subjects. One of the several significant differences he found between the two groups was that there were four times as many low birth weight subjects than control subjects in institutions such as psychiatric hospitals, institutions for the mentally retarded, the physically handicapped, the blind, and so forth. Alm also noted that there were twice the number of low birth weight subjects attending special classes, but that there were no significant differences between low birth weight subjects and controls on variables such as criminality, income and public welfare.

Drillien (1958, 1959, 1961, 1964) was responsible for many early investigations into the development of low birth weight individuals. Two of her earlier studies (1958, 1961) involved a follow-up of 69 low birth weight subjects who had weighed 3 lb (1,360 grams) or less at birth. Like Alm, she found high proportions of low birth weight subjects in special placements. For example, 18% were in special classes, a further 18% were in schools for the physically handicapped, and 10 % were said to be 'ineducable'. Only 24% were in regular educational programmes, and all but two of these were in the lower levels of their school grades.

These earlier studies were disheartening in finding relatively high mortality rates and, for those very low birth weight infants (less than 1,500 grams) who managed to survive, a high incidence of severe handicaps. However, with advances in medical technology, and the growing number and sophistication of neo-natal intensive care units (NICU), the prognosis for infants of very low birth weight (VLBW) has improved greatly in recent years, although the picture still remains somewhat confused.

Stewart and Reynolds (1974) using the Stanford–Binet Form LM found that 92% of 65 VLBW children they assessed up to age 7 years 10 months had an IQ score of 80 or more. Caputo, Goldstein and Taub (1981) compared 38 children who had been 2,500 grams or less at birth with a control group of 26 full–term children. Subjects were 7 to 9.6 years when assessed on the WISC-R. They found that the low birth weight children had significantly lower Performance IQ scores. Weiner, Rider, Oppel and Harper (1968) however, found that low birth weight subjects and controls were significantly different on both Verbal and Performance IQ, whilst Rubin, Rosenblatt and Balow (1973) also found low birth weight children to have significantly lower Stanford–Binet IQ and WISC full scale IQ scores.

In one of the more recent studies Nickel, Bennett and Lamson (1982) followed up 25 children aged between 6 and 18 years who had weighed under 1,000 grams at birth. Seven (28%) of these children had one or more major neurologic or sensory handicaps. These authors also found these children displayed weaknesses in arithmetic reasoning, reading comprehension as well as fine and gross motor skills and, to a lesser degree, perceptual skills. Several other recent studies (e.g., Alden, Mandelkorn, Woodrum, Wennberg, Parks & Hodson, 1972; Pape, Buncie, Ashby & Fitzhardinge, 1978) have investigated the outcome of infants whose birth weights were 1,000 grams or less. They have assessed Developmental Quotient (DQ) in children up to 24 months of age and found that ¼ to ⅓ of these children have DQs below the average range.

As Hunt (1981) has pointed out, comparisons across studies are not easy to make for various reasons. Differences in the characteristics of and numbers of the populations studied, differences in definitions of low birth weight, variations in the ages of children assessed at follow-up, and in the kinds of assessments and measuring instruments used, and differences in defining what constitutes 'handicapped' and 'normal' outcome, all contribute to the difficulty of comparing and reviewing the studies in the recent literature. In addition, some studies have used control or comparison groups, while others have not. As a general statement, one can say that the prognosis for infants of very low birth weight has improved greatly since the early discouraging follow-up studies such as those of Drillien and others referred to earlier in this paper.

The present study concerns the later cognitive functioning of children who were under 1,500 grams at birth. Specifically, it compares their performance on a number of cognitive scales to that of a full-term, appropriate birth weight group of control subjects.

Method

Subjects
The subjects were 40 children of English-speaking white middle-class backgrounds ranging in age from 3.0 years to 6.7 years. There were 22 females and 18 males in the total group.

Experimental (Low birth weight) group
This group consisted of 21 very low birth weight subjects who had been cared for in the NICU at the Queen Victoria Hospital, Adelaide. Their ages ranged from 3.0 years to 6.3 years. Criteria for selection were that they:
1. were of very low birth weight, i.e., less than 1,500 grams;
2. their gestational age at birth was less than 34 weeks (mean G. A. for the group was 29.2 weeks);
3. were from white, English-speaking, middle-class backgrounds; and
4. had no gross behavioural, physical or psychological problems.

Control (full-term) group
The control group consisted of 19 subjects ranging in age from 3.2 years to 6.7 years, and were selected so that their ages matched as closely as possible those of the experimental group. Criteria for selection were that the children:

Table 2.1 Average scaled scores on the six MSCA scales for the control and experimental groups*

Scale	Experimental group		Control group
Verbal (V)	43.2	(46.2)	54.2
Perceptual-performance (P)	51.0	(55.0)	57.2
Quantitative (Q)	47.7	(51.0)	56.8
Memory (Mem)	43.3	(46.0)	53.6
Motor (Mot)	44.1	(47.9)	51.6
General Cognitive Index (GCI)	94.14	(100.62)	105.68

*Figures in parenthesis refer to the average scaled scores of the experimental group after correcting for gestational age.

1. had been greater than 2,500 grams but less than 4,000 grams at birth;
2. had been full-term deliveries or delivered within two weeks of the due date;
3. were from white, English-speaking, middle-class backgrounds;
4. had no gross behavioural, physical or psychological problems; and
5. had experienced no major complications or problems at or immediately after birth.

Apparatus
The McCarthy Scales of Children's Abilities (MSCA) were administered to all 40 children. The MSCA is a standardised test of mental or cognitive abilities for children of preschool and early childhood ages (i.e., ages 2.5 to 8.5 years), containing 18 separate subtests grouped into six scales. These scales are Verbal (V), Perceptual-Performance (P), Quantitative (Q), Memory (Mem) and Motor (Mot). (Each of these scales has a mean of 50 and a standard deviation of 10 points.) The final scale is the General Cognitive Index (GCI) which is composed of the first three scales (V, P and Q). The GCI has a mean of 100 and a standard deviation of 16, and thus relates closely to both the Stanford-Binet and Wechsler IQs. (McCarthy, 1972).

Procedure
All children selected for the present study were assessed on the MSCA by one of the authors (M. C.), at either the Queen Victoria Hospital or the Adelaide Children's Hospital so that testing conditions were similar for each subject.

Table 2.2   T-values of comparisons of control and experimental groups on the six MSCA scales.

Variable	Control vs Experimental (uncorrected data)	Control vs Experimental (data corrected for prematurity)
V	4.19 ****	3.03 ***
P	2.11 *	.73 (n.s.)
Q	4.10 ****	2.60 *
Mem	4.67 ****	3.48 ***
Mot	2.28 *	1.14 (n.s.)
GCI	4.76 ****	2.93 **

* $p < .05$
** $p < .01$
*** $p < .005$
**** $p < .0005$
n.s.: not significant

RESULTS

Data from the experimental group were in two forms; these two forms being compared independently with data from the control group. One set of data from the experimental group was in its standard form, based on the actual chronological age of the subjects in that group. Another set of data from the experimental group was corrected for gestational age by allowing for the varying degrees of prematurity of the subjects within this group. Subjects were designated a 'corrected chronological age' and indexed scores for the six MSCA scales were then adjusted accordingly. (Table 2.1).

As can be observed from the figures presented in Table 2.1 this correction for prematurity has raised the mean scores of the experimental group, but they are still lower than the corresponding mean scores of the control group.

Independent t-tests were conducted comparing these two forms of data from the experimental group with data from the control group.

Table 2.2 shows the t values for both the uncorrected data and the adjusted data in comparison to the control group data for the six MSCA scales.

DISCUSSION

As a group, the VLBW subjects scored significantly more poorly on the six MSCA scales than control group subjects. Even when their scores were adjusted to allow for their respective degrees of prematurity, the VLBW subjects still scored more poorly on four out of the six scales. Differences remained highly significant on the Verbal and the Memory scales ($p < .005$) and also the GCI scale ($p < .01$).

The Verbal (V) and Memory (Mem) Scales

On the Verbal scale, there was a difference in the means between the two groups of 11 points in favour of the control group. This is just over one standard deviation. Even when an adjustment was made for prematurity, this difference was 8 points and was significant at the .005 level. This finding concurs with the majority of previous researchers (e.g., De Hirsch, Jansky & Langford, 1964, 1966; Field, Hallock, Ting, Dempsey, Dabiri & Shuman, 1978; Phillips, 1968; Rubin et al., 1973; Weiner et al., 1968), although they used different tests of verbal ability and their low birth weight samples included children who had been up to 2500 grams at birth. In contrast, Caputo et al. (1981) found no such significant differences between their low birthweight subjects ($\leqslant 2500$ gm) and controls either on the WISC-R Verbal IQ or on any of the Verbal subscales of the WISC-R.

The Memory scale was one other scale on which differences between VLBW children and control group subjects were most marked. There was a difference in the means of the two groups on this scale of 10.3 points (see Table 2.1). When subjects' scores were adjusted for prematurity, this difference became 7.6 points, a difference that was significant at the .005 level (see Table 2.2). A more specific analysis of the results of subjects on this scale revealed that VLBW subjects fared more poorly on memory tasks that require more than mere immediate recall or, as it is often referred to, ultra-short-term memory. Where the VLBW subjects were required to listen carefully and hold the information in memory either momentarily or for some time, or where it was necessary to manipulate or transform the auditory input while holding it in memory, they performed significantly more poorly than control subjects.

It is interesting to note that when deficits on the Verbal scale were analysed in specific detail, VLBW children performed significantly more poorly than controls on tasks which required relational or transformational thinking ability, such as providing an opposite analogy or an antonym. Bearing in mind the above discussion on specific memory deficits, it would be interesting to ascertain whether these sorts of difficulties are due to receptive or expressive impairments. Presumably, the children tested understood the requirements of the tasks involved, so any deficits in this regard may not be receptive. As far as it is known, no other investigators have indicated such specific difficulties in the cognitive abilities of VLBW children, and this is an area which obviously needs further thorough investigation.

The GCI Scale

The difference in the mean GCI scores of the VLBW and control groups was 11.5 points, a difference comparable to that found by Dann, Levine and New (1958, 1964) who used the Stanford-Binet Intelligence Scale to assess the intellectual functioning of their subjects. Other investigators (e.g., Caputo et al., 1981; Rubin et al., 1973; Weiner et al., 1968), using mainly the Wechsler or Stanford-Binet scales, have also found the intellectual or cognitive functioning of VLBW subjects to be impaired to varying degrees when compared to groups of control subjects. In the present study, the difference between the means of the VLBW and control groups was reduced to 5.0 points when the VLBW group's scores were adjusted for prematurity. This 5-point difference was still significant at the .01 level.

The Perceptual-Performance (P) and Quantitative (Q) Scales

Results on the P scale are not as striking as on the other scales. Initially, there was a significant ($p < .05$) difference of 6.2 points between the means of the two groups. However, when the VLBW group's scores were adjusted for prematurity, this difference became only 2.2 points, and was not significant. In contrast, other investigators (Caputo et al., 1981; Lis, 1969; Weiner et al., 1968) who used the Bender-Gestalt Test to assess visually-based perceptuo-motor functioning found that low birth weight children performed more poorly than controls in this area of functioning.

The difference between the VLBW subjects and controls on the Q scale was initially quite marked (9.1 points, $p < .0005$; see Tables 2.1 and 2.2). However, when adjustments were made to scores to allow for prematurity, this difference was reduced somewhat and was not so significant (5.8 points, $p < .05$). Several other groups of researchers (Caputo et al., 1981; Nickel et al., 1982; Taub, Goldstein & Caputo, 1977; Weiner, 1968; Weiner et al., 1968) have concluded that low birth weight or short gestation subjects were impaired to some degree on tests of quantitative or arithmetic reasoning and mathematics achievement.

Conclusions

In concluding, it needs to be pointed out as other authors have done (e.g., Dann et al., 1964; De Hirsch et al., 1966; Frances-Williams &

Davies, 1974; Phillips, 1968; Taub et al., 1977; Weiner et al., 1968) that although the VLBW subjects in this study did, in general, score significantly more poorly than controls on the MSCA, many of them still achieved scores that would be considered to be within the normal ranges for these six scales. Indeed, when allowances were made for prematurity, the VLBW group's scores were more comparable to those of the control subjects. In addition, the sample size of the present study was relatively small, so one needs to be wary of drawing any definitive conclusions from these results. More controlled longitudinal follow-up studies of VLBW children are required before definitive findings can emerge, and further research into the existence or otherwise of rather more *specific* cognitive deficits amongst these children is needed. The deficits found in the VLBW subjects in this study warrant further investigation, particularly those concerning memory functioning and 'cognitive transformations', as such findings seem not to have been made before.

References

Alden, E. R. Mandelkorn, T., Woodrum, D. E., Wennberg, R. P., Parks, C. R. & Hodson, W. A. (1972). Morbidity and mortality of infants weighing less than 1,000 grams in an intensive care nursery. *Pediatrics, 50,* 40–9.

Alm, I. (1953). *The long term prognosis for prematurely born children.* Uppsala: Almquist and Wicksell.

Caputo, D. V., Goldstein, K. M. & Taub, H. B. (1981). Neonatal compromise and later psychological development: a 10-year longitudinal study. In Friedman, S. L. & Sigman, M. (Eds), *Preterm birth and psychological development,* New York: Academic Press.

Dann, M., Levine, S. Z. & New, E. (1958). The development of prematurely born children with birthweights or minimal postnatal weights of 1,000 grams or less. *Pediatrics, 22,* 1037–53.

Dann, M. Levine, S. Z. & New, E. (1964). Long-term follow-up of small premature infants. *Pediatrics, 33,* 945–60.

De Hirsch, K., Jansky, J. J. and Langford, W. S. (1964). The oral language performance of premature children and controls. *Journal of Speech and Hearing Disorders, 29,* 60–9.

De Hirsch, K., Jansky, J. J. & Langford, W. S. (1966). Comparisons between prematurely and maturely born children at three age levels. *American Journal of Orthopsychiatry, 36,* 616–28.

Drillien, C. M. (1958). Growth and development in a group of children of very low birth weight. *Archives of Disease in Childhood. 33,* 10–18.

Drillien, C. M. (1959). Physical and mental handicaps in the prematurely born. *Journal of Obstetrics and Gynaecology of the British Commonwealth, 66,* 721–33.

Drillien, C. M. (1961). The incidence of mental and physical handicaps in school-age children of very low birth weight. *Pediatrics, 27*, 452–64.

Drillien, C. M. (1964). *The growth and development of the prematurely born infant.* Edinburgh: Livingstone.

Field, T., Hallock, N., Ting, G., Dempsey, J., Dabiri, C. & Shuman, H. H. (1978). A first-year follow-up of high-risk infants: formulating a cumulative risk index. *Child Development, 49*, 119–31.

Frances-Williams, J. & Davies, P. A. (1974). Very low birth weight and later intelligence. *Developmental Medicine and Child Neurology, 16*, 709–25.

Hunt, J. V. (1981). Predicting intellectual disorders in childhood for preterm infants with birth weights below 1501 gm. In Friedman,'S. L. & Sigman, M. (Eds), *Preterm birth and psychological development.* New York: Academic Press.

Lis, S. (1969). Visuo-motor development and its disturbances in a sample of prematures born with the weight below 1250 grams. *The Slow Learning Child, 16*, 73–84.

McCarthy, D. (1972). *Manual for the McCarthy Scales of Children's Abilities.* New York: The Psychological Corporation.

Nickel, R. E., Bennett, F. C. & Lamson, F. N. (1982), School performance of children with birth weights of 1,000 grams or less. *American Journal of Diseases of Children, 136*, 105–10.

Pape, K. E., Buncie, R. J., Ashby, S. & Fitzhardinge, P. M. (1978). The status at two years of low-birth-weight infants born in 1974 with birth weights of less than 1,001 grams. *Journal of Pediatrics, 92*, 253–60.

Phillips, C. J. (1968) The Illinois Test of Psycholinguistic Abilities: a report on its use with English children and a comment on the psychological sequelae of low birth-weight. *British Journal of Disorders of Communication, 3*, 143–9.

Rubin, R. A., Rosenblatt, C. & Balow, B. (1973). Psychological and educational sequelae of prematurity. *Pediatrics, 52*, 352–63.

Sameroff, A. J. (1981). Longitudinal studies of preterm infants: a review of chapters 17–20. In Friedman, S. L. & Sigman, M. (Eds), *Preterm birth and psychological development.* New York: Academic Press.

Stewart, A. L. & Reynolds, E. O. R. (1974). Improved prognosis for infants of very low birth weight. *Pediatrics, 54*, 724–35.

Taub, H. B., Goldstein, K. M. & Caputo, D. V. (1977). Indices of neonatal prematurity as discriminators of development in middle childhood. *Child Development, 48*, 797–805.

Weiner, G. (1968). Scholastic achievement at age 12–13 of prematurely born infants. *Journal of Special Education, 2*, 237–50.

Weiner, G., Rider, R. V., Oppel, W. C. & Harper, P. A. (1968). Correlates of low birth weight. Psychological status at eight to ten years of age. *Pediatric Research, 2*, 110–18.

3

Search for Sounding Objects by One-Year-Old Infants

Jeff Field and Carolyn Field
University of Auckland

Just like adults, infants are often in a situation where they have to search for a person or object that is not directly visible to them at one point in time. The success of their search will depend upon the information available to them about where to search and upon the strategies they adopt for finding the target, or, in other words, their search skills. In recent years research and discussion about infants' search skills and the information that they make use of in search has really blossomed (see, for example, Harris, 1983; Wellman & Somerville, 1982). These research efforts have focussed heavily on infants' use of visual information during search and very few studies have as yet addressed the issue of infants' use of auditory spatial information in search.

Our experiments are specifically concerned with the auditory guidance of what may be called distal search. By distal search we simply mean the ability to reach for, or locomote to, the precise location of an object. Previous investigations of infants' use of sound in their distal search can be classified into three categories that we will call visual deprivation, locomotory search, and manual search studies.

Visual deprivation experiments have involved either blind infants or sighted infants presented with sounding objects in darkness. Studies of the development of blind infants' sound-guided reaching for objects have revealed that such behaviour emerges spontaneously at about an average of 10 months, well after the development of visually-guided reaching in normal infants (Fraiberg, 1977).

There have been at least two reports of infants' use of sound in their locomotory search for their mothers (Rieser, Doxsey, McCarrell &

Brooks, 1982; Zucker & Corter, 1981). Both of these studies have involved 9-month-old subjects and both suggest that while sound can guide search to an initial place, subsequent hiding of the sounding object in a new location is associated with the same kind of perseverative responses that appear in such two-choice tasks with silent objects at 9 months of age.

Our work falls into the category of manual search studies and three reports have claimed to show that infants can use sound cues in their manual search by the end of the first year (Bigelow, 1983; Freedman, Fox-Kolenda, Margileth, & Miller, 1969; Uzgiris & Benson, 1980). In the most recent of these reports of sound-guided manual search Bigelow (1983) observed 7- to 19-month-old infants in a two-phase experiment. In phase I infants received up to five different Piagetian object permanence tasks, ranging from partial hiding to the successive invisible displacements of objects, where the objects were always silent. In phase II she used the same tasks, but with the addition of sound to the toys that were hidden. A distraction task, where the infants did not observe the actual hiding of the toys, was also randomly inserted in Phase II. Bigelow concluded that infants began to use sound to guide their search in stage IV of object permanence development. She also concluded that successful search for an invisibly-hidden, sounding object precedes the ability to search for sounding objects that are seen to disappear before being invisibly displaced.

Despite the apparent consistency of findings from these manual search studies, it can be argued that they have failed to show conclusively that infants begin to use sound localization in order to search for hidden objects around one year of age. In all cases the studies failed to include matched, silent, hiding trials in an appropriately counterbalanced order with sound trials. In other words, once they have been 'warmed' to search in a test situation, infants under about one year of age may search without even having seen whether, or where, something was hidden (see, for example, Wellman & Somerville, 1982). Thus, in these earlier studies it has not always been possible to differentiate visually-directed search from sound-guided search. Furthermore, in all three studies no reliable assessments were reported of the subjects' ability to orient in the direction of the hidden, sounding objects immediately prior to initiating searches. Such orientation data would have indicated whether the infants were localizing the sounds accurately or not.

In the present experiment we retained some features of a traditional Piagetian object permanence task, but also made some procedural improvements over some of the earlier research. First, in our hiding task, where a toy was hidden initially in a box and then under a cloth that was placed over the box, the box was not returned to the infant, but placed to one side, effectively providing two potential search locations for the subjects, in a box or under a cloth. Second, we rated whether infants were looking toward the box or cloth locations, prior to initiating their search. Third, and most important of all, control groups were used in which infants had to locate a silent object under the same conditions as those available to infants provided with a sounding object. Finally, the order of presentation of search tasks involving either visible or invisible object disappearance was properly counterbalanced to control for possible practice effects.

Twelve-month-old infants were selected for this initial study since the literature (Uzgiris & Benson, 1980) suggested that the kind of task we planned to use is a reasonably difficult one at that age, even without any sound cues to the location of the target. The specific questions of interest in our study were:

1. Whether search performance would be enhanced by the provision of a sounding object compared with a silent one.
2. Whether the frequency of successful searching on a task where an object's hiding was seen would be less than under conditions of non-observed hiding, when the object was invisibly displaced after it had been hidden.

METHOD

Subjects

Twenty-six, healthy one-year-old infants, with no recent history of ear infections, were recruited from middle class suburbs for the experiment. Satisfactory data could not be collected from two of this initial group, one because she was too distressed and the other because of technical problems during her testing. The 24 remaining infants were allotted to two groups of 12 subjects containing equal numbers of males and females, but their allocation was otherwise random. The control group who experienced only silent objects had a mean age of 54.1 weeks (range, 52.6 to 56.1 weeks) and the experimental group averaged 53.7 weeks (range, 52.0 to 56.7 weeks).

Apparatus

The infants were seated on their parents' laps, facing the experimenter across a small table that supported a grey, felt-covered, presentation tray. Three small toys were used as stimulus objects interchangeably between search conditions, depending upon each infant's interest. Attached to each toy was a very small earphone speaker (Ashidavox Earstick Es-24) that was connected by a thin grey wire to a hidden cassette tape recorder. This gave the experimenter control of either of two recorded sounds associated with the toys; a music box lullaby, or bell-ringing sounds.

During each trial, one of the objects was placed in a felt-lined box (12.5 cm in length and width x 12 cm height). A lengthwise slit in the box, through which the wire passed from the object to the cassette player, always faced the experimenter. A large opaque white cloth, measuring 75 cm square, occluded the object during the test trials. The cloth was large enough to lie on the table and cover the wire connected to the recorder at one side of the table. Each testing session was videotaped for later scoring of behaviour with a camera positioned behind and to the right of the experimenter.

Design and procedure

All infants were familiarised initially with both the sounding toys and the box and cloth. They were next given two warm-up hiding trials with each object being hidden completely, either in the box, or under the cloth. All subjects were able to locate the objects over several such complete-hiding trials, thereby showing no perseverative errors on the task.

Every subject subsequently experienced what will be denoted as four pretest, four observed disappearance and four non-observed disappearance trials. The pretest trials followed the same procedure as that used in the observed disappearance trials, except that silent toys were used for all subjects. Each pretest and disappearance trial began when the infant had fixated the object for 2 s. The toy was then lowered into the box and the cloth placed over it. The experimenter then reached under the cloth with both hands, one hand lifted the object from the box and the other placed the box on one side of the table, while the object, hidden by the cloth, was placed on the other side of the table. The presentation tray was then pushed forward so the cloth and box were both within easy reach of the subject. The time taken from the toy disppearance to the tray being pushed forward to within reach of the subject was about 7 s. If the infant found the object, he or she was rewarded with lots of praise. If the subject did not search for the toy within 20 s, it was exposed and manipulated to gain the infant's attention, before moving on to the next trial.

The procedure for the non-observed disappearance task was similar to the foregoing except that infants did not see the manipulations involved in hiding the toys. It was similar to the distraction task used by Freedman et al. (1969). Trials again began after the infant had fixated the object for 2 s. On a command from the experimenter, the parent and infant turned 180° away from the task setting to face a poster on the wall. During this distraction time of approximately 7 s, the experimenter hid the object under the cloth. As soon as the subject was again facing the experimenter, he or she was encouraged to search. While the control group had to search for silent toys on these trials, for the experimental group the toys sounded continuously, except during the distraction period. The sound was turned off as the infant was turned away and reinstated at the moment the infant was centred, upon turning back.

The order of presentation of the observed and non-observed disappearance trials was counterbalanced within each sound condition. Half of the infants in the control (no sound) and experimental (sound) groups received the observed disappearance trials last and half received the non-observed disappearance trials last. The left or right positioning of the object on each trial was also varied according to a pre-selected, counterbalanced order. There was an intertrial interval of approximately 20 s.

The videotapes of the test sessions were scored with the audio-track turned off and with the scorer blind to each infant's group identity. The following variables were scored for each trial: location of initial search (box, cloth, or specified other); the location of second searches; whether the search was successful; the latency of successful searches; and the direction of visual regard immediately prior to search, if this differed from the direction of manual search.

A search was defined as either the infant manipulating the box or cloth (picking up the box and looking into it or turning it over, picking up the cloth, or patting the surface of the cloth), or looking into the box. A successful search referred to cases where infants exposed the object within 20 s of presentation time and fixated the object within 2 s of exposure. Interobserver reliability was assessed by having a second, independent observer score the behaviours of six randomly chosen subjects. Percentage agreement on the judgement of successful trials was 98.6%, and for search location it was 97.2%.

Results and Discussion

On the tasks involving the observed hiding of a toy the infants search initially at the box location (see Table 3.1 (a)). The first of two

Table 3.1   Percentage of trials where (a) initial searches were made at the box and (b) objects were eventually located successfully.

Group	Pretest (no sound)	Observed Disappearance	Non-observed Disappearance
		Task	
		(a) Initial search at the box	
No sound	81%	77%	57%
Sound	94%	91%	59%
		(b) Successful search	
No sound	32%	49%	62%
Sound	29%	46%	56%

Note: Each percentage is based upon a total of 48 trials.

ANOVAs incorporating the factors of sound condition, order, sex and search task was carried out on the frequency of initial searches at the box location, irrespective of whether or not successful searching eventuated. There was a significant main effect for task, $F(2, 16) = 17.020$, $p < .001$. This was due to less initial searching at the box on the non-observed disappearance than both the pretest (Tukey q, $p < .01$) and the observed disappearance task ($p < .01$). As the data in Table 3.1(a) suggest, the subjects' initial choice of the box was significantly above chance in both the sound and no sound groups for the pretest and observed disappearance trials (in all cases $p < .03$, with a two-tailed binomial test). For both sound conditions of the non-observed disappearance task, however, the infants' distributions of initial search at the box or cloth locations were not significantly different from chance (in both cases $p < .9$).

The lack of any difference between the sound and no sound groups in rates of eventual search success was confirmed by a second ANOVA that yielded main effects for sex, $F(1, 16) = 6.768$, $p < .05$, and hiding task, $F(2, 32) = 7.213$, $p < .01$. Females made significantly more successful searches than males and multiple comparisons using the Tukey procedure revealed significantly more successful responses on the non-observed disappearance task compared to the pretest ($p < .01$). It should be noted that the percentages given in Table 3.1(b) reflect the fact that the great majority of infants showed inconsistent success across their four trials of each search task.

Why was there such a bias towards initial search at the box location on trials involving disappearance of a toy? It seems likely that infants may have been influenced mainly by the previous disappearance of the target toy into the box and also probably by the greater attention-getting qualities of a large, moving container than an amorphous cloth. The visual orientation data support this suggestion. Infants in the experimental group did not look toward the sound source in the cloth before searching in the box. Thus, we were left in doubt as to whether the infants even localised the sound on the majority of trials. There was no evidence of a generalised increase in attention to the task on sound trials, nor was there any change in the latency to search, or in the incidence of corrected search on sound trials. Like some earlier researchers (Bigelow, 1983; Freedman et al., 1969) we presumed the infants would be able to perceive the general direction of the toy sounds without too much difficulty. This presumption should be avoided in future studies.

We can conclude that the 12-month-old infants in this experiment did not search more successfully for hidden, sounding objects than for hidden, silent objects. This finding clearly fails to support the conclusions of Bigelow (1983) and Freedman et al., (1969) who used the results of infants' search for sounding objects on non-observed hiding trials, without comparing these with trials where silent objects were used. It is obvious that the kind of Piagetian search tasks used in both the present and previous studies cannot provide a sensitive test of the role of sound cues in search. None of the earlier studies have checked whether adults could accurately localise the sounds of the search targets, let alone infants. We asked two blindfolded adults to point to the side of the sound sources when they were randomly placed in the positions used with the infant subjects. Although accurate in their judgements of lateral location, both adults expressed difficulty in carrying out the auditory lateralization judgements and often needed several seconds to make their decisions. Several important methodological refinements are therefore essential in future research and these are included in our current studies of this topic. First, there needs to be a clear determination that infants' search performance is greater than that due to chance or purely visual information. Second, the hiding locations should have equal salience for infants. Finally, the sound sources should be arranged to maximise the probability that infants can localise them prior to making any searches.

References

Bigelow, A. E. (1983). The development of the use of sound in the search behaviour of infants. *Developmental Psychology, 19*, 317–21.

Fraiberg, S. (1977). *Insights from the Blind*. New York: Basic Books.

Freedman, D. A., Fox-Kolenda, B. J., Margileth, D. A., & Miller, D. H. (1969). The development of the use of sound as a guide to affective and cognitive behaviour—A two phase process. *Child Development, 40*, 1099–1105.

Harris, P. L. (1983). Infant cognition. In M. M. Haith & J. J. Campos (Eds) *Handbook of child psychology: Vol. 2. Infancy and developmental psychobiology*. (pp. 689–782). New York: John Wiley & Sons.

Rieser, J. J., Doxsey, P. A., McCarrell, N. S., & Brooks, P. H. (1982). Wayfinding and toddlers' use of information from an aerial view of a maze. *Developmental Psychology, 18*, 714–20.

Uzgiris, I. C., & Benson, J. (1980). *Infants' use of sound in search for objects*. Paper presented at the International Conference on Infant Studies, New Haven, Connecticut.

Wellman, H. M., & Somerville, S. C. (1982). The development of human search ability. In M. E. Lamb & A. L. Brown (Eds), *Advances in developmental psychology: Vol. 2*. (pp. 41–84). Hillsdale, N. J.: Lawrence Erlbaum & Associates.

Zucker, K. J., & Corter, C. M. (1981). *Infants' use of sound in search for mother during brief separation*. Paper presented at the biennial meeting of the Society for Research in Child Development, Boston.

4

Failure on Piagetian Tasks: Misinterpretation of the Question?

Ron Gold
Deakin University

This paper deals with the question of why young children fail Piaget's number conservation and class-inclusion tasks. In the conservation task, the child is shown two rows of counters aligned in one-to-one correspondence, and is asked whether they contain the same number of counters. When he has replied correctly that they do, the length of one of the rows is changed, and the original question repeated. The child now says that one row (usually the longer one) contains more than the other. In the class-inclusion task, the child is shown, say, a picture of eight boys and two girls. When he is asked 'Are there more boys or more children?' he replies 'More boys'. Clearly, in each of these tasks, the child does not understand the question that is asked of him, at least in the way that an adult would understand it. The issue is, however, *why* he does not understand it.

Piaget considered that the child's problem is that he is perceptually dominated and—the other side of the same coin—that he lacks *reversible thought*. In the conservation task he cannot overcome the perceptual 'pull' of the contrast in row lengths that is produced by the transformation. He becomes able to solve the task when he acquires reversibility by *compensation:* he comes to appreciate that the change in row length is exactly compensated by the concomitant change in row density. Solution of the class-inclusion task requires that the child have 'boys' and 'children' in his mind simultaneously; he must thus be able mentally to decompose 'children' into 'boys' and 'girls' at the same time as he combines 'boys' and 'girls' to form 'children'. It is this simultaneous carrying out of an action and its inverse that defines reversibility by *inversion*. Lacking reversible thought, the young child

30

can perform only one of these actions at a time. The contrast between the subclasses 'seduces' him, and it is these sets that he compares when answering the question.

It is evident that in the absence of the knowledge which Piaget saw as being produced by reversible thought, no concept of conserved number or included class can reasonably be said to be present. A child who believes that when a row of counters is expanded the change in length (say) more than compensates for the change in density cannot reasonably be said to have the concept of conserved number (in that particular situation at least). And a child who cannot simultaneously consider an included set and the set that includes it cannot reasonably be said to have the concept of included class (again, in that situation). So Piaget's analysis comes down to saying that the young child fails the conservation and class-inclusion tasks because he lacks the very concepts of conserved number and included class. He does not understand the question asked of him because he *cannot* understand it, because it deals with a concept that he does not have.

This 'conceptual deficit' view of failure on the conservation and class-inclusion tasks has proved controversial. A number of authors have suggested that the young child does in fact have the concepts of conserved number and included class, and that he fails the tasks only because he cannot cope with the difficult and unusual communicational demands which they make on him. In the case of conservation it has been suggested, for example, that changing the length of one of the rows of counters leads the child to assume that the experimenter's question is actually asking about length and not about number. And in the case of class-inclusion it has been proposed that the request to compare a class with one of its subclasses is such an unusual one that the child assumes that the experimenter really wants him to compare the two subclasses. According to these suggestions, it is not that the child *cannot* understand the question asked of him, but merely that he *mis*understands it. He thinks that he is being asked a different question, and *that* is the question he answers.

What types of experimental evidence might help to distinguish this 'misinterpretation' position from the conceptual deficit position? This paper focusses on one strategy that has been tried. It involves comparing children's performance on the conservation or class-inclusion task with their performance on a new task that has three characteristics. First, it is highly similar in form to the conservation or class-inclusion task. Secondly, from a Piagetian point of view, it tests for a concept that is clearly much simpler than that which is tested for by the conservation or class-inclusion task. And thirdly, it can plausibly be considered as furnishing just as much opportunity for misunderstanding the question as does the conservation or class-inclusion task. Suppose it is now found that errors on this new task in fact take a very similar form to, and occur just as often as, those which are made on the conservation or class-inclusion task. It would then be parsimonious, the argument goes, to see the two types of error as being essentially one and the same thing; the two tasks would in effect be measuring the same ability. Piaget's theory could not explain this, because from its point of view the new task makes much simpler demands than does the conservation or class-inclusion task. But the misinterpretation position would have an explanation of the result: it occurs because the two tasks present the same opportunity for misunderstanding the question, and *this* is what is important.

An example relating to class-inclusion comes from studies (Grieve & Garton, 1981; McGarrigle, Grieve & Hughes, 1978; Trabasso, Isen, Dolecki, McLanahan, Riley & Tucker, 1978) which have employed a double class hierarchy. The child might, for example, be shown toy farm animals standing in two fields. In one field are three black horses and one white horse; in the other field are two black cows and two white cows. (See Figure 4.1) Now one could, of course, use such a display to give the usual class-inclusion task: focussing on just the horses, one would ask 'Are there more black horses or more horses?' But one could also use the display to give what might be called a 'between-sets' task, in which the child has to compare a subclass and a superclass from different fields: thus the child would be asked 'Are there more black horses or more cows?'

It turns out that young children make errors on this type of task. Their errors seem to take the form of answering a question different from that which was asked. In particular, the children appear to change the question so that it refers to two sets at the same level of the class hierarchy. Thus they change the question by leaving out the adjective ('More horses or more cows?'), by overgeneralising the adjective ('More black horses or more black cows?') or by adding a contrasting adjective ('More black horses or more white cows?').

This result has been adduced as evidence for the misinterpretation view of class-inclusion failure and against Piaget's view. The between-sets error is so similar to the class-inclusion error, the argument has been, that we must see them as caused by the same underlying difficulty. Piaget's theory cannot explain the findings because, from his point of view, the two tasks test for very different abilities. In particular, the

Fig. 4.1 Display used in a typical between-sets trial

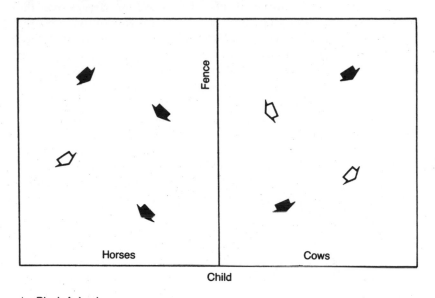

♦ Black Animals
◊ White Animals
Arrow indicates direction animal is facing

between-sets task does not involve any inclusion relation, so that re-versibility by inversion is not required. According to Piaget's theory this should make the between-sets task appreciably easier than the class-inclusion task. But the misinterpretation position—or a specific form of it, at least—could explain the findings. It is possible that young children have a general tendency to misinterpret any question that asks them to compare two sets at different levels of a class hierarchy. Performance on the two tasks would then be so similar simply because both give the same opportunity for this type of misinterpretation.

An example relating to number conservation comes from a study by Donaldson and McGarrigle (1974). These authors gave young children a task bearing a considerable resemblance to that of Piaget; the only difference was in the type of transformation that was performed. The children were presented with two rows of toy cars placed on shelves, one above the other. One row contained four cars, the other, five. The rows were aligned in one-to-one correspondence, in such a way that the unmatched car protruded at the end of its row. The experimenter asked the child which shelf had more cars on it and, this question having been answered, placed a set of four garages over the row of four cars, and a set of six garages over the row of five cars; one garage in the latter set was thus left empty. The experimenter then repeated the original question. It was found that the transformation caused many of the children to alter their judgement: while they correctly chose the row with five cars when the garages were absent, they chose the row with four cars when the garages were present. Here, apparently, they were basing their quantity judgements on the relative fullness of the two sets of garages.

Donaldson (1982) adduced this result as (one source of) evidence against Piaget's view of number conservation failure and for the misinterpretation hypothesis. Although she did not state her reasoning explicitly, she was apparently following a similar line of argument to that outlined above for the case of the between-sets task.

The conclusions which have been drawn in these studies may be criticised. One can argue that the findings support the misinterpretation hypothesis and contradict Piaget's position only if the new task is as difficult as the conservation or class-inclusion task. But in fact the relationship between the two types of task was not looked at very carefully in the studies concerned. In one study the Piagetian task was not given at all. In other studies both tasks were given, but quite a number of other questions were asked of the child as well, and it is impossible to tell whether performance was being influenced by the giving of these other questions.

It was decided to carry out further studies on the issue. First, three studies on the relationship between the number conservation task and Donaldson and McGarrigle's task (to be referred to below as the 'covering' task), are reported.

Experiment 1

METHOD

Subjects
In the first study the participants were 24 boys and 20 girls, ranging in age from 51 months to 65 months with a mean of 56.3 months.

Materials
Two sets of materials were used: model animals (horses and cows, painted either black or white) and model vehicles (cars and trucks,

painted either red or green). The models were displayed on two shelves, one above the other. For half the sample the covering task was given using animals and the conservation task was given using vehicles; the rest of the sample got the materials the other way round.

Procedure

Each child got two trials of each task; both trials of one task were given before those of the other commenced. Half the children got the tasks in one order, the other half in the other order.

A trial of the covering task began when the experimenter placed five (say) white horses in a row on one shelf and five black horses in a row on the other shelf. The two rows were in one-to-one correspondence. After the child had counted the rows, he was asked 'Do the two rows have the same number of horses?' and 'Does one row have more horses than the other?' Half the children got the 'same' question first, half the 'more' question first. When these questions had been answered correctly, the child was told to watch while some 'sheds' were put over the horses. (The covering structures were referred to as 'garages' when vehicles were the materials.) A set of five sheds was placed over one row of horses and a set of six sheds over the other. The earlier questions were then repeated.

A conservation trial took the same form as a covering trial, except for the transformation performed: one row was expanded and the other contracted.

RESULTS

A child was scored as having passed a trial if he responded correctly to both the 'same' question and the 'more' question. For each task the children tended either to pass both trials or to fail both trials. Accordingly non-parametric statistics were used, a child being credited with having passed a task if he passed both trials of that task.

There were no sex differences or order effects, so the data were collapsed across these categories. Thirty-one children passed the covering task and 21 passed the conservation task. Thirteen passed the covering task but failed the conservation task, while three showed the reverse pattern of performance. The McNemar test indicated that the covering task was significantly easier than the conservation task ($\chi^2 = 5.06$, 1 d.f., $p < 0.025$, 1-tailed test).

In this study, then, the covering task turned out to be easier than the conservation task. One problem, though, was that the tasks used were 'equality' tasks: there were the same number of objects in each row. Donaldson and McGarrigle's task, however, had been an inequality task. So it was necessary to carry out another experiment in order to check that the result was not limited to the equality situation.

Experiment 2

Method

Subjects
The participants were 12 boys and 12 girls, ranging in age from 50 months to 63 months, with a mean of 56.7 months.

Procedure
This second experiment followed the same procedure as the first except that there were now four objects in one row and five in the other. In the covering task, the experimenter placed a row of four sheds/garages over the row of four objects and a row of six sheds/garages over the row of five objects. In the conservation task the row of four objects was expanded and the row of five objects contracted in such a way as to make the former protrude equally at each end of the latter.

Results

The same scoring criteria were used as before. There were no sex differences or order effects, so the data were collapsed across these categories. Twenty-three children passed the covering task and 14 the conservation task. Nine passed the covering task but failed the conservation task, while no child did the reverse. The McNemar test indicated that the covering task was significantly easier than the con-servation task ($X^2 = 7.1$, 1 d.f., $p < 0.005$, 1-tailed test).

So the result was not just limited to the equality situation. But there was one more thing that needed checking. It was at least conceivable that the children were finding the covering task to be easier, not be-cause of the different type of transformation involved, but just because the misleading perceptual cue was less 'eye-catching': it is possible that the presence of a single unfilled shed/garage is simply less salient than is a difference in row lengths. In the next experiment, therefore, every attempt was made to ensure that the misleading cue in the covering task would be brought to the child's attention very strongly.

Experiment 3

METHOD

Subjects
The participants were 12 boys and 12 girls, ranging in age from 46 months to 59 months, with a mean of 52.6 months.

Procedure
The misleading cue in the covering task was emphasised in two ways. First, the number of empty sheds/garages was increased to two. There were four objects in each row—this study used equality tasks again—and a set of six sheds/garages was put over one row and a set of four sheds/garages over the other. Secondly, the child's attention was drawn explicitly to these empty sheds/garages: before asking the test question the experimenter pointed to them and said 'So we have two empty sheds/garages, two extra sheds/garages'. In the conservation task there were also four objects in each row.

RESULTS

There were no sex differences or order effects. Seventeen children passed the covering task and six the conservation task. Eleven children passed the covering task but failed the conservation task while no child did the reverse. The McNemar test indicated that the covering task was significantly easier than the conservation task ($\chi^2 = 9.1$, 1 d.f., $p < 0.005$, 1-tailed test).

It seems, then, that the conservation task poses the child appreciably more problems than does the covering task. This finding is consistent with Piaget's theory. It follows that children's performance on the covering task cannot be taken as evidence that Piaget's theory of number conservation is wrong and the misinterpretation position correct.

The next study relates to the relationship between the class-inclusion task and the between-sets task.

Experiment 4

METHOD

Subjects
The participants were 56 5- and 6-year-olds (ranging in age from 60 months to 84 months, with a mean of 73.6 months) and 76 8- and

9-year-olds (ranging in age from 96 months to 119 months, with a mean of 107.7 months). There were 60 boys and 72 girls.

Materials

The materials used were toy animals—horses, cows, pigs and sheep —painted either black or white.

Procedure

Each child received two trials of each task. Half the children received the tasks in one order, the other half in the other order. The stimuli for a typical between-sets trial were as described earlier; half the children were asked 'Are there more black horses or more cows?', while the other half were asked 'Are there more cows or more black horses?' In the corresponding class-inclusion trial, half the children were asked 'Are there more black horses or more horses?', while the other half were asked 'Are there more horses or more black horses?'

RESULTS

For each task the children tended either to pass both trials or to fail both trials. Accordingly, non-parametric statistics were used, a child being credited with having passed a task if he passed both trials of that task.

There were no sex differences. Because of the somewhat different pattern of order effects obtained with the younger vs older children, the results for these groups will be presented separately.

In the case of the 5- and 6-year-old children, there were no order effects. Ten children passed the between-sets task but failed the class-inclusion task while two children did the reverse. The McNemar test indicated that the between-sets task was significantly easier than the class-inclusion task ($X^2 = 4.08$, 1 d.f., $p < 0.025$, 1-tailed test). With the 8- and 9-year-old children, there were no order effects on the between-sets task but there was an order effect on the class-inclusion task: this task became significantly easier when it was given second. This order effect meant that a within-subjects analysis would be biased against the hypothesis that the between-sets task is easier than the class-inclusion task. Such an analysis nevertheless supported the hypothesis. Twenty children passed the between-sets task but failed the class-inclusion task while five children did the reverse. The McNemar test indicated that the between-sets task was significantly easier than the class-inclusion task. ($X^2 = 7.84$, 1 d.f., $p < 0.005$, 1-tailed test).

DISCUSSION

So it seems that the class-inclusion task poses the child greater problems than does the between-sets task. This finding is consistent with Piaget's theory. It follows that children's performance on the between-sets task cannot be adduced as evidence against Piaget's explanation of class-inclusion failure and for the misinterpretation hypothesis. It may be that one can attribute the between-sets error to a tendency by young children to misinterpret questions asking for a comparison between two sets at different levels of a class hierarchy. But it does not seem that the same factor could also provide a full explanation of the class-inclusion error.

If the findings preclude this particular form of the misinterpretation explanation of class-inclusion failure, this is not to say that they preclude other forms of the misinterpretation hypothesis. One could devise a misinterpretation hypothesis that would be consistent with the data. And the same thing is true for the case of the covering and number conservation tasks. So the general conclusion is that, in both cases, the findings do not give us any basis for making a firm choice between Piaget's conceptual deficit view and the misinterpretation position.

References

Donaldson, M. (1982) Conservation: What is the question? *British Journal of Psychology, 73,* 199–207.

Donaldson, M., & McGarrigle, J. (1974) Some clues to the nature of semantic development. *Journal of Child Language, 1,* 185–94.

Grieve, R., & Garton, A. (1981) On the young child's comparison of sets. *Journal of Experimental Child Psychology, 32,* 443–58.

McGarrigle, J., Grieve, R., & Hughes, M. (1978) Interpreting inclusion: A contribution to the study of the child's cognitive and linguistic development. *Journal of Experimental Child Psychology, 26,* 528–50.

Trabasso, J., Isen, A., Dolecki, P., McLanahan, A., Riley, C., & Tucker, T. (1978) How do children solve class-inclusion problems? In R. Siegler (Ed.), *Children's thinking: What develops?* Hillsdale, N. J.: Erlbaum.

5

The Effect of Context on the Memory Performance of Children

Chris Pratt and James Pearson
The University of Western Australia

During the last decade there has been increasing interest among developmental psychologists and educationists in the effect of context on children's performance on cognitive tasks. With respect to this Donaldson (1978) has described two different types of context, *embedded* and *disembedded*, in which children are required to demonstrate cognitive skills such as memory. Embedded contexts are those in which the child deals 'with people and things in the context of fairly immediate goals and intentions and familiar patterns of events' (p. 76) whereas, disembedded contexts are those where children operate outside the supportive context of familiar meaningful events. According to Donaldson, children of preschool age are affected to a great extent by context and experience most difficulty when presented with tasks in disembedded contexts.

Brown and DeLoache (1978) and White (1980) have also commented on the effects of context and, in particular, have made reference to the negative effects of laboratory tasks on young children's cognitive performance. These authors have stressed the importance of considering the ecological validity of the tasks that are presented to children.

Although memory has long been regarded as an important cognitive skill (Binet & Henri, 1895; Sattler, 1982), there has been little research into the effect of context on memory (Cavanaugh & Perlmutter 1982; Paris 1978). One study by Istomina (1977), however, is cited by Brown and DeLoache (1978) and Meacham (1977) because it appears to lend support to the claim that young children will demon-

40

strate their best memory performance in familiar, meaningful situations.

Istomina examined the memory performance of 3- to 7-year-old children in two different conditions. The conditions were a *shopping game* in which children were required to remember and purchase several items from a shop and a *memory test* in which children were required to remember a list of items similar to those in the shopping game. These conditions are clearly equivalent to those Donaldson refers to as embedded and disembedded respectively. Istomina reports that children in the shopping game, the embedded context, recalled more items on average than children in the memory test, the disembedded context. These results are interpreted as providing evidence that the goal of remembering was more salient for the children in the meaningful context of the shopping game.

There are several procedural problems concerned with differences that arise between the shopping game and the memory test that cast doubt on the validity of the conclusions that have been drawn. They include the presence of items on display in the shop which may have acted as cues for recall; the involvement of two adults in the shopping game compared with only one in the memory test; the memory test being conducted in the classroom and the shopping game in separate rooms; and the tendency for other children in the shopping game to prompt the child who was trying to remember the items to be purchased.

It is possible that any one or a combination of these specific differences may have led to superior performances in the shopping game rather than some general difference arising from differing degrees of meaningfulness in the two conditions.

Furthermore, some of the children in both conditions had the list of items repeated to them. Istomina does not give any details, however, about the number of children who had the list repeated or the possible effects of this.

The purpose of the experiments reported in this paper therefore was to examine the effect of context on memory performance in children in situations that take account of the problems encountered in the Istomina study.

In the first study the memory performance of kindergarten and second grade children was examined in two conditions, a shopping game and a memory test, while in the second study the effects of repetition, situation and the number of adults were investigated.

Experiment 1

Method

Subjects

The subjects were 20 kindergarten and 20 second grade children drawn from the pre-primary and primary classes of a Government school in a predominantly middle-class area of Perth, Western Australia. The mean ages for each of the two groups were 4.8 (range 4.3 to 5.2) and 6.7 (range 6.3 to 7.1). There were eleven girls and nine boys in the kindergarten group and an equal number of girls and boys in the second grade group.

Procedure

All the testing was conducted in two adjoining rooms. In the shopping game, a shop was created in one room using props including a cash register and shopping basket. However, props that would have acted as specific cues for recall, such as grocery items, were not used. A kitchen in a house was created in the other room using props including a stove, cupboards and table and chairs. In the memory test condition the same two rooms were used but all the props were removed and replaced with a testing table and two chairs in each room.

Each child in the shopping game was taken from the classroom by the researcher and introduced to the shopkeeper who was at the checkout in the shop. The child was told that he or she would be asked to come to the shop later. The child was then taken to the other room where he or she played 'house' with the researcher, who then asked the child to go to the shop to buy some items from the shopkeeper.

A list of nine items was then presented verbally at a rate of one word per second. The list was presented twice with a ten second interval between presentations. The items in the list were *salt, coffee, matches, lettuce, nuts, apple, bacon, pins* and *brush*. Following the second presentation, the child was sent to the shop where the assistant noted down the items that were requested. Following this each child was given the items and then returned to the researcher.

In the memory test, each child was taken from the classroom by the researcher and introduced to the researcher's assistant who was sitting in one room behind a table. It was explained that they would have to remember a list of words and tell it to the assistant.

The child was then taken to the adjoining room where the researcher presented the nine item list of words. The list was the same as that

Table 5.1   Mean recall scores for young children in the shopping task and memory test conditions.

	Age Group	
Condition	Pre-School	Grade 2
Shopping game	3.5	4.3
Memory Condition	3.8	4.2

used in the shopping conditions and the conditions for presentation were the same. Following the second presentation, the child was sent to the assistant who wrote down the words that were recalled.

All children participated in the shopping game or memory condition individually and half the children at each age level were assigned to each condition.

Results And Discussion

The mean recall scores for children in each condition are shown in Table 5.1. Although the mean recall scores for children in the older group are slightly higher than the mean scores for younger children, a 2(Age) × 2(Context) ANOVA revealed that there were no significant effects for age, context, or age × context.

The failure to obtain a significant effect for context in this study, particularly for the younger children, would appear to fail to support the assertion by Brown and DeLoache that young children will demonstrate better memory performance in situations that are more meaningful to them. Furthermore, this study has not replicated the findings reported by Istomina. One possible explanation may be that, from the child's perspective, the two conditions in this study did not differ with respect to meaningfulness.

Observations of the children in the shopping game indicated that they understood the game and became involved in it, talking for example about 'buying' the items or forgetting to get (an item) from the 'shop'. It is possible, however, that the memory test was also meaningful to the children, insofar as it involved telling another adult the list of words. This may be an easier task to understand than telling the same adult the list. In Istomina's study only one adult was involved in the memory test, whereas two were involved in the shopping game. Furthermore, in the Istomina study, the shopping game took place in separate rooms, whereas the memory task took place in the classroom while children were engaged in their normal classroom activities. In this experiment, however, both conditions involved quiet rooms that were separate from the classroom. There is also the problem that in the Istomina study some children had the list repeated while others did not, while in this experiment all children were presented with the list twice.

Experiment 2

The purpose of the second experiment therefore was to investigate systematically the effects of the differences that may account for Istomina's findings. That is, the second experiment examined the effects of the situation (classroom vs quiet testroom), the number of adults involved (1 vs 2) and the number of presentations of the list (1 vs 2).

METHOD

Subjects
The subjects were 32 kindergarten and 32 second grade children drawn from a Government pre-school centre and primary school in a mostly middle-class area of Perth, Western Australia. The mean ages of the two groups were 4.9 (range 4.3 to 5.3) and 6.10 (range 6.4 to 7.5) respectively. There were equal numbers of girls and boys in each group.

Procedure
Children at each age level were assigned to one of eight conditions (conditions a to h). Approximately equal numbers of girls and boys were assigned to each condition. In all conditions children were informed that they were going to do a test to find out how many things they could remember. The list of items was presented at a rate of one word per second. There was a pause of approximately 30 seconds between the end of presentation of the list and recall which was prompted by the question, 'What can you remember?'.

In conditions (a), (b), (c) and (d) children were presented with the list only once. Children in conditions (a) and (b) were tested in the classroom, where they had been involved in ongoing classroom activities. (Condition (a) was essentially a replication of the 'memory test' condition in Istomina's experiment.) The experimenter, the only adult involved in condition (a), presented the list items and recorded the child's recall performance.

Table 5.2   Mean recall scores for children in experiment 2.

(a) Pre-school				
	Nil Repetition		One Repetition	
	1 Adult	2 Adults	1 Adult	2 Adults
Classroom	2.00	3.00	3.50	2.25
Testroom	3.25	3.50	5.25	3.50

(b) Grade 2				
	Nil Repetition		One Repetition	
	1 Adult	2 Adults	1 Adult	2 Adults
Classroom	4.75	4.50	5.00	4.50
Testroom	4.00	4.00	5.00	4.75

Condition (b) involved two adults, the experimenter and a female assistant. After the experimenter had presented the list of items, each child was required to walk to the assistant in another part of the classroom. The assistant asked the child 'What can you remember?' and recorded the recalled items.

Conditions (c) and (d) were similar to conditions (a) and (b) respectively, except that the testing was conducted in two adjacent quiet testrooms. In both conditions, children were brought individually from their classroom to the testrooms. In condition (c), the testing was carried out with one adult, the experimenter, and made use of one room only. In condition (d), after presentation of the list, the child was required to walk from the experimenter in one room to the assistant in the adjacent room.

Finally, conditions (e), (f), (g) and (h) were the same as conditions (a), (b), (c) and (d) respectively, in all but one respect. In conditions (e), (f), (g) and (h), the list of items was presented to each child twice. Following the first presentation, there was a delay of ten seconds before the items were presented again, in the same order and at the same rate as the first presentation.

RESULTS AND DISCUSSION

The mean recall scores for the children in each condition are shown in Table 5.2. A 2(age) × 2(situation) × 2(number of adults) × 2(number of presentations of list) ANOVA was conducted on the children's recall scores. This revealed a significant main effect for age, $F(1,63) = 20.753$, $p < 0.05$, and a significant main effect for repetition, $F(1,63) = 4.457$, $p < 0.05$. There were also two significant interaction effects, for age × situation $F(1,63)=6.531$, $p < 0.05$, and for repetition × number of adults $F(1,63) = 4.457$, $p < 0.05$. There were no other main effects or interaction effects.

The significant difference between the mean recall scores of pre-school children and Grade 2 children confirms the superiority of the recall performance of older school-age children over younger, pre-school children. This finding is consistent with the developmental trend in children of increasing recall performance with age that has been found in other memory research (e.g., Kail 1983).

The significant age × situation interaction suggests that older children are better able to attend selectively to relevant information and as a result their recall performance is less affected by the distractions present in the classroom than that of younger children. The recall performance of the older children is greater in both the classroom and testroom situations, and the difference between the mean recall of the two age groups is greater in the classroom situation.

The adverse effect that visual and auditory distractions exert on children's recall performance has been shown by Hagen (1972). Such distractions were prevalent in the classroom situation of this experiment, which bore a close resemblance to the setting in which Istomina (1977) conducted her investigation of young children's recall performance in the test situation.

Although there is insufficient detail reported in the Istomina study to be certain, it is likely that the detrimental effects of the distractions present in the memory condition led to the differences in performance, rather than the meaningfulness of the shopping game.

Not only was the mean recall performance of pre-school children in the classroom situation of the present experiment relatively poor, but the behaviour of some pre-school children in the classroom situation was different to that of children of the same age group in the testroom situation. A number of children were reluctant to take part in the recall task as it disrupted their on–going classroom activities and many children appeared to devote their attention to other children's classroom activities, rather than to the recall task.

The significant main effect for number of list presentations indicates that both age groups of children were able to benefit from the list being repeated once. Thus, just as Donaldson (1981) had shown that repetition of items improves the memory performance of adults, this experiment shows that pre-school and Grade 2 children also benefit from repetition of items to be recalled.

Furthermore, the number of adults × number of list presentations interaction suggests that the optimal conditions for recall in the context of this experiment were one adult and one repetition of the list. Contrary to the suggestion made above with respect to experiment 1 that two adults may have made the task more meaningful for children, the results of this experiment indicate that, when the list is repeated once recall is at a higher level if only one adult is involved.

GENERAL DISCUSSION

The results of these two experiments question the claim that children's memory performance will be influenced by the meaningfulness of the context or embeddedness of the task. The results of experiment 1 certainly question the interpretation placed on Istomina's findings that memory performance is superior in a shopping game because it is more meaningful. Further, the results of experiment 2 suggest that, in part, the differences Istomina found may have resulted from specific procedural differences including the amount of distractions involved in each situation.

Generally the results of this study indicate that careful consideration must be given to the use of such terms as *meaningful contexts* and *embedded* and *disembedded* tasks. The aspects of a context that make it meaningful for a child and the characteristics of a task that result in it being classified as embedded or disembedded are not yet clear. The terms are frequently used to refer to global differences rather than specific ones. It is important therefore that further research into the effects of specific aspects of context and task presentation on cognitive performance is conducted so that those factors that enhance the performance of young children can be determined and a clearer understanding of the importance of context can be gained.

References

Binet, A. and Henri, V. (1895). La mémoire des mots. *L'Anée Psychologique,* 1, 1–23.

Brown, A. L. and Deloache, J. (1978). Skills, plans and self-regulation. In Siegler, R. (Ed.), *Children's thinking: what develops?* Hillsdale, N. J.: Lawrence Erlbaum Associates.

Cavanaugh, J. C. and Perlmutter, M. (1982). Metamemory: A critical examination. *Child Development, 53,* 11–28.

Donaldson, M. (1978). *Children's Minds.* Glasgow: Collins.

Donaldson, W. (1981). Context and repetition effects in recognition memory. *Memory and Cognition, 9,* 308–16.

Hagen, J. W. (1972). Strategies for remembering. In S. Farnham-Diggory (Ed.), *Information processing in children*. New York: Academic Press.

Istomina, Z. M. (1977). The development of voluntary memory in preschool-age children. In M. Cole (Ed.), *Soviet Developmental Psychology*. N.Y.: Sharpe.

Kail, R. (1983). *The development of memory in children*. San Francisco: Freeman, (2nd Edition).

Meacham, J. A. (1977). Soviet investigations of memory development. In R. V. Kail & J. W. Hagen (Eds), *Perspectives on the development of memory and cognition*. Hillsdale, N. J.: Lawrence Erlbaum Associates.

Paris, S. G. (1956). The development of inference and transformation as memory operations. In P. A. Ornstein (Ed.), *Memory development in children*. Hillsdale, N. J.: Lawrence Erlbaum Associates.

Sattler, J. M. (1982). *Assessment of children's intelligence and special abilities*. Boston: Allyn and Bacon.

White, S. H. (1980). Cognitive competence and performance in everyday environments. *Bulletin of the Orton Society, 30*, 29–45.

6

Children's Collaboration and Conflict in Dyadic Problem Solving

Peter D. Renshaw and Alison F. Garton
Murdoch University

The importance of social interaction for cognitive development has been highlighted primarily by Vygotsky (1978), and to a lesser extent by Piaget (1932). Vygotsky's theory suggests that cognition develops in the process of social interaction and the first theme in Vygotsky's theory is the movement from the social to the individual, from the interpsychological to the intrapsychological plane. A second theme is the movement from initially spontaneous and unconscious problem-solving behaviour to a self-directed and consciously monitored process (Garton, 1984). Critical to the emergence of self-direction and conscious monitoring is speech, and Vygotsky saw that the provision of a social context for problem-solving forced children to formulate their ideas verbally and thereby enabled them to begin the process of acquiring the power of self-directed monitoring. Although Vygotsky provided a provocative framework for studying social interaction and cognition, there have been very few attempts to demonstrate in detail how the process operates, one notable exception being the mother–child interaction studies reported by Wertsch (e.g., Wertsch, McNamee, McLane & Budwig, 1980).

While Piagetian theory directs our attention to conflict between children, Vygotsky directs our attention to collaboration. However, as Wertsch has pointed out, many of Vygotsky's central theoretical concepts are difficult to define and the concept of collaboration is no exception. Collaboration may be seen as the absence of conflict or disagreement, but this is an extremely restrictive definition. The alternative is not to dichotomise collaboration and conflict, but to examine the types of disagreements that arise in collaborative problem-

Fig. 6.1   A model of the process of establishing a collaborative problem-solving dyad

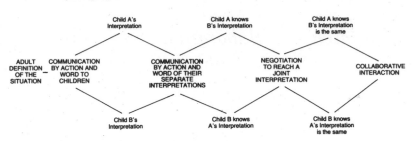

solving and the ways such disagreements are resolved. Forman and Cazden (1983), in their study of collaborative problem solving between children define collaboration as '(requiring) a mutual task in which the partners work together to produce something neither could produce alone.' The emphasis in this definition is on production—a product that neither could have produced alone. However, when Vygotsky defined the zone of proximal development, he stated that it was:

> The distance between the actual developmental level as determined by independent problem solving and the level of potential development as determined through problem solving under adult guidance or in collaboration with more capable peers. (p. 86).

Here the notion of collaboration has connotations of guidance and suggests that one of the pair has the capability, and could have produced the outcome alone. Forman and Cazden's definition does not agree with the definition implied by Vygotsky in the quotation above and, when they measure levels of collaboration, they focus on processes rather than products.

The purpose of the present paper is to clarify the concept of collaboration, to describe the types of social interactions that are constituents of collaboration and to examine the type of conflict resolution used in collaborative activities. Central to our purpose is the notion of an intersubjective situation definition which Wertsch (1983) employed in clarifying the concept of collaboration between an adult and a child. What happens, however, when two children are required to collaborate on a goal–directed problem-solving task? Here the negotiation of an intersubjective situation definition involves numerous tasks of interpretation and communication that are set out in Figure 6.1. This figure illustrates the complexity that confronts children when they are given a problem to solve together. It is essential for collaboration that the two children reach the point where each knows that the other has the same interpretation of the task problem. When this joint (or intersubjective) interpretation is reached, then the conditions have been established for the resolution of disagreements in a mutually satisfying manner. Each child knows he or she can appeal to a rule or definition that the other child will accept, and in this sense their collaboration is guided by their reference to a rule that transcends each of them.

In contrast, children who do not reach or negotiate an intersubjective definition cannot appeal to a rule that transcends them. Each child can only appeal to their own interpretation of the situation, which either the other child cannot understand adequately or it conflicts with his interpretation. The resolution of disagreements in such a dyad cannot be mutually satisfying since one child must capitulate and accept the other's interpretation. Moreover their attempts to work together would be likely to generate many disagreements since each is working on an interpretation that the other does not share.

METHOD

Subjects
The subjects in the study were children in Grades 2 (7-year-olds) and 4 (9-year-olds) of a suburban primary school. This paper focuses on three pairs of males and three pairs of females from each class.

Task
In each interaction session, the children were asked to work towards the solution of a goal-directed problem. The problem solving task used was an attribute task that required the children to make a line of blocks initially according to a 'one difference' rule (i.e., each block had to be different from the previous block on one dimension, such as shape, size or colour), and subsequently to a 'two-difference' rule. This task has a number of advantages for studying collaborative problem solving: there are many decisions to be made and the problem solving activity can be recorded as the children make choices and lay out the blocks. It also provides the opportunity for children to observe each other's choices and judge the adequacy of their partner's choices, enabling disagreement with and challenge of the choices.

Procedure
The pairs of children were videotaped as they worked together on the attribute block task in the presence of an unobtrusive experimenter.

Table 6.1   Second and fourth grade dyads' interpretation of the rule

	Difference	Pattern	None
2nd Grade Males	1	1	1
Females	2	1	0
4th Grade Males	3	0	0
Females	3	0	0

The children were taught the necessary rule by the experimenter, who demonstrated it verbally, and by using both a positive and a negative example and asking each child to explain why the example was right or wrong. Every effort was made to ensure the children understood the rule before they were allowed to begin working together. In addition, the children were told to talk to each other and to decide together which block should be placed next.

Data Analysis
The analysis to be reported here is of children's initial patterns of interaction during their first session of problem solving. This early interaction was defined as the period during which the first six blocks were placed. The videotapes of this initial interaction were transcribed in detail, with both verbal and non-verbal behaviours being recorded. Interobserver disagreements were resolved by repeated viewing of the videotapes until consensus was reached. In addition to analysing the initial period of the first interaction session, all instances of disagreements between the children were identified wherever they occurred through both the interaction sessions. A disagreement was defined simply as any instance of conflict or dissent expressed by one of the children. Typical markers of dissent were 'No, not that', or 'Don't do that'. It was not necessary for the dissent to be reciprocated for the episode to be coded as a disagreement.

Results And Discussion

(a) Interpretation of the Adult Rule
Although the rule was explained at length to the children, a variety of different rules emerged when they began working together. The rules could be classified into three types: *difference rules*, which were the same as the adult rule or variants of it; *pattern rules*, which involved placing the blocks according to a colour × shape design, or pretending that the block configurations represented certain objects; *no obvious*

Table 6.2   Levels of collaboration established by the dyads

		Joint	Disjoint	No attempt
2nd Grade	Males	1	1	1
	Females	2	1	0
4th Grade	Males	1	2	0
	Females	2	0	1

rule, which indicated that no discernible or underlying rule or plan was observed beyond getting the blocks down in a line. The frequencies of rule use by the dyads are shown in Table 6.1.

(b) Children's Communication of their Separate Interpretations of the Rule.
The actions of the children immediately after they began the task were crucial in establishing their level of collaboration. In particular, the dyads differed markedly in their attempts to establish a joint understanding of a rule. Only in two dyads—a 2nd Grade female dyad and a 4th Grade female dyad—was there evidence of explicit attempts to establish a joint understanding. In the majority of the dyads, children did not plan together, but a joint understanding of the rule did emerge in some pairs as partners monitored each other's choices. In other cases, children attempted to monitor the choices made but these attempts did not result in agreement about the appropriate rule, and the children continued to place blocks apparently without understanding the choices made by their partners. In two instances, there was no evidence either of planning or monitoring and it appears that children in those dyads did not attempt to understand their partner's view. Table 6.2 summarises the levels of collaboration achieved by the dyads.

Overall then, as shown in Table 6.2, half of the groups established a joint interpretation of the rule, either by planning together or successfully monitoring their partner's choices. These groups are referred to as JOINT in the discussion below. The other half failed to establish a common interpretation of the rule either because their monitoring efforts failed (the DISJOINT groups) or they did not attempt to understand their partner's view.

There are striking differences in the way the joint and disjoint dyads began their interaction. First, in both of the joint groups, the interaction began with a question—'Shall we put these at the end?' (2nd Grade female dyad), and 'This one?' (4th Grade female dyad). Here, the function of the child's speech was to invite the participation of the

Table 6.3   Number of disagreements in each dyad classified as joint, disjoint, and no attempt

	Joint	Disjoint	No attempt	
2nd Grade				
Male	–, 3	17	2	$\bar{x} = 7.3$
Female	8, 12	5	–	$\bar{x} = 8.3$
4th Grade				
Male	7	17, 11	–	$\bar{x} = 11.7$
Female	7, 1	–	0	$\bar{x} = 2.7$
	$\bar{x} = 6.3$	$\bar{x} = 12$	$\bar{x} = 1$	$\bar{x} = 7.5$

partner in decisions, and in this way, a common understanding of the rule began to emerge.

In contrast, the two disjoint groups had a pattern of interaction that excluded participation of the partner in decisions. The first utterances in both these groups were assertions—'Put this blue one here' (2nd Grade male dyad), and 'That's not it' (4th Grade male dyad). The subsequent interaction in these groups failed to establish joint understanding of a rule, although in both, attempts were made.

(c) Collaborative Interaction: The Resolution of Disagreements
Our model of the process of establishing collaboration would suggest that a joint interpretation of a rule would reduce disagreements and such disagreements as did arise would be successfully resolved by appeal to a common understanding between the partners. Table 6.3 shows the number of disagreements that occurred in the two interaction sessions for each of the dyads.

The average number of disagreements was least in the two no-attempt dyads ($\bar{x} = 1$) and this reflects the lack of social interaction that occurred in these two groups. The comparison between the joint ($\bar{x} = 6.3$ disagreements) and disjoint dyads ($\bar{x} = 12.5$ disagreements) confirms our prediction that dyads who had a common interpretation of a rule would have fewer disagreements than dyads who failed to establish a common rule.

The dyads varied not only in the quality of disagreements but also in the characteristics of the resolution process. In analysing the resolution process, we focussed on four characteristics—the number of utterances, whether the resolution involves an appeal to a common rule, or whether it involves an appeal to subjective feelings, and whether the partners show evidence of agreeing and being satisfied

Table 6.4   Characteristics of the resolution process in joint and disjoint dyads

	Number of utterances	Rule appeal	Subjective appeal	Partner agreement
Joint				
2nd Grade	6	Yes	No	Yes
4th Grade	6	Yes	No	Yes
Disjoint				
2nd Grade	30	No	Yes	No
4th Grade	4	Yes*	No	No

* Appeal to the rule by only one of the dyad who dominates the interaction.

with the resolution. An example from the different dyadic types in each grade is shown in Table 6.4.

These qualitative differences can be illustrated further by comparing a disagreement from a 2nd Grade joint group with one from a 2nd Grade disjoint group. With the 2nd Grade joint dyad, the disagreement concerned how the blocks should be patterned and what colour should go first. J laid the basis of the resolution when she says 'No, pretend that's the white (pointing to a yellow rectangle), red, white, blue'. J in this manoeuvre suggested that they arrange the colours red, white and blue. This appeared to win her partner over and both began to place blocks according to the suggested pattern, and they chanted alternately the next colour to be placed:

C. red first
J. and the yellow
C. yeah the yellow. Then the blue
J. and then the red

Thus, the disagreement is resolved to the satisfaction of both girls by one of them providing an adequate rationale.

The disagreement in the 2nd Grade disjoint dyad was very long involving 30 utterances. The reason for the disagreement is captured in the delightful piece of dialogue below:

R. Looks a bit like a train
J. Does to me but we won't be making a train . . .
R. I know we won't . . .
J. We'll be making something else. So put it there
R. No, keep that there . . .
    No, don't put that there

Neither of the children will let the other know what he is making so there is no common basis for resolving their dispute. They can only appeal to subjective feelings like the following from J: 'Put it there, it's better, see look' or 'No, it's not sorta like, it's sorta like this'.

Conclusion

Our purpose in this paper was to clarify the notion of collaboration by developing a process model that specified what to observe as children work together and the type of mutual understanding that children need to achieve for collaboration to occur. From our model, we made predictions regarding the relative occurrence of disagreements in various dyads and the quality of their resolution. Although the number of dyads is small, our predictions were confirmed by the data and can be seen as initial validation of the model. Our next step will be to apply the model to a larger sample of dyads to determine its generalisability.

In terms of specific findings, two trends are worth highlighting now. No developmental differences in terms of the occurrence of collaboration were recorded between the 2nd and 4th Grade dyads. One of the more collaborative groups was in fact a 2nd Grade dyad who based their collaboration on their use of a pattern rule rather than the difference rule supplied by the adult. That is, they both reinterpreted the adult at a similar developmental level and worked within their existing competencies rather than being drawn on to the more difficult task of working together with the difference rule. Secondly, it is interesting to note that the two most collaborative groups were female and the most competitive form of interaction was observed with the males. While not wishing to perpetuate male and female stereotypes, it does seem that girls are more skilful collaborators.

Finally, the relationship between our findings and the theoretical framework offered by Vygotsky (1978) needs to be elaborated. Vygotsky claimed that the provision of a social context for problem solving elicited from children their otherwise implicit strategies. This was seen as the first step towards a more controlled and purposeful use of such strategies. While our study does not address the second issue, it certainly demonstrates that children feel the need to explain and justify their choices. That is, the implicit strategies were externalised and communicated to their partner. In all but two of the dyads, there are numerous examples of children explaining choices to their partner or having their choices challenged and then being required to justify them. So it may be that the provision of a social context sets the scene for more powerful problem solving strategies and greater individual control of these strategies.

References

Forman, E. A. & Cazden, C. B. (1983). Exploring Vygotskian perspectives in education: The cognitive value of peer interaction. In J. V. Wertsch (Ed.), *Culture, communication and cognition: Vygotskian perspectives.* New York: Cambrige University Press.

Garton, A. F. (1984). Social interaction and cognitive growth: Possible causal mechanisms. *British Journal of Developmental Psychology*, 2, 269–74.

Piaget, J. (1932). *The moral judgement of the child.* London: Routledge and Kegan Paul.

Vygotsky, L. S. (1978). *Mind in society.* Cambridge, MA: Harvard University Press.

Wertsch, J. V. (1983). The zone of proximal development: Some conceptual issues. In B. Rogoff & J. V. Wertsch (Eds), *Cognitive growth in children: The zone of proximal development.* San Francisco: Jossey-Bass.

Wertsch, J. V., McNamee, G. D. McLane, J. & Budwig, N. A. (1980). The adult–child dyad as a problem-solving system. *Child Development*, 50, 1215–21.

7

Scholastic Ability in Left-Handers

Lesley E. Tan
Melbourne College of Advanced Education—
Institute of Early Childhood Development
David A. Hay
La Trobe University

Introduction

For many years, research has suggested that left-handedness is associated with intellectual deficit or other neurological signs (Bradshaw
& Nettleton, 1983; Porac & Coren, 1981). Most of the studies had involved comparisons of clinical samples with normal controls, but in
the seventies, several large surveys measuring ability and hand preference in normal populations raised doubts about the relationship. In
only one of these studies did left-handers score lower than right-
handers (Calnan & Richardson, 1976) and the differences were not
large. In all others there were no overall differences between handedness groups (Hardyck, Petrinovich & Goldman, 1976; Heim & Watts,
1976; Kocel, 1977; Newcombe & Ratcliffe, 1973; Roberts & Engle,
1974, reported in Hicks & Kinsbourne, 1978). There is thus an inconsistency between the findings about left-handedness and intellectual
deficit which derive from the two different types of investigation.
Findings from samples from clinical populations are that left-handers
are in excess in retarded or learning-disabled groups, but population
studies of normal subjects find that left- and right-handers do not
differ in ability or achievement.

An intriguing hypothesis to explain this inconsistency was proposed
by Annett and Turner (1974). Using Annett's (1972) genetic model of
handedness, they suggested that left-handers comprise two different
populations. In one, left-handedness is associated with the 'absence of
a genetic determinant' (the Right Shift, RS, factor), which also means
that normal language development does not occur in the left cerebral

hemisphere, whereas in the other, neuropsychological development is normal. Annett excluded pathology from her hypothesis, regarding handedness as determined by chance but with different distributions in the two genetically different groups (RS− and RS+). The RS− group are more likely to be left-handed and retarded in language development and would predominate in clinical samples. Thus one might expect left-handers to be generally similar to right-handers in a normal population but over-represented among the lowest achievers and Annett and Turner's (1974) study provided support for this.

Attracted by this hypothesis, Hardyck (1977) undertook a reanalysis of his large (n = 7688) sample of primary school children. He reported his results as differences between the percentages of left- and right-handers in low ability groups. When 'below −1 SD' was used as the criterion, left-handers were in excess only seven times out of the 12 test × age group comparisons, and for 'below −2 SD', left-handers were in excess eight times out of ten. This appeared to support the Annett hypothesis. However, Hardyck also applied his analysis to high achievement groups and found some indication that left-handers were over-represented in these also, and suggested that Annett and Turner's data, and his own, were probably best explained as due to sampling error. However, more recently Geschwind (1983, Geschwind & Behan, 1982) has reported that correlates of left-handedness may include migraine, auto-immune disease and superior mathematical talent as well as dyslexia and other learning disorders and argued that the distribution of ability is dissimilar between right- and left-handers, with the latter possibly over-represented among the ablest groups for certain skills as well as among those with cognitive defect. An increased incidence of left-handedness has been found among maths teachers and tertiary maths students (Annett & Kilshaw, 1982) and among a group of extremely mathematically-talented students (Benbow & Benbow, 1984).

We report here analyses of data carried out for the purpose of testing Annett and Turner's (1974) hypothesis by seeing if a relationship between left-handedness and poor scholastic performance was present among low achievers to an extent not found in the general sample. Furthermore it was hoped that evidence pertaining to Geschwind's theory might also be obtained.

METHOD

The Australian Studies in School Performance (Keeves & Bourke, 1976) used criterion-referenced tests to assess basic numeracy and reading ability in large nationally representative samples of school children. The tests were developed to assess to what extent students in the normal educational system had adequate numeracy and reading skills. A stratified random sampling design was used to obtain 6628 10–year-olds and 6247 14–year-olds from all Australian states. Due to some incomplete data, our report is based on samples of 6494 (3267 boys and 3227 girls) and 5898 (2986 boys and 2912 girls) respectively. For each subject, the teacher who knew him or her best completed a questionnaire which included information on whether or not remedial help was needed in numeracy or reading, and on the student's handedness (right, RH or left, LH).

In the context of the ASSP project, subjects were said to have achieved mastery if 80% or more of the items were answered correctly. A low achieving group was identified in this study for each of the four age × test subgroups, as those whose scores were in the bottom 18 to 20% of the distribution. High achieving groups were also identified as those with all answers correct (10–year-old numeracy) or not more than one incorrect (the other three subgroups), these represented the top 5 to 10% of the distribution.

RESULTS

Data from boys and girls were treated separately as differences in laterality and in abilities may occur between the sexes; 8.7% of boys and 7.3% of girls were LH. Mean scores and standard deviations for numeracy and reading tests are shown in Table 7.1. Differences between RH and LH 10–year-olds' means were negligible, but for the 14–year-olds left-handers scored lower than right-handers. Only in the case of boys' reading, was the difference statistically significant, $t = 2.4$, $df = 2984$, $p < .01$, one-tailed, and in the other three, differences just failed to reach significance ($p < .10$ in each case). Differences in standard deviations were also analysed—these were similar for RH and LH 10–year-olds, but in three of the four comparisons of 14–year-olds' scores, the variance of left-handers exceeded that of right-handers ($p < .01$ in each case).

Students having problems were identified in two ways, either as not achieving mastery or in need of remedial help. On this basis left-handers were more likely to have problems; they were significantly in excess among 10–year-old boys and 14–year-old girls with problems of numeracy and among 14–year-olds with reading problems (Table 7.2). In Table 7.2, sixteen comparisons are made (sex × age × type of test × type of index) and although the differences are significant for

Table 7.1 Scores (mean ± s.d) of 10- and 14-year-olds on school performance tests by handedness (For whole sample: numbers given in text)

	Handedness	Girls		Boys	
		Numeracy	Reading	Numeracy	Reading
10y.o.	RH	26.6 ± 5.4	23.4 ± 4.2	26.5 ± 6.0	22.3 ± 4.8
	LH	26.4 ± 5.2	23.3 ± 4.4	26.4 ± 6.0	22.3 ± 5.0
14y.o.	RH	26.2 ± 5.4b	27.3 ± 4.0b	26.4 ± 5.8	27.0 ± 4.3a,b
	LH	25.5 ± 6.4	26.7 ± 4.7	25.8 ± 5.8	26.3 ± 4.9

a difference between means significant, $p < .05$
b difference between s.d. significant, $p < .01$

Table 7.2   Proportions of RH and LH students having problems with numeracy and reading

	Handedness	n	Numeracy		Reading	
			% lack mastery	% need remediation	% lack mastery	% need remediation
10y.o. girls	RH	2860–2957	25.2	19.6	40.7	14.7
	LH	262– 268	25.8	18.7	41.0	17.4
10y.o. boys	RH	2823–2925	26.6	23.0	50.8	26.3
	LH	325– 333	28.5	28.0*	50.9	27.2
14y.o. girls	RH	2559–2721	25.0	12.2	26.3*	9.6
	LH	171– 182	32.4*	15.0	33.1	14.0*
14y.o. boys	RH	2591–2770	24.3	18.6	28.1	21.2
	LH	198– 213	29.6	21.2	36.8**	25.5

* $p < .05$ ** $p < .01$

only five of these, in absolute terms there is a larger proportion of LH students than RH students having problems in 15 of the 16. Table 7.3 shows the proportions who lacked mastery in at least one of the two skill areas. Significantly fewer LH 14–year–olds were performing adequately on both numeracy and literacy than right-handers, though there was no such effect in 10–year–olds.

The proportions of left-handers in the low achieving groups are shown in Table 7.4. LH students are significantly over-represented in three cases, and there is a general tendency in this direction as the proportion of left-handers is greater seven times out of eight. When subgroups having perfect or near-perfect scores were analysed (Table 7.5), no significant differences were found and no general trend was apparent (there are more LH among high scorers five out of eight times).

DISCUSSION

Comparisons of RH and LH students within age × sex groups showed that left-handers were more often among those low in basic numeracy and reading ability. Not all differences were significant, but most pointed in the same direction. At age 10 differences were slight, but by 14 years a tendency for left-handers to score lower was apparent. Our data confirm, and may reconcile, the findings of Annett and Turner (1974) and Hardyck (1977). They support Annett's hypothesis that a sub-population of left-handers has an etiology different from most LH and associated with intellectual deficit. These people are mainly responsible for the relationship between left-handedness and mental defect, cognitive disability, etc. in clinical groups. In normal populations they are over-represented in low ability groups.

A new finding here is the significantly higher variance of LH score distributions of 14–year–olds. Excess left-handers at both the low and the high ends must balance out so that the LH means are not significantly lowered, despite the LH low scores. We interpret our data to imply that the distribution of ability in left-handers is not the same as in right-handers. Various pieces of evidence, reviewed by Bradshaw and Nettleton (1983) suggest that left-handers may excel on certain aspects of cognition. If, as is generally agreed, the organisation of cerebral function differs between RH and LH populations, then different patterns of abilities might be expected with LH superiority for some and RH superiority for others. Geschwind (1983) argued strongly that left-handers tend to be over-represented among both high and low achievers. This led Benbow and Benbow (1984) to investigate

Table 7.3 Students lacking mastery in either numeracy or reading

Age	Handedness	Girls				Boys			
		Total N	lack mastery n	%		Total N	lack n	mastery %	
10	RH	2949	1372	46.5		2922	1602	54.8	
	LH	267	124	46.4		332	182	54.8	
14	RH	2712	990	36.5**		2767	1006	36.4**	
	LH	181	85	47.0		212	96	45.3	

** $p < .01$

Table 7.4 Proportions of LH students in low scoring groups (lowest 20%) compared with remaining 80% of students

Age	Test	Girls				Boys			
		lowest 20%		others		lowest 20%		others	
		N	%LH	N	%LH	N	%LH	N	%LH
10'	Numeracy	566	8.1	2661	8.4	613	11.9	2654	9.8
	Reading	413	10.9	2814	8.0*	719	11.7	2548	9.8
14	Numeracy	567	7.9	2345	5.9	601	9.5	2383	6.5*
	Reading	558	7.3	2354	6.0	636	9.3	2350	6.6*

* $p < .05$

Table 7.5 Proportions of LH students in high scoring groups compared with remaining students

Age	Test	Girls				Boys			
		highest		others		highest		others	
		N	%LH	N	%LH	N	%LH	N	%LH
10	Numeracy	92	5.4	3135	8.4	185	12.4	3082	10.1
	Reading	287	10.1	2940	8.2	271	12.5	2996	10.0
14	Numeracy	251	8.3	2661	6.1	349	5.7	2637	7.3
	Reading	199	7.5	2713	6.2	176	6.3	2810	7.2

handedness in their samples of exceptionally mathematically talented youth, and they found twice the normal incidence of left-handers. Our data provide no clear support for this idea, but the tests used were not designed to select the most able students.

Relationships between ability and handedness occurred mostly in the 14-year-old data, suggesting that handedness effects appear around adolescence. Since girls mature earlier, these effects might be expected in 10-year-old girls rather than boys, but our data were equivocal in this regard, and the only comparable study (Calnan & Richardson, 1976) found no significant handedness × sex interaction in 11-year-olds. However Porac and Coren (1981) compiled the results of 29 studies and concluded that handedness and cognitive skills covaried in adults but not in children.

Theories such as Annett's and Geschwind's seek to relate the causes of left-handedness to the effects. Using ideas derived from these, we present an alternative framework. Environmental factors, such as cultural pressures against left-hand use, must be taken into account as well as genetic and pathological factors in the etiology of left-handedness. Furthermore these are not seen as mutually exclusive (Bradshaw & Nettleton, 1983; Tan, 1980), but as a first approximation we suggest that there are at least two general tyes of left-hander. For one, damage or abnormality of the left cerebral cortex is the link between a change of hand preference from the RH norm and language or other intellectual disability. Ability levels of this group extend into the normal range but tend to be lower overall. The other type is associated with a different organisation of cerebral function (not damage), and the underlying cause is probably genetic. Among this group the distribution of abilities differs from that typical of right-handers, and special mathematical, spatial, musical or other talents may occur. It is likely that left-handedness has advantages which are responsible for this condition with its probable genetic basis remaining in human populations at a frequency of approximately one in ten. A genetically determined condition would not remain at such a high frequency if it were deleterious. As the organisation of cerebral function and the effects of factors such as sex and maturational change which interact with handedness become better understood, further insights into these aspects of individual differences will become possible.

References

Annett, M. (1972). The distribution of manual asymmetry. *British Journal of Psychology, 63*, 343–58.

Annett, M. & Kilshaw, D. (1982). Mathematical ability and lateral asymmetry. *Cortex, 18,* 547–68.

Annett, M. & Turner, A. (1974). Laterality and the growth of intellectual abilities. *British Journal of Educational Psychology, 44,* 37–46.

Benbow, C. P. & Benbow, R. M. (in press). Biological correlates of high mathematical reasoning ability. In G. J. DeVries, J. P. C. DeBruin, H. M. B. Uylings & M. A. Corner (Eds), *Sex differences in the brain—The relation between structure and function. Progress in brain research.* Vol. 61.

Bradshaw, J. L. & Nettleton, N. C. (1983). *Human cerebral asymmetry.* Englewood Cliffs, NJ: Prentice-Hall.

Calnan, M. & Richardson, K. (1976). Developmental correlates of handedness in a national sample of 11-year-olds. *Annals of Human Biology, 3,* 329–42.

Geschwind, N. (1983). Biological associations of left-handedness. *Annals of Dyslexia, 33,* 29–40.

Geschwind, N. & Behan, P. (1982). Left-handedness: association with immune disease, migraine and developmental learning disorder. *Proceedings of the National Academy of Sciences, 79,* 5097–5100.

Hardyck, C. (1977). Laterality and intellectual ability: A just not noticeable difference? *British Journal of Educational Psychology, 47,* 305–11.

Hardyck, C. Petrinovich, L. F. & Goldman, R. D. (1976). Left-handedness and cognitive deficit. *Cortex, 12,* 266–79.

Heim, A. W. & Watts, K. P. (1976). Handedness and cognitive bias. *Quarterly Journal of Experimental Psychology, 28,* 355–60.

Hicks, R. E. & Kinsbourne, M. (1978). Handedness differences: human handedness. In M. Kinsbourne (Ed.), *Asymmetrical function of the brain.* New York: Cambridge University Press.

Keeves, J. P. & Bourke, S. F. (1976). *Australian studies in school performance. Vol. I. Literacy and numeracy in Australian schools: a first report.* Canberra: Australian Government Publishing Service.

Kocel, K. (1977). Cognitive abilities: handedness, familial sinistrality and sex. *Annals of the New York Academy of Science, 299,* 233–42.

Newcombe, F. & Ratcliff, G. G. (1973). Handedness, speech lateralisation and ability. *Neuropsychologia, 11,* 399–407.

Porac, C. & Coren, S. (1981). *Lateral Preferences and Human Behavior.* New York: Springer-Verlag.

Tan, L. E. (1980). Unpublished M. Ed. thesis, Monash University, Australia.

8

Adolescents' Organisational Strategies for Planning Errands

Simone Volet, Jeanette Lawrence and Agnes Dodds,
Murdoch University

Everyday, practical cognition is goal–directed and responsive to the changing elements of a task. Busy people must organise and plan their work to meet conflicting demands on time and effort. Recent studies have shown that professional adults use overall strategic plans to maximise efficiency and satisfaction, and to minimise effort (Dodds & Lawrence, 1983; Hayes-Roth & Hayes-Roth, 1979; Scribner, 1984). Yet little is known about adolescents' cognitive organisation and planning although their school and social activities seem to demand some coordination and juggling. We were interested in whether adolescents, like busy adults, plan, adapt and monitor their activities to meet task demands and opportunities.

Hayes-Roth and Hayes-Roth (1979) described the efficiency with which college subjects cognitively structured, prioritised and re-ordered a list of errands on a hypothetical town map. Effective planning activities in their protocol data could be identified as *a priori* metaplanning and on–the–job running repairs and adaptations.

Metaplanning constitutes the kind of early conceptual overview that produces efficient work, and identifies a person's prior analysis of a task, to select goals, strategies and criteria for developing and evaluating plans (Miller, Galanter & Pribram, 1960).

Yet prior cognitive organisation does not capture all the efficiency people display when they plan well. Operational, on–the–job planning occurs in response to task features and individualised cognitive reshuffling. The Hayes-Roths coined the term 'opportunistic planning', to describe intentional and effective moves that on surface reading appear like random, uncoordinated changes, but involve alternative plans.

Good planners alter goals and modify intentions when new possibilities arise in the flow of events or from their own flexible thinking.

Age-related differences in cognitive organisation reveal adolescents' failure to meet Polya's (1957) definitional and planning criteria for effective problem solving. Pitt (1983) found that 15-year-olds used inadequate and ineffective ways of defining task demands on formal operational problems. Ineffective planning and poor organisation contributed to processing errors. Half Meyer and Rebok's (1983) 13-year-olds generated incomplete plans for a simple card sort, compared with only a few adults. Some adolescents exhibited the kind of opportunistic, active planning that is effective in adults.

From such indications of the effectiveness of adults' prior and running organisation, and the ineffectiveness of younger subjects, we extended the Hayes-Roths' planning model to compare group performances on a similar errand planning task. We developed a coding system to identify planning moves in verbalisations of different groups.

Metaplanning, the most abstract planning activity, described subjects' overall approaches for organising and prioritising errands. Single errand planning involved organisation of individual errands concretely located in time and space, on the map and any work on a specific feature of an overall plan. Random execution signified no or minimal organisation, and identified subjects' erratic moves unrelated to any other moves or overall purposes.

While the Hayes-Roths saw opportunistic planning as an alternative to overall, prior planning, our scheme accounts for on-the-job plans which can either replace general overall plans, or be used in their service. For example a person may make an overall approach, but once into it, realise that the plan can be modified by chunking or re-organisation of its features. In a first study, we compared adolescents' with adults' spontaneous planning, then experimentally intervened to induce better planning in adolescents.

Study one

METHOD

Subjects were nine women undergraduates, and nine (two female, seven male) bright students from a Year Ten extension class (mean age, 15.1). They were told they had an 'afternoon off work' in Perth, with a map and a list of possible errands to complete within certain

Table 8.1   Percentage of women's and adolescents' planning propositions in four types

	Group	
	Women	Adolescents
Planning Proposition		
Overall Metaplanning	14	6
Opportunistic Planning	12	5
Contextual Planning	73	71
Random Execution	–	19
Total of Planning Propositions	341 = 100%	197 = 100%

time constraints, while thinking out loud. A scheme of four moves was used to code planning segments of the verbal data. Each segment of 18 transcribed protocols was coded with only one of eight original categories. Two independent judges coded 13 protocols with perfect interjudge agreement of 89% of 1082 codings, Cohen's kappa, k = .85 (Tinsley & Weiss, 1975).

RESULTS

Adolescents were less efficient and poorer in planning and adaptability than women, with only two completing the task successfully compared with eight women. Adolescents made 22 errors of omission or failure to meet constraints, while only one woman made one minor error.

Group plans were distributed differently over metaplans, opportunistic plans, single errands, and unplanned random moves, with about 70% of all moves as single errand plans, $\chi r^2 = 25.2$, $p < .01$, Friedman's two way analysis of variance. Fewer of adolescents' plans (6%) than women's (14%) were abstract metaplans, $z = 2.67$, $p < .01$, and fewer were opportunistic plans (5% 12%), $z = 2.33$, $p < .05$, (Ferguson, 1966). Unplanned, random moves were 19% of adolescents' statements but none of the women's.

There were qualitative differences in group metaplans and subsequent moves. Eight efficient women's metaplans were based either on time constraints or personal priorities. In contrast, only five adolescents expressed any plans that involved standing back from the task, and four of these only made plans for single errands so that each errand had to be re-planned. Hence they made more errors. Four other adolescents who made no plans, but worked randomly also made errors.

While flexible opportunistic plans of the women were triggered by their own cognitive simulations of the task and prior experiences, opportunistic plans of four adolescents were almost exclusively triggered by features of the task.

In summary, these bright youngsters made few over-all plans, and were inclined to meet each errand as an isolated task. It was difficult for them to organise their work or to make full use of the information given to them.

A second study was carried out to determine if adolescents would demonstrate planning under more favourable conditions. Errands were made more attractive and familiar, and task constraints more obvious. Subjects were given the chance to demonstrate organisation of the work in two trials under three experimental conditions.

Organisation and performance of adults and children have been raised under several conditions. Pitt's (1983) 15-year-olds performed better when forced to plan. Training in self-testing and management (Brown, Campione & Day, 1981), and Polya-type planning, monitoring and evaluation (Bash and Camp 1980; Washbourne, Lawrence & Kurzeja, 1985), has raised cognitive performance of normal, retarded and impulsive as well as college students.

If adolescents could show better organisation under prompts to make their best plan, or with opportunity to practice, then we would be less likely to accept the early 15-year-olds' planning deficiencies, and more confident about improving adolescents' natural cognitive organisation. In addition, we could observe if subjects demonstrated any natural planning and monitoring, and whether these moves affected performance.

Study two

METHOD

Subjects were all 29 students (mean age, 15.3) from a Year Ten class at a boys' high school, in central Fremantle. Boys were randomly divided into three planning conditions for two trials. Boys in a prompt and practice group were instructed to plan the afternoon's activities for the first trial, and prompted to do a 'best plan' on their second trial. Practice only subjects performed the task twice under the same standard instructions, and prompt only subjects were urged to do a best plan on the first trial, and then perform the second trial under standard instructions. The errand task was situated in the city of Fremantle, as shown in Figure 8.1.

Fig. 8.1 A Free Afternoon in Fremantle

You are given a free afternoon from school at 12 noon. Your school is in Ellen Street. You can plan to spend the rest of the day as you like in the Fremantle shopping area. However, as there is a bus strike, your father will pick you up at 4 pm sharp at the corner of Phillimore Street and Market Street, and take you home.

- You would like to call at a friend's place close to the Esplanade and have lunch with him at 12.30 pm.
- Your uncle is in Fremantle Hospital and you would like to visit him for half an hour.
- Your mother has asked you to pay the phone bill at Telecom or at the post office. Telecom is closed from 12 noon to 2 pm and the post office closes at 1.30 pm.
- You want to pick up your watch at the jeweller's in Market Street. It is open from 2.30 pm to 5.00 pm.
- You need information for a school project and can obtain it either at the Fremantle Museum which opens at 1.30 pm or at the Maritime Museum which closes at 1.30 pm.
- You would really like to have a few video games.
- There is a good film at Port Cinema, and you don't want to miss it. There are sessions starting at 1.30 pm, 3.00 pm and 4.30 pm.
- As well, you have been asked to post an urgent letter for a teacher.

Work on the city plan, using only the places and facilities marked on the map. Please think out loud what you are thinking or doing. Anything that comes into your mind is important.

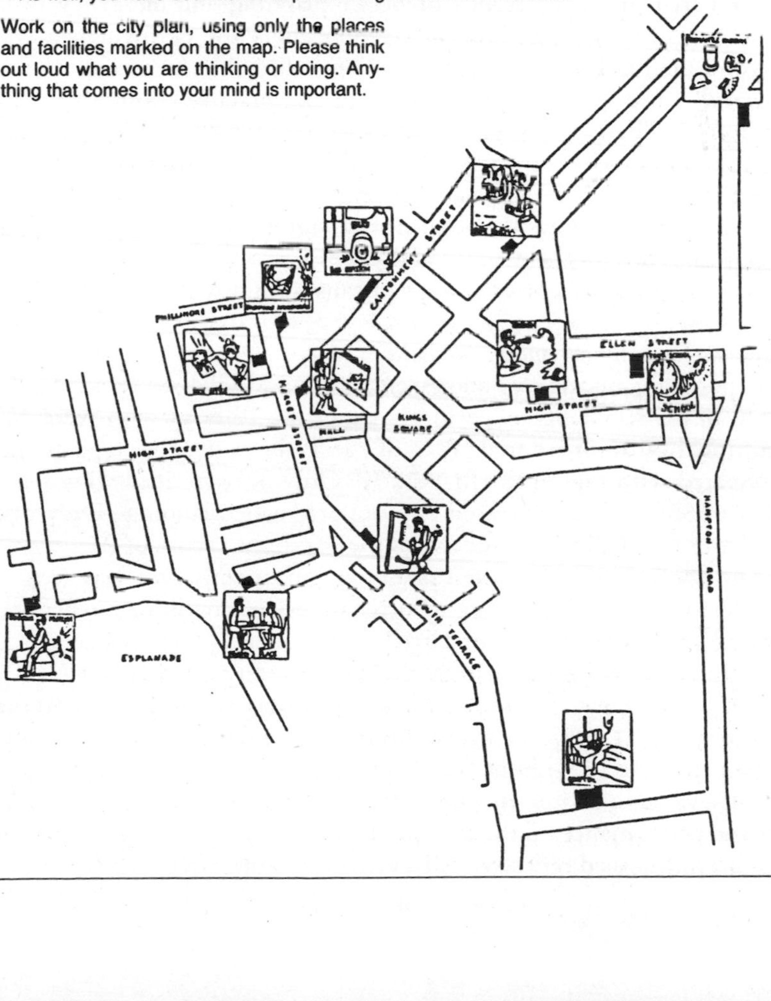

Verbalisations and experimenter observations yielded a maximum performance score of 22 on each trial, a metaplan score (0 to 2) and frequencies of all subjects using opportunistic plans on each trial and spontaneous evaluations at the end of trial one. Two judges independently coded eight protocols with 88% agreement.

RESULTS

Effect of prompt and practice

Efficiency could be raised under condition of prompt and practice, but not to perfect coverage of the errands. Boys did not demonstrate high levels of metaplanning or opportunistic planning under any experimental conditions. Yet prompt and practice conditions on the second trial produced trends of better planning and efficiency even with the small sample. The interaction effect for performance was beyond the .05 level, $F(1,26) = 3.81$, $p < .062$, but indicated a trend towards a stronger effect when prompt and practice conditions were combined. There was improvement on their own performance for the prompt and practice subjects $F(1,26) = 4.3$, $p < .05$, but no improvement for either of the single conditions. Trends in metaplanning were in a similar direction, although not at significance level. The mean metaplan score for the prompt and practice group improved from 0.7 to 0.9, while the other two groups' means went down from 0.6 to 0.2.

Spontaneous planning and performance

The poor organisation of adolescents in the original study was replicated in the spontaneous performance of the 19 boys who were not prompted on the first trial. Five of the 19 boys used metaplanning, compared with one in the first study. Only 37% in Study Two and 44% in Study One expressed any opportunistic planning. Only one boy completed all the errands with the maximum score of 22.

The effectiveness of natural planning and organisation was seen in the performance of ten boys who regardless of condition, expressed overall metaplans on the first trial. Their mean performance (18.3) was significantly higher than that of the 19 with no metaplans (16.1), $F(1,27) = 4.69$, $p < .05$. Opportunistic planning was expressed on the first trial by 11 subjects whose mean performance score (18.9) was higher than the 18 without (15.6), $F(1,27) = 14.41$, $p < .001$.

Self-evaluation after the first trial was the best indicator of improved performance on the second. Twelve subjects who regardless of condition, showed reflective self-evaluation work after their first trial, performed better on the second trial (mean score, 19.58) than the 17 who expressed no self-evaluation (mean, 17.58), $F(1,27) = 6.21$, $p < .05$. Nine out of 12 self-evaluators had expressed a metaplan on the first trial, compared with only one of 17 non self-evaluators, $\chi^2 = 14.86$, $p < .001$. On the second trial, eight self-evaluators expressed a metaplan, but no non self-evaluators. In addition, 67% of self-evaluators used opportunistic planning on both trials compared with 18% of the non self-evaluators, $\chi^2 = 7.2$, $p < .01$.

Further, of the seven worst performers on the first trial, four who spontaneously evaluated their work showed the highest improvement of all on the second trial, with a mean improvement score of 5.5 compared with 1.48 for the rest.

CONCLUSION

The task of organising an afternoon's errands allowed us to examine adolescents' spontaneous and induced planning on partially constrained problems. In two studies, adolescents did not perform well on errand-planning tasks, and very few displayed any organisational strategies. It was not easy to get adolescents to organise their cognitive work. It is possible that our urging to plan was not strong enough inducement to do better. When it did occur, spontaneous use of planning strategies was related to better performance.

The best indicator of improved performance was an adolescent's monitoring and checking of his own work. The effectiveness of students' self-evaluation is like Brown and Smiley's (1978) students' better processing when trained to use task-specific monitoring strategies. It would seem that we observed the kind of executive monitoring that Brown, Campione and Day (1980) argue is a mark of efficient cognitive organisation. Our trends also are in line with the Bash and Camp (1980) argument that performance improvements follow when children are trained in verbalised reflective monitoring.

Piaget's (1976) later writings give particular importance to the more mature thinker's ability to engage in conscious self-regulation. We are finding that university students who monitor their learning progress are better able than their peers to make up learning deficits. In a series of interviews with five women undergraduates the influence of cognitive organisation was observed. Three who planned and monitored study for an examination achieved better results than the two who were unable to reflect and manage their cognitive organisation and academic performance (Volet, 1985).

Since most of young people's tasks are done on the spot, without a great deal of training in strategic management, our data need to be extended to see if the lack of natural disposition to plan and monitor pervades other problem situations. Perhaps in everyday tasks, like school work and home chores, youngsters call up sets of pre-packaged plans or strategies which save the effort of generating specific plans (Goodnow, in press). Perhaps the strong influence of personal goals is the key to understanding good planning in young subjects. Educational and family interventions in youngsters' lives may not be conducive to the development of personal goals and self-management. We are exploring ways to observe adolescents' and adults' plans and self-regulation on constrained tasks like learning to use a computer, and school-related tasks like working on projects. We need to discover the kinds of personal, social and environmental constraints under which efficient cognitive organisation is exhibited by busy young people.

References

Bash, M. A. S., & Camp, B. W. (1980). Teacher training in the think aloud classroom program. In G. Cartledge & J. F. Milburn (Eds), *Teaching social skills to children: Innovative approaches*, (pp., 143–78). Oxford: Pergamon Press.

Brown, A. L., Campione, J., & Day, J. (1980). Learning to learn: On training students to learn from text. *Educational Researcher, 10*(2), 14–21.

Brown, A. L., & Smiley, S. S. (1978). The development of strategies for studying texts. *Child Development, 49*, 1076–1088.

Dodds, A. E., & Lawrence, J. A. (1983). Heuristics for planning university study at a distance. *Distance Education, 4*(1), 40–52.

Ferguson, G. A. (1966). *Statistical analysis in psychology and education.* New York: McGraw-Hill.

Goodnow, J. J. (in preparation). Some everyday forms of intelligent behavior: Organising and reorganising. To appear in R. Sternberg & R. Wagner (Eds), *Practical intelligence: Origins of competence in the everyday world.*

Hayes-Roth, B., & Hayes-Roth, F. A. (1979). A cognitive model of planning. *Cognitive Science, 3*, 275–310.

Meyer, J. S., & Rebok, G. W. (1983). *Acting to plan and planning to act in children's problem solving.* Paper presented at the 1983 Biennial Meeting of the Society for Research in Child Development, Detroit.

Miller, G. A., Galanter, E., & Pribram, K. H. (1960). *Plans and the structure of behaviour.* New York: Holt, Rinehart & Winston.

Piaget, J. (1976). *The grasp of consciousness.* Cambridge, Mass: Harvard University Press.

Pitt, R. B. (1983). Development of a general problem-solving schema in adolescence and early adulthood. *Journal of Experimental Psychology: General, 112*(4), 547–84.

Polya, G. (1957). *How to solve it*. Princeton, NJ: Princeton U. Press.

Scribner, S. (1984). Cognitive studies of work. *The Quarterly Newsletter of the Laboratory of Comparative Human Cognition, 6*(1 & 2), whole number.

Tinsley, H. E., & Weiss, D. J. (1975). Interrater reliability and agreement of subjective judgments. *Journal of Counselling Psychology, 22*, 4.

Volet, S. E. (1985). *Profiles of five university students' studying processes*. Unpublished manuscript, Murdoch University.

Washbourne, M., Lawrence, J. A. & Kurzeja, D. (1985). *Adult mediated-training of problem-solving skills in children*. Murdoch University.

SECTION 2
LANGUAGE AND READING
DEVELOPMENT

Research on language development has traditionally been concerned with phonological, syntactic, and semantic development in preschool aged children. In recent years, however, attention has begun to be focused on language development in somewhat older children. Example topics include children's increasing ability to reflect on the structural features of language and to comprehend figurative uses of language. A related development is the increasing tendency of researchers to view reading as a derived skill that builds upon spoken language. This has resulted in a greater emphasis being placed on exploring possible relationships between different aspects of language development and learning to read.

The five chapters in this section reflect these current trends in child language research. The first two chapters are concerned with the development of children's understanding that speakers in certain situations intend their utterances to be interpreted in a nonliteral manner. The remaining three chapters focus on interrelationships between growth in language and literacy acquisition.

In their chapter on children's comprehension of metaphor, Wales and Coffey present the results of a study in which children ranging from 6 to 9 years of age were asked to interpret metaphors, similes, and noun pairs. In addition to the expected developmental trends, the results indicate that figurative expressions which related attributes within the same domain are easier to interpret than expressions relating attributes from different domains. Moreover, comprehension of metaphors and similes is facilitated by substitutions of their verbs by verbs that increase the salience of 'necessary' attributes.

Working within the framework of Ackerman's two-stage process model of children's comprehension of irony, Chan and Cole describe a study they conducted to determine whether verbal cues and cartoons would assist children in comprehending the meaning of ironic utterances. Children in grades 1 and 3 were asked to interpret short stories that varied in the relation between the contextual and utterance information provided in the story, and in whether the story was presented with a cartoon that illustrated the contextual information in the story. Results indicate that while pictorial cues facilitated the comprehension of irony, verbal cues do not seem to help children interpret ironic utterances.

Tunmer and Nesdale investigate the nature of the relationship between phonemic segmentation skill and learning to read. First grade children were administered tests of verbal intelligence, phonemic segmentation ability, and reading achievement. The results of their study indicate that the relation of phonemic segmentation ability to accuracy of naming pseudowords (a measure of phonological recoding) is non-linear; that phonemic segmentation tests that include digraph words may provide inaccurate estimates of phonemic segmentation ability; and that phonemic segmentation ability affects reading comprehension indirectly through phonological recoding.

In her chapter on syntactic processing in children varying in reading skill profile, Bowey presents the results of a study which aimed to determine whether impairments in oral language syntactic processing were associated with reading comprehension difficulties. On the basis of initial screening tests, fourth-grade children were each assigned to one of four groups that varied in the level of, and relative balance between, decoding and comprehension skills. Results indicate that performance on each of two tests of oral language syntactic processing is associated with the level of reading skill achievement, rather than with the relative balance of decoding and comprehension skills.

To discover whether twins are characterised by the same pattern of reading difficulties as are singletons, Hay, Collet, Johnston, O'Brien and Prior compare the reading profiles of twins and singletons who failed to achieve mastery of literacy. The most significant finding of the study is that 14-year-old twin boys were differentiated from singletons by a much higher incidence of speech problems and reading reversals, as well as by some difficulties with social behaviour in the classroom. These differences are explained in terms of lateralisation and concentration problems specific to twins.

WILLIAM E. TUNMER

9

On Children's Comprehension of Metaphor

Roger Wales and Guy Coffey
University of Melbourne

The set of approaches to metaphor is large in number and include among linguistic notions that metaphor is a consequence of the relaxation of selection restrictions (Katz, 1972), or involves the transfer of semantic features from one item to another (Levin, 1977). Among psychological studies the dominant emphasis has been on general cognitive rather than specifically linguistic issues, although Matic and Wales (1982) have established that syntactic variables such as word class (noun vs verb) and word position fundamentally influence the interpretation of novel metaphors as do more general cognitive pragmatic issues such as the relative concreteness of the item. Within the general cognitive approaches there are two dominant ones: the 'Comparison theory' and the 'Interaction theory'. The Aristotelian view that metaphors are implicit comparisons has been developed recently by a number of writers (e.g., Kintsch, 1974; Miller, 1981). A metaphor of the form 'A is a B' (where A is the 'topic' and B the 'vehicle') is, Miller says, 'a comparison with the parts left out' (p. 226) and is comprehended by a process of paraphrasing the metaphor as a comparison statement. The 'ground' (the meaningful relationship between the topic and vehicle), is said to be found by discovering which features the topic and vehicle share. This theory, while appealing in its simplicity, has been trenchantly criticised. The comparison theory's critics (e.g., Ortony, 1979, 1981; Tourangeau & Sternberg, 1981, 1982; Verbrugge & McCarell, 1977) dispute that the topic and vehicle must necessarily be related on the basis of shared features; they suggest the matched features are more often similar (literally or non-literally) than identical and that sometimes feature matching does not occur at

81

all, rather the vehicle introduces an attribute to the topic. Furthermore, it is pointed out that since any entities or ideas share, at a high level of abstraction, some common characteristic, the comparison theory does not explicate why some topic/vehicle pairs produce metaphors and others anomaly, nor does it tell us why some shared features are irrelevant to the reading of a metaphor. The comparison theory also does not account for metaphors' asymmetry (A is a B = B is an A) and leaves their ability to reveal unsuspected semantic and conceptual relations unexplained. Two recent developmental studies of children's comprehension of metaphor, Billow (1975) and Cometa and Eson (1978), adopted the comparison theory as their conceptual framework and consequently operationalised its flaws. These studies found positive correlations between classificatory ability and metaphor comprehension, but as the theoretical meaningfulness of this relation is based on the untenable 'shared feature' assumption, probably all that was shown was that both these skills increased with age.

The theoretical models of metaphor provided by Ortony (1979, 1982) and Tourangeau and Sternberg (1981, 1982) sought to redress some of the comparison theory's shortcomings. Ortony does not dispute that the process of making comparisons is of fundamental importance to comprehending metaphors, but contends that the nature of the similarities thus drawn differs from likenesses established by comparisons involving literal language use, as in a statement of literal similarity. Ortony says that while interpretation of literal similarity statements involves finding shared highly salient predicates of the terms compared, interpretation of intra-sentential metaphors and similes of the form 'A is (like) a B' entails either matching, on the basis of similarity (not necessarily identity), a highly salient attribute of the vehicle with a low salience attribute of the topic, or introducing a salient attribute of the vehicle to the topic. Ortony operationally defined 'salience' as the 'subjects estimates of the prominence of a particular attribute with respect to a concept to which it does or could apply' (p. 162). As the matching or transference of attributes often occurs across ontologically distinct domains or realms of experience (e.g., the percepts of the different sense modalities, or physical versus psychological phenomena), the matched attributes may themselves be metaphorically related and the transferred attribute transformed before its application to the topic. According to Ortony, there are two principal sources of metaphoricity: firstly it is derived from the salience imbalance of matching attributes (relatively high salience attribute of vehicle, low salience for topic,) second, is the domain incongruence of the topic and vehicle. Tourangeau and Sternberg's 'interaction model' also emphasises the importance of the non-literality of the similarities between the topic and vehicle. The interpretation of metaphors, they claim, involves construing a belief system in the topic's domain which corresponds to certain of the vehicle's salient attributes and the structural relationships between these attributes. They suggest that there is no single basis for finding attribute or structural correspondences—it may entail discovering relations between features applicable to both domains (e.g., dual function terms), or the mapping of attributes of the topic and vehicle onto a common abstract dimension, or a variety of other processes. Studies with adults by Tourangeau and Sternberg (1981) and Verbrugge and McCarrell (1977) provide some support for the interaction model.

Both Ortony and Tourangeau and Sternberg's theories contend that relating features across incongruent domains is an important aspect of interpreting metaphor. Few developmental studies of metaphor comprehension, however, have investigated the effect of domain incongruence on the comprehensibility of metaphors, or whether young children's apparent difficulties in interpreting metaphors in any way reflect an inability or a disinclination to relate features across domains. A study by Winner, Rosensticl and Gardner (1976) did take the domain relation between the topic and vehicle into account, but did not manipulate this variable in a manner which would reveal its role in comprehension. Winner et al. investigated the ability of 6- to 14-year-old children to comprehend psychological-physical metaphors (which relate a psychological experience to a physical event) as compared with cross-sensory metaphors (which synaesthetically relate an experience in one sensory modality to another sensory modality). This study found that comprehension of metaphors became prevalent at about 10 years of age, and that understanding was more frequent for cross-sensory than psychological-physical items amongst 7-, 8- and 10-year-olds but not amongst the youngest or oldest children. The predominant forms of response given by the 6- to 8-year-olds related the topic and vehicle by contiguity, or by focusing on incidental aspects of the topic to which the vehicle's attributes could be literally applied, thus avoiding across domain transfer. This developmental progression of metaphor comprehension displays a roughly similar pattern to other comparable studies (e.g., Billow, 1975, Cometa & Eson, 1978, Pollio & Pollio, 1979) although the proportion of metaphoric responses at each age varies considerably between studies; such disparities are no doubt partly due to differences in the semantic and syntactic structure of the items each study presented for interpretation. These disparities should warn us against searching for a reified 'metaphoric ability' which is distinct from normal linguistic and cognitive processing, and which is generalised across metaphors' multifarious forms. With this admonition in mind, the present study sought, firstly, to isolate some of the sources of difficulty young children have in comprehending metaphor, and secondly, to investigate the developmental progression of their understandings and misunderstandings of metaphor.

In an attempt to define clearly the parameters of the metaphors provided for interpretation, the present study controlled those linguistic and cognitive variables which theory or empirical research suggest are likely to affect metaphor's comprehensibility. In the first phase of our study syntactic structure, and the domain relations between the topic and vehicle, were systematically varied. Other variables, such as linguistic context, the directiveness of the verb (e.g., *is* vs *is like* vs *moves like*, etc.), the presence or absence of adjectival modification, the concreteness of topic and vehicle, the amount of factual information needed for interpretation, and the metaphor's frequency of usage in adult speech, were held as constant as possible. Children aged from 6 to 9 years were asked to interpret items of the syntactic forms '*A is a B*', '*A is like B*' and the word pair '*A–B*', where all *A*s and *B*s are nouns typically understood by 6-year-olds, and all *B*s are concrete. The domain relations between *A*s and *B*s were of three forms: physical domain–physical domain (i.e., topic and vehicle possess attributes in the same domain, and perceptual and/or functional attributes of both terms are related), psychological–physical, and cross-sensory. The domain relations were varied in an attempt to assess whether metaphor comprehension difficulties stem from difficulties in perceiving nonliteral similarities across domains. In our study the 'same-domain' items' topic shares or can receive perceptual and/or functional attributes of the vehicles without alteration of these attributes; i.e., the vehicle's attributes can be applied directly to the topic. For example, in the same-domain metaphor, 'the river is a snake' we can transfer a predicate of snake, 'long and winding' and apply it without transformation to the topic, 'the river', whereas in the cross-domain (psychological–physical) metaphor, 'her happiness is a kite', the kite's characteristic of 'soaring high' etc. cannot be literally ascribed to happiness.

Experiment 1

METHOD

Subjects

The subjects consisted of 42 children, half of whom were of mean age 6.11, range 6.0–7.10 and half of mean age 8.9, range 8.0–9.7. Selection was random with the qualification that the children were all native speakers of English.

Design

A 2 × 3 × 2 repeated measures design was used with one between subject variable (age) and two within subject variables (figurative type and domain type). The design was chosen as it possesses the advantage that subjects serve as their own control on the within subject variables (Winer, 1971) and because a completely randomised factorial design would have required many more subjects. The two within subject variables were nested, meaning that at each level of figurative type there were two levels of domain type. The experimental items were formulated from a pool of 40 topic–vehicle pairs consisting of 20 same-domain noun pairs and 20 cross-domain pairs (10 psychological-physical and 10 cross-sensory). These noun pairs were randomly assigned to one level of figurative type so that each had an equal probability of being converted into a metaphor, a simile, or of remaining a noun pair. Each subject received 40 items. The item generation procedure was carried out separately for each subject so that, across subjects, a given topic–vehicle was not tied to any one level of figurative type. As it was possible that the order of presentation of the sets of metaphors, similes and noun pairs would affect how each was interpreted, a Latin square design was adopted, to counterbalance for order effects (Winer, 1971) and to allow any effect of them to be detected.

Instructions to the children

These are detailed below, since in such tasks so much can depend on how the task demands are communicated. [For noun pairs the instructions in square brackets replaced those which are italicised.] The interviewer said:—

'I'm interested in how children understand words. We're going to play a game with words. *I'll read you a sentence and then I want you to say what you think it could mean.*

[I'll say two words and I want you to think about both of them

together, and then say what they could mean.] Just say what you think of even if it sounds a bit funny. For example what do you think—'*the grass is (like) a carpet*' could mean?' [grass and carpet]
Non-directive prompts were given, such as—
'Is there anything else it could mean?'
Then the interviewer said—
'Now we'll just think about "carpet". If I didn't know what "carpet" is, what could you tell me about it?'
The same question was then asked about grass, then—
'If you remember what you said "carpet" can mean and also what "grass" can mean, then what do you think—
"*the grass is (like) a carpet*" means?' [grass and carpet].
The procedure was repeated for a second example—
'*The man is a lamp post*' [man and lamp post].

The reasons for asking the subjects to separately 'define' the topic and vehicle in the examples were twofold. Firstly it was a task the children could confidently perform. Secondly, it probably helped orient the children toward thinking about words' various denotations.

Scoring
The tape recordings of the sessions were transcribed and each subject's 40 responses were scored. Responses were scored 'metaphoric' or 'non-metaphoric' according to whether the form of the relationship established between the vehicle and topic was consistent with that which adults establish in their metaphoric interpretations. The emphasis, therefore, was on the formal qualities of the interpretation rather than its content; a child's interpretation of a metaphor may differ in content from adults' responses. For example, an adult may be more likely to interpret 'the thought is like fairyfloss' as meaning that the thought is light and nebulous than 'the thought is yummy ... a really beautiful thought'.

Results

The mean number of metaphoric responses to same-domain and cross-domain items for each age group (by subjects and collapsed across figurative type) is presented in Table 9.1.

From the F-Ratios of the subject and item analyses of variance min F was calculated (Clark, 1973) and was found to be significant both for the domain type effect, $min\ F(1,66) = 26.54$, $p < .01$ and for the age effect, $min\ F(1,49) = 25.12$, $p < .01$, but the interaction effect did not

Table 9.1   Mean number of metaphoric responses across domain type and age

Age	Same-Domain	Cross-Domain
6–7 Years	6.24	1.52 (.95)
8–9 Years	13.67	6.67 (1.57)

Note—Maximum possible score = 20

reach significance, *min* $F(1,70) = 2.32$, $p > .1$. Scheffé's comparisons showed that the effect of domain type was significant at both the younger and older age levels, $F(1,40) = 5.36$, $p < .01$ and $F(1,40) = 7.95$, $p < .01$ respectively, and the effect of age significant at both the same and cross-domain levels, $F(1,40) = 8.44$, $p < .01$ and $F(1,40) = 5.85$, $p < .01$ respectively.

The distribution of means across figurative type (collapsed across domain type) is shown in Table 9.2.

A 3 (figurative type) × 2 (age) ANOVA found that the effects of figurative type and age were significant, $F(2,80) = 10.23$, $p < .001$ and $F(1,40) = 25.58$, $p < .001$ respectively. There was no figurative type × age interaction effect. Scheffé's comparisons indicate that the younger age group's mean for similes, but not metaphors, was significantly greater than the noun-pair's mean, $F(2,60) = 2.68$, $p < .05$, and that for the older group both the metaphor and simile's means were significantly greater than the noun-pair's mean, $F(2,60) = 3.48$, $p < .01$, and $F(2,60) = 3.38$, $p < .01$ respectively. There was, however, no significant difference between metaphors and similes at the younger age level, $F(2,60) = 1.29$, $p > .1$, or the older level. At each level of figurative type the difference in means across age was significant at the .01 level. The figurative type × age interaction was not significant.

The overall developmental pattern exhibited—a marked increase in the frequency of metaphoric interpretations between the ages of 6 and 9—is consistent with the results of other developmental studies of figurative language comprehension (Billow, 1975; Cometa & Eson, 1978; Winner et al., 1976; Winner et al., 1980). Children of 6 and 7 years of age comprehended on average 32.9% of same-domain metaphors and 1.9% of cross-domain metaphors as compared with 68.6% and 32.6% respectively for the 8- and 9-year-olds. The results for cross-domain items tally with Winner et al.'s (1976) finding that 5% of 6-year-olds' responses to cross-domain metaphors and

Table 9.2   **Means and standard deviations of metaphoric responses across figurative type and age**

Age		Metaphor	Simile	Noun-Pair
6–7	$\bar{X}$	3.90	5.14	2.57
years	SD	2.58	3.98	2.97
8–9	$\bar{X}$	11.05	10.95	7.71
years	SD	5.21	5.40	5.90

Note—Maximum possible score = 20
    Scores doubled as each subject received twice as many metaphors as similes and noun-pairs.

48% of 10-year-olds' responses were metaphoric, and thereby further highlight the relative comprehensibility of the same-domain metaphors. The pronounced domain type effect suggests that children, especially the younger ones, had difficulty in finding cross-domain correspondences or were not orientated toward doing so. The second phase of our study was designed to explore these possibilities further.

Although domain type had an overriding effect on sentential item comprehensibility, analysis of items indicated that, even with domain relation held constant, there was considerable variation in rates of metaphoric responding across sentential items. It is evident from our data that two of the same-domain sentential items with the four highest rates of metaphoric responding and all four of the lowest rating items were common across age. The correlation between each same-domain sentential item's rate of metaphoric responding across age was moderately high, $r = .76$. (Calculation of this correlation for cross-domain items was prevented by floor effects on 6- to 7-year-olds' scores).

Viewed *in toto*, the results do not easily accord with a linear, stage theory of 'metaphoric understanding'. It is apparent that the frequency of metaphoric interpretations was contingent on the domain type of the metaphor. It is also clear that 'metaphoric understanding' was not something 'possessed' by the older children and absent in the younger children; the developmental trends are better characterised by saying that the older children were more often capable of, or orientated towards, successfully applying strategies which led to metaphoric interpretations. The dilemma now unfurled is that of why subjects successfully employed strategies which led to metaphoric interpretations for some metaphors but not for others. Experiment 2 addressed this issue.

Experiment 2

Method

Subjects

Sixteen children, ten 6- and 7-year-olds (mean age, 6.11), and six 8- and 9-year-olds (mean age, 8.3), all of whom were subjects in Experiment 1, participated in all three tasks of Experiment 2. Subjects were selected on the basis that they had interpreted at least five same-domain metaphors and similes metaphorically and at least five non-metaphorically in Experiment 1.

Design

Experiment 2 was divided into three tasks. The first task investigated the subjects' knowledge representations of the vehicles of metaphors and similes they interpreted in Experiment 1. If, as Ortony (1979) argued, a metaphoric ground is formed by drawing a highly salient attribute from the vehicle, then it is reasonable to infer that comprehension of a metaphor is conditional upon, or at least expedited by, the interpreter possessing a representation of the vehicle's schema in which the attribute relevant to interpretation is salient. In Task 1 the salient attributes of vehicles from metaphors and similes of Experiment 1 were elicited by free association. Within subject comparisons were made between the saliently represented attributes of vehicles from same-domain sentential items interpreted metaphorically (Veh. (SD.M)) and non-metaphorically (Veh. (SD.N)). It was expected that Veh. (SD.M), significantly more often than Veh. (SD.N), would represent as salient the attribute necessary to form a metaphoric interpretation of the item from which they were drawn (from hereon this attribute is designated as the 'necessary attribute').

Results

Salient attributes of vehicles from cross-domain metaphors interpreted non-metaphorically (Veh. (CD.N)) were also elicited to clarify the reasons for the domain effect of Experiment 1. It is possible that this effect, which we have hitherto suggested was a consequence of difficulties in grasping cross-domain correspondences, was at least partially caused by non-salient representations of the cross-domain items' necessary attributes. The mean number of salient necessary attributes for Veh. (SD.N) fell below the mean for both Veh. (SD.M)

Table 9.3   The mean number of vehicles with salient necessary attributes for each vehicle type

Veh. (SD.M)	Veh. (SD.N)	Veh. (CD.N)
3.75	1.69	3.00

Note—Maximum possible score = 5

and Veh. (CD.N) as shown in Table 9.3. Most necessary attributes of Veh. (SD.M) and Veh. (CD.N) were represented as salient and most necessary attributes of Veh. (SD.N) were non-salient.

Wilcoxon T Tests found that salience scores of Veh. (SD.M) and Veh. (CD.N) were significantly greater than for Veh. (SD.N), $T(16) = 0$, $p < .005$, and $T(16) = 8.0$, $p < .005$ respectively, and that scores for Veh. (SD.M) were significantly greater than for Veh. (CD.N), $T(16) = 17.0$, $p < .005$. This illustrates that the distribution of salience scores for Veh. (SD.M) was above that of Veh. (CD.N)'s distribution which was above Veh. (SD.N)'s distribution. If the elicitation tasks provided a valid measure of attribute salience, then the results suggest that subjects more frequently interpreted same-domain metaphors and similes metaphorically when the necessary attribute was subjectively represented as a salient feature of the vehicle than when it was 'non-salient'.

Task 1's results offer some clues as to why same-domain items of Experiment 1 were found to vary considerably in their comprehensibility; this variation was probably at least partly due to differences across these items in subjects' representations of necessary attributes' salience level. The results do not, however, afford such an 'explanation' of variation in cross-domain item comprehensibility as salience level did not predict frequency of metaphoric responding for these items.

Task 2 of Experiment 2 further investigated the domain type effect by isolating one aspect of the process of comprehending cross-domain metaphors. It is presumably a necessary antecedent condition for the comprehension of (novel) cross-domain metaphors that the interpreter is aware that there are semantic correspondences between the different sense-modalities and realms of experience.

In Task 2 subjects were required, as in Gardner's (1974) study, to choose which adjective of a pair of polar adjectives corresponds to an element in another domain, but unlike that study the element was verbally rather than perceptually presented—the task involved answering orally presented questions, e.g., 'Is a bright colour loud or quiet?' (for the metaphor 'the red is a shout'). All questions invoked domain relations which were implicated in the interpretations of one of the cross-domain metaphors of Experiment 1. If subjects exhibited an ability to correctly answer questions with domain relations equivalent to cross domain metaphors and similes these children had responded to non-metaphorically, then their non-metaphoric interpretations cannot be attributed to lack of awareness of inter-domain relationships. The children were asked to provide reasons for their answers to determine whether an ability to form cross-domain relations precedes a metalinguistic awareness of these relations.

The mean number of correct answers to the 10 domain-relation questions was 8.56 and the scores ranged from six to 10. A sign test indicated that scores were significantly above the chance level (p < .001). This level of correct responding held for 6- to 7-year-olds alone: the mean was 8.60. Children had difficulties, however, justifying their choices; 'explanations' for their answers either paraphrased their answer, expanded on one term of the answer or related the domain correspondence to a concrete event in which the questions' terms are correlated.

The high rate at which the subjects were able to correctly answer the domain relation questions, all of which corresponded to metaphors or similes they answered non-metaphorically, indicates that difficulties in comprehending cross-domain metaphors were not simply due to the subjects' inability to discern cross-domain correspondences. Furthermore, such an inability is not a factor which discriminates the younger from the older subjects, and therefore was not responsible for their differing frequencies of metaphoric interpretations. These results, coupled with those of Task 1 which showed that the difficulty with cross-domain items cannot be wholly ascribed to the saliency of the necessary attributes, lead to the conclusion that children frequently failed to metaphorically interpret cross domain metaphors and similes even when they represented the necessary attribute as a salient feature of the vehicle, and when they were capable of apprehending the domain correspondences which these expressions establish.

Task 3 investigated whether metaphoric interpretations are facilitated by promoting the salience of the relevant attributes of the vehicle. Ortony (1979) has suggested that verbs which specify the dimension on which the metaphoric relation is formed, foreground the necessary attribute. Following Ortony's proposal the necessary attributes of metaphors and similes of Experiment 1 were promoted by replacing the verb 'to be' with a more 'directive' verb, that is, a verb which specified a particular sensory modality or function (e.g., to look, to sound, to act), thus 'the butterfly is a rainbow' becomes 'the butterfly looks like a rainbow'. (Notice that to be grammatically well formed the translation must include 'like', an alteration which in itself should not affect comprehensibility as means for metaphors and similes did not differ in Experiment 1). Subjects were given the 'directive verb' form of sentential items which they gave non-metaphoric interpretations to in Experiment 1. It was expected that the number of metaphoric responses would be significantly greater for directive verb items than for a control group of untranslated items.

Each subject's set of five metaphors and similes from which their Veh. (SD.N) of Task 1 were drawn, was translated into 'directive verb similes'. The verb supplanting 'to be' was 'to look', 'to sound', 'to feel', 'to move' or 'to act', according to whether the ground was within respectively the visual, auditory or haptic domains, or described movement in physical space or functional characteristics. Each subject interpreted the set of five directive verb similes, derived from their Veh. (SD.N), plus 'control group' items comprising any same-domain metaphors or similes answered non-metaphorically in Experiment 1 other than those which had been translated. Although the control group variable was rather crude, it did provide a rough estimate of whether the subjects' performance on Experiment 1's items had improved over time, and how much an improvement in the level of comprehension of directive verb similes, relative to the original items, could be attributed to the directive verb itself.

Directive verb similes received a mean of 2.31 metaphoric responses. Therefore nearly half (46.3%) of these items which, in their original form in Experiment 1 were interpreted non-metaphorically, were responded to metaphorically. The control group items received 25% metaphorical interpretation. A sign test on the proportion of the control and experimental group scores bordered on significance ($p < .06$). Considering the small numbers of subjects involved the result can be taken as indicative of a strong trend towards the directive verb transformation facilitating comprehension, although such a claim needs to be checked by further work.

GENERAL CONCLUSIONS

The results of both experiments can now be collated. At each level of age and figurative type, the mean number of metaphoric responses was higher for same-domain items than for cross-domain items. Further experimentation found that metaphoric responding to same-domain sentential items tended to coincide with the necessary attributes being represented as salient in the vehicle's schema and non-metaphoric responding with their non-salient representation. In contrast, the vehicles of cross-domain sentential items which were non-metaphorically interpreted had necessary attribute representation predominantly at a high salience level. These findings supported the notion that the accessibility of the necessary attribute importantly influences the comprehensibility of same-domain metaphors and similes, while suggesting that difficulties in comprehending cross-domain items cannot be attributed to this factor.

The high level of correct responding to the domain-relation questions (Task 2) indicated that, if the domain type effect was primarily due to difficulties in discerning cross-domain correspondences, then the basis of these difficulties was not an incognisance of how attributes are related across domains. Given this result, and the finding that for most of the non-metaphorically interpreted cross-domain sentential items sampled the necessary attribute was represented as salient, two reasons for cross-domain items' low mean were postulated. These reasons were that subjects were possibly not orientated toward establishing cross-domain correspondences, or not consistently able to co-ordinate the interpretative process of looking for cross-domain relations and searching for attributes which can participate in these relations.

References

Billow, R. M. (1975). A cognitive developmental study of metaphor comprehension. *Developmental Psychology, 11*, 415–423.

Clark, H. H. (1973). The language-as-a-fixed-effect fallacy: A critique of language statistics in psychological research. *Journal of Verbal Learning and Verbal Behavior, 12*, 335–59.

Cometa, M. S. & Eson, M. E. (1978). Logical operations and metaphor interpretation: A Piagetian model. *Child Development, 49*, 649–59.

Davidson, D. (1979). What metaphors mean. In S. Sacks (Ed.), *On metaphor*. Chicago: University of Chicago Press.

Gardner, H. (1974). Metaphors and modalities: How children project polar adjectives onto diverse domains. *Child Development, 45*, 84–91.

Katz, J. J. (1972). *Semantic theory*. New York: Harper & Row.

Kintsch, W. (1974). *The representation of meaning in memory*. Hillsdale, N. J., Erlbaum.

Levin, S. R. (1977). *The semantics of metaphor*. Baltimore, Md., John Hopkins University Press.

Malgady, R. G. (1977). Children's interpretation and appreciation of similes. *Child Development, 48*.

Malgady, R. G. & Johnson, M. G. (1976). Modifiers in metaphors: Effects of constituent phrase similarity on the interpretation of figurative sentences. *Journal of Psycholinguistic Research, 5*, 43–52.

Matic, M. & Wales, R. J. (1982). Creating interpretations for novel metaphors. *Language and Communication, 2*.

Miller, G. A. (1981). Images and models, similes and metaphors. In A. Ortony (Ed.), *Metaphor and thought*. Cambridge: Cambridge University Press.

Ortony, A. (1979). Beyond literal similarity. *Psychological Review, 3*, 161–180.

Ortony, A., Reynolds, R. E. & Arter, J. A. (1978). Metaphor: Theoretical and empirical research. *Psychological Bulletin, 85*, 919–43.

Paivo, A. (1981). Psychological processes in the comprehension of metaphor. In A. Ortony (Ed.), *Metaphor and thought*. Cambridge: Cambridge University Press.

Pollio, M. R. & Pollio, H. R. (1979). A test of metaphoric comprehension and some preliminary developmental data. *Journal of Child Language, 6*, 111–20.

Tourangeau, R. & Sternberg, R. J. (1981). Aptness in metaphor. *Cognitive Psychology, 13*, 27–55.

Tourangeau, R. & Sternberg, R. J. (1982). Understanding and appreciating metaphors. *Cognition, 11*, 203–44.

Verbrugge, R. R. & McCarrell, N. S. (1977). Metaphoric comprehension: studies in reminding and resembling. *Cognitive Psychology, 9*, 494–533.

Winer, B. J. (1971). *Statistical principles in experimental design*. New York: McGraw-Hill.

Winner, E., Rosenstiel, A. & Gardner, H. (1976). The development of metaphoric understanding. *Developmental Psychology, 12*, 289–97.

Winner, E., Engel, M. & Gardner, H. (1980). Misunderstanding metaphor. What's the problem? *Journal of Experimental Child Psychology, 30*, 22–32.

10

Children's Understanding of Ironic Utterances

Lorna K. S. Chan and Peter G. Cole
The University of Western Australia

Most models of language acquisition deal with naturally occurring direct speech acts and rarely contain constructs which explain how children come to understand ironic utterances. Explanations of these nonliteral locutions are neglected in models of language acquisition because standard rules of representational, referential and associative meaning do not apply in such cases. Comprehension of ironic utterances requires that standard semantic rules be reversed or reordered and higher order mental operations be used to gain access to appropriate meanings.

Research indicates that children do comprehend some forms of irony even at an early age (Ackerman, 1983). Not only do most young children come to understand simple irony, but they use it appropriately in everyday communication. They play verbal jokes on one another, use sarcasm, exaggeration, understatement, overstatement and deliberate ambiguity for their particular purposes. They employ these rhetorical forms of language in order to convey ironic meaning (Kaufer, 1981).

Irony is often cited as an example of an indirect speech act. Irony can be grouped with metaphor, insinuation and other indirect forms into a class of acts that use variant or non-standard semantic rules for interpretation. In such contexts 'the speaker's utterance meaning and the sentence meaning came apart in various ways' (Searle, 1975, p. 59). This disparity of utterance meaning and sentence meaning cannot be resolved by simple transformation rules. The meaning does not always lie, for example, in the opposite of the literal interpretation, or in an assertion that does not confirm the literal interpretation (Searle,

1975) because numerous locutions that employ understatement or overstatement point to the inadequacy of such contrivances. The understanding of irony lies beyond such simple transformation rules.

One of the most persuasive interpretations of irony can be found in the work of Kaufer (1981). According to Kaufer, irony is the use of an evaluative communicative mode that acts to redirect the listener away from literal and descriptive analysis. Kaufer suggests that the user of irony makes an evaluative argument that violates contextual expectations with the intention of persuading the listener that the evaluative argument has been deliberately misapplied. The listener is thereby persuaded to accept the view that the literal interpretation is false and that some other evaluation or judgement must be inferred from context. The clarity of the speaker's irony depends upon the appropriate juxtaposition of contrastive elements and the speaker's understanding of his listener's knowledge of this rhetorical form of language in the particular context. The listener's comprehension depends on his knowledge of the speaker's intentions and his understanding of the stylistic form of ironic utterances.

Ackerman (1982, 1983) has proposed a model of children's comprehension of ironic utterances. In Ackerman's view, in order to interpret an ironic utterance, a listener has to compare the utterance and context, note the contradiction and infer that the speaker is aware of the contradiction and intends the utterance to be interpreted in a nonliteral manner. Then the listener has to reinterpret and make an inference about the intended meaning of the utterance. Ackerman has identified two separate sequential stages in children's interpretation of irony. The first relates to the detection of contradiction or conflict in contextual expectation. The second refers to the inference of appropriate meaning based on recognition of the contradiction or conflict.

There is little doubt that certain contextual conditions and speaker cues facilitate children's comprehension of irony. Contextual discrepancy and intonation typically have an effect on understanding of this form of discussion (Ackerman, 1983). It is also true that contextual discrepancy and stressed intonation affect the processes of detection and inference of irony in different ways. The purpose of the present study was to explore relationships among such variables and extend the study of children's understanding of indirect speech acts that has been initiated by Ackerman. In particular, we sought to determine if verbal cues and cartoons would assist children to comprehend the meaning of ironic utterances.

METHOD

Subjects

Forty children participated in this experiment. Ten boys and ten girls were randomly selected from each of the first and third grades at a primary school in Perth, Western Australia. The mean age of the first graders was 6.0 years while that of the third graders was 8.2 years. None of the children had any known physical or intellectual handicaps.

Design

This experiment employed a 2 (Grade: First and Third) × 2 (Mode of Presentation: Verbal Only and Verbal-Pictorial) × 3 (Context Relation: Literal, Nonliteral, Explicit Nonliteral) mixed factorial design. The last factor was a within-subjects factor.

Materials

Nineteen paragraph frames of two sentences each were constructed, each containing a short narration of an incident. The first sentence denoted the setting and context of an incident and the second contained a statement that included an utterance. Eighteen of the paragraph frames were used in the experiment. One additional frame was used for pretraining. Examples of these paragraph frames are presented in Table 10.1.

Two versions of the first sentence were written for each paragraph frame. For the first version the contextual information provided in the first sentence was consistent with the utterance information in the second sentence. In the other version, the contextual information provided in the first sentence contradicted the literal interpretation of the utterance in the second sentence. Hence the utterances in the second sentence of the paragraph frames could be interpreted in either a literal or nonliteral (ironic) manner, depending upon the particular context variation.

Further, two versions of the second sentence were constructed for each paragraph frame. The two versions differed in the inclusion or exclusion of a modifier aimed to make the speaker's ironic intent more or less explicit. Six modifiers were used, each repeated three times (see examples in Table 10.1).

Combining these different versions of the first and second sentences, three sets of stories were produced from the eighteen paragraph

Table 10.1 Sample stories and questions

Story 1

John was sitting on the floor, (covered in porridge)[a] (with a new T-shirt on).[b] His father said to him (in a joking way),[c] 'My word, you look beautiful today!'

Questions

1 Did John look beautiful? (fact question)
2 Did the father think John looked (beautiful)/(terrible)?[d] (speaker attitude question)

Story 2

The children were waiting to go into the classroom (but had not lined up)[a] (all lined up in a straight line).[b] Their teacher (teased them and)[c] said, 'My, what a lovely straight line you have made.'

Questions

1 Was the line straight? (fact question)
2 Was the teacher (pleased)/(not pleased)[d] with the children? (speaker attitude question)

---

[a] nonliteral context
[b] literal context
[c] modifier
[d] alternate forms of the question

frames. In the literal set, each paragraph was made up of a combination of the context variation which was consistent with the utterance information in the second sentence, not including modifiers. The nonliteral set consisted of paragraphs combining the context variation that contradicted the literal meaning of the utterance with that version of the second sentence in which modifiers were excluded. The paragraphs in the explicit nonliteral set were the same as the nonliteral stories but included as well a modifier in the utterance sentence to highlight the speaker's ironic intent in using the utterance.

In addition to context relation, the mode of presentation of these stories was also manipulated. For each paragraph frame, two cartoons were prepared, each illustrating a different version of the first sentence. The cartoons were used to highlight the contextual information. A total of 36 cartoons was produced.

Two 'yes–no' questions were devised for each paragraph frame, one being a fact question and the other a speaker attitude question. The fact question asked whether the literal information in the utterance was true or not. These questions were essentially paraphrases of the utterances, put in an interrogative form. The correct answers for these questions were always 'yes' for the literal stories and 'no' for the nonliteral ones. The speaker attitude questions asked about the propositional intention or attitude the speaker wanted to communicate in making the utterance and thus, in the case of the nonliteral stories, addressed the ironic intent of the speaker in using the utterance. Two forms of the speaker attitude question were written for each paragraph frame such that one necessitated a 'yes' and the other a 'no' answer.

Six lists of stories were created for use in the experiment. There were six literal, six nonliteral and six explicit nonliteral stories in each list. Context type was counterbalanced across the lists. Each story was matched with the appropriate form of the speaker attitude question such that the numbers of *yes* and *no* answers were balanced for each of the three kinds of stories. These procedures were adopted to ensure that the correct answers to the fact and speaker attitude questions differed on at least half the occasions. The order of presentation of the eighteen stories in each list and the order of asking the two questions in each story were randomised across subjects.

Procedure

Subjects in each grade level were randomly assigned to each of the two modes of presentation conditions and randomly allocated one of the six lists of stories and questions. All subjects were tested individually and were all given the pretraining story (a literal version) as an illustration of the procedure. In the verbal mode condition subjects were read the 18 stories and at the end of each story they answered the two questions orally. In the verbal–pictorial mode condition subjects were shown the associated cartoon while the story was read to them. The spoken answers were recorded.

RESULTS

Preliminary analyses indicated no significant differences in the mean scores for the six lists of stories, so the list factor was not included in any subsequent analysis.

The data were analysed using two separate $2 \times 2 \times 3$ repeated measures analyses of variance, one on the number of correct responses to the fact questions and the other on the number of correct responses to the speaker attitude questions. Both analyses were conducted on the computer programme MULTIVARIANCE (Finn, 1972). The means and standard deviations of the two dependent measures obtained in the various conditions for the two groups of subjects are depicted in Table 10.2.

Table 10.2 Means and standard deviations of scores on the two types of questions for grade, mode of presentation and context relation

Mode of Presentation		Fact Questions			Speaker Attitude Questions		
		Literal	Explicit Non-literal	Non-literal	Literal	Explicit Non-literal	Non-literal
Grade One							
Verbal Only	$\bar{x}$	5.6	4.3	4.3	4.9	3.9	3.3
	SD	0.52	1.64	1.49	1.29	0.99	1.64
Verbal-Pictorial	$\bar{x}$	5.6	5.2	5.7	5.3	3.9	4.7
	SD	0.52	1.03	0.48	0.82	1.20	1.06
Grade Three							
Verbal Only	$\bar{x}$	5.3	4.6	4.1	4.9	3.2	3.0
	SD	0.82	1.26	1.29	1.10	1.99	2.00
Verbal-Pictorial	$\bar{x}$	5.7	5.5	4.9	4.7	5.1	4.0
	SD	0.67	0.71	1.10	1.16	0.99	0.94

Fact questions

Both the interactions of context relation with mode of presentation and context relation with grade attained significance. The significant Mode of Presentation × Context Relation interaction was concentrated in the contrast between the literal and combined nonliteral stories, $F(1, 36) = 4.45$, $p < .05$. Examination of the means revealed that children in the verbal only presentation condition were less able to give correct responses to the fact questions in both types of nonliteral contexts than in the literal ones, whereas children in the verbal-pictorial presentation condition demonstrated similar levels of competence in all three types of contexts. Clearly, the pictures were effective in helping the children to reject the literal interpretation of the utterances. The interaction of grade with the nonliteral versus explicit nonliteral contrast was also significant, $F(1,36) = 4.64$, $p < .04$. Results indicated that the Grade 3 subjects performed better than the first graders on the explicit nonliteral stories, but the reverse was true for the nonliteral stories. There was no significant grade level main effect. Both the mode of presentation and context relation main effects were significant, $F(1,36) = 10.34$, $p < .01$ and $F(2,35) = 7.16$, $p < .01$, respectively, but these are more appropriately interpreted as conditional effects (Finn, 1974).

Speaker Attitude Questions

The analysis revealed a significant Grade × Mode of Presentation × Context Relation interaction. This significant second-order interaction was concentrated in the nonliteral versus explicit nonliteral contrast, $F(1,36) = 6.06$, $p < .02$, but not in the literal versus combined nonliteral comparison. Examination of the means revealed that regardless of grade level, subjects in the verbal only presentation condition gave fewer correct responses in the two types of nonliteral contexts than in the literal contexts. In the verbal-pictorial presentation condition, however, the facilitative effect of the cartoons was observed for both the nonliteral and explicit nonliteral stories among the third graders but only for the nonliteral stories among the first graders. The grade level main effect failed to attain significance. Both the mode of presentation and context relation main effects were significant, $F(1,36) = 9.87$, $p < .01$ and $F(2,35) = 6.44$, $p < .01$, respectively, but the significant three-way interaction necessitated interpretation of the effects of the three factors as conditional on one another and not as independent average effects (Finn, 1974).

DISCUSSION

The present experiment was modelled on Ackerman's two-stage process that distinguishes between detection and inference. The fact questions focused on detection of a contradiction between the contextual information and the literal interpretation of the utterance information. The speaker attitude questions, on the other hand, focused on interpretation of the speaker's intent in making the utterance. Overall, children in the present experiment were less capable with inference than with detection, as indicated by the fewer correct responses to the speaker attitude questions relative to the fact questions, across all conditions.

Both first and third graders were less competent in interpreting ironic utterances relative to their performance in the literal contexts. This is evident in the significant literal versus combined nonliteral contrast on both the fact and speaker attitude questions. There were fewer correct responses to the two types of questions for the nonliteral and explicit nonliteral stories than for the literal stories. This finding is consistent with Ackerman's conclusions and can be explained as the result of children's relative unfamiliarity with ironic solution possibilities when confronted with a contradiction between contextual and utterance information.

The present study also examined the effects of pictorial cues and verbal cues on children's comprehension of ironic utterances. The use of cartoons helped the children to make correct rejections of the literal interpretation of the utterance information in the two nonliteral contexts. When the stories were orally read to the children without the aid of cartoons, fewer correct responses to the fact questions were observed in the two nonliteral contexts than in the literal context. However the use of cartoons in addition to the verbal presentation was found effective in increasing the number of correct responses in the nonliteral contexts to a level similar to that observed for the literal stories. The cartoons illustrated the contextual information and hence made the incongruence of the utterance information with the contextual information more apparent.

The cartoons and the verbal cues (modifiers) used in the present study were expected to serve different purposes. The cartoons provided illustrations of the contextual information and in the case of the nonliteral contexts served to make the incongruence of the contextual and utterance information more apparent. In such cases the cartoons facilitate judgement about the inappropriateness of the literal interpretation of the utterance information, that is, cartoons were predicted to assist the detection process. Further, detection of inconsistency between contextual and utterance information seemed a necessary precedent to appropriate inference of the speaker's ironic intent. Hence the cartoons were expected to affect indirectly the inference process as well. On the other hand, the verbal cues aimed to make explicit the speaker's intent to be ironic and hence were expected to highlight the ironic function of the utterance. These modifiers were thus assumed to provide powerful cues only for the inference process.

These assumptions have been partially supported by the present findings. The mode of presentation main effect on both types of questions provided evidence for the facilitative effects of the cartoons on both the detection and inference processes. The pictorial presentations facilitated detection of the disparity and hence directed the children's attention to making appropriate inferences regarding the speaker's intent. The effects of the verbal cues were tested through the contrast between nonliteral and explicit nonliteral contexts. This particular contrast failed to attain significance on both types of questions. The results tend to suggest that the verbal cues by themselves, in general, would not help interpretation of irony, probably because of their lack of effect on the detection process which was considered a necessary precedent to the inference process. This conclusion is consistent with Ackerman's (1983) model for children's comprehension of nonliteral function which proposes that detection may precede and is necessary but not sufficient for inference.

Verbal cues used in conjunction with cartoons had differential effects on the first and third grade children, as indicated in the significant Grade × Mode of Presentation × nonliteral versus explicit nonliteral contrast interaction on the speaker attitude questions. It was indicated earlier that the verbal cues by themselves were not sufficient to aid comprehension of irony. However, the third grade children in the present study benefited from the verbal cues used in conjuction with cartoons. This was demonstrated by the third graders who made more appropriate inferences of the speaker's ironic intent in the explicit nonliteral contexts relative to the nonliteral contexts in the verbal-pictorial presentation condition. On the other hand, the first grade children in the present study made less effective use of such verbal cues. The first graders in the verbal–pictorial presentation condition made more correct inferences of the speaker's ironic intent than those in the verbal only condition for the nonliteral stories, but such was not the case for the explicit nonliteral stories. It seems likely that for first grade children, the inclusion of modifiers in addition to the use of illustrations could have interfered with information processing. Optimal processing of information amongst first graders may require less complex forms of emphasis, perhaps supplied solely by a pictorial mode. Rohwer and Harris (1975) have also observed that fourth-grade children receiving simultaneous presentation of oral, printed and pictorial information performed less well in prose learning than those receiving only oral plus pictorial information. The first grade children in Ackerman's (1983) study were also observed to have made relatively little use of stressed intonation, which was assumed to affect only the inference process.

An unexpected finding was the lack of significant mean differences between the first and third grade children on both fact and speaker attitude questions. It seems likely that the questions were not sensitive to developmental differences in children's understanding of oral language. Further studies are required to test for age differences in children's comprehension of ironic utterances.

References

Ackerman, B. P. (1982). Contextual integration and utterance interpretation: The ability of children and adults to interpret sarcastic utterances. *Child Development, 53*, 1075–83.

Ackerman, B. P. (1983). Form and function in children's understanding of ironic utterances. *Journal of Experimental Child Psychology, 35*, 487–508.

Finn, J. D. (1974). *A general method for mutlivariate analysis.* New York: Holt, Rinehart & Winston.

Finn, J. D. (1972). *MULTIVARIANCE: Univariate and multivariate analysis of variance, covariance and regression.* Ann Arbor: National Educational Resources.

Kaufer, D. S. (1981). Understanding ironic communication. *Journal of Pragmatics, 5*, 495–510.

Rohwer, W. D., Jr, & Harris, W. J. (1975). Media effects on prose learning in two populations of children. *Journal of Educational Psychology, 67*, 651–7.

Searle, J. R. (1975). Indirect speech acts. In P. Cole & J. Morgan (Eds), *Syntax and Semantics, Vol. 3: Speech Acts.* New York: Academic Press.

11

Phonological Awareness and Learning to Read

William E. Tunmer and Andrew R. Nesdale
The University of Western Australia

Several studies involving a wide variety of tasks and procedures have examined the development of young children's ability to segment spoken words into their constituent phonemic elements (see Nesdale, Herriman & Tunmer, 1984, for a review of research). Much of this research has been stimulated by the possibility that children's awareness of the phonemes which constitute spoken words may be an important prerequisite for being able to learn to read. Some researchers even go so far as to suggest that lack of phonological awareness may be the most important barrier to reading acquisition yet discovered (Gough & Hillinger, 1980). In support of this claim, predictive correlations have been reported between measures of phonological awareness obtained before reading instruction began and later reading achievement. Recently reported training studies provide further support for the view that phonological awareness is causally related to learning to read (e.g., Bradley & Bryant, 1983). While it is becoming increasingly clear that phonological awareness plays a critical role in helping the child to become a skilled reader, the exact relation of this skill to reading remains to be specified. A major aim of the present study was to attempt to determine more precisely the nature of this relation.

Recent research by Gough, Juel, and Roper-Schneider (1983) suggests that in the first stage of reading acquisition children rely primarily on a strategy in which new words are learned by sight. However, beginning readers must eventually come to realise that there are systematic correspondences between the elements of spoken and written language to identify words not seen before and to begin to attain levels of practice that make fluent reading possible. It has been argued that phonological recoding, or the application of grapheme-phoneme correspondence rules, acts as a self-teaching mechanism which enables the child to develop automaticity and speed in recognizing words visually (Jorm & Share, 1983). Speed at the word recognition level is essential for comprehending text, since if word recognition is slow and capacity-draining, it will adversely affect the integration of text into larger, more meaningful 'chunks' of information. Evidence in support of this claim comes from studies which show that speed and accuracy of naming pseudowords, a commonly used measure of phonological recording ability, is one of the tasks that most clearly differentiates good from poor comprehenders of text (e.g., Perfetti & Hogaboam, 1975).

Two predictions stem from these considerations. First, since the beginning reader must figure out what phonemes go with what graphemes to acquire phonological recoding ability, a *nonlinear* relationship between phonological awareness, the ability to recognise phonemic elements, and phonological recoding (as measured by accuracy of pronouncing pseudowords) would be expected. That is, if phonemic segmentation ability is a necessary (but not sufficient) condition for acquiring the grapheme-phoneme correspondences, one would expect to find children who are phonologically aware, but who cannot read pseudowords; but not find children who are not phonologically aware but who *can* read pseudowords. Secondly, if the effects of phonological awareness on reading acquisition are mediated by phonological recoding skill, the relationship between phonemic segmentation and pseudoword naming should be stronger than that between phonemic segmentation and reading comprehension, since pseudoword naming requires both phonemic segmentation ability and knowledge of the grapheme-phoneme correspondence rules, whereas reading comprehension involves, in addition, text level processes such as comprehension monitoring.

Another issue explored in the present study concerns the relationship between the development of phonological awareness and reading instruction. There are at least two possibilities, the first being that reading instruction greatly influences the development of phonological awareness and the second, that phonological awareness develops largely independently of reading instruction, possibly being closely related to other aspects of cognitive and/or linguistic development. The first view predicts that type of reading instruction (e.g., code-emphasis vs. meaning-emphasis) should produce differences in the development of phonological awareness, whereas the second view does not.

One task that has been used to assess phonological awareness in children is the phoneme tapping task developed by Liberman, Shankweiler, Fischer, and Carter (1974). In this task the child is asked to segment spoken words of up to three phonemes in length. A possible difficulty associated with a test of this sort, however, is that for beginning readers it may confound the segmentation of phonemes with the segmentation of graphemes. The child may tap out the number of letters in a familiar word rather than the number of phonemes. This would result in 'overshoot' errors on words which contain digraphs, or letter pairs which represent single phonemes (e.g., *sh, th, ch, oa, oo*). For example, the child would incorrectly tap four times for a word like *book*, instead of three.

To examine this possibility, Tunmer and Nesdale (1982) developed a phoneme tapping task which was composed equally of real words and pronounceable pseudowords with half of the words in each category containing digraphs (e.g., *with, man, gith, zan*). The results obtained from administering this test to a sample of kindergarten and first grade children indicated that a large proportion of the first graders showed a much greater tendency to overshoot on both the real and pseudowords containing digraphs. It appeared that these beginning readers used their developing knowledge of the grapheme-phoneme correspondence rules to generate a graphemic representation of the word, and then tapped out the graphemes rather than the phonemes. That is, they relied on a 'spelling' strategy in performing the task. On the basis of these findings, Tunmer and Nesdale concluded that phonemic segmentation tests of the type used by Liberman et al. might provide inaccurate estimates of phonological awareness if they included digraph words. In view of the research which has linked phonological awareness to early success in reading acquisition, a prediction that follows from this suggestion is that tests of phonological awareness comprising nondigraph words should be more strongly associated with reading achievement than those comprising digraph words.

A related prediction is that poor decoders (i.e., those beginning readers who have yet to master the grapheme-phoneme correspondence rules, as reflected in their performance on a pseudoword naming task) should perform better on familiar nondigraph real words than on nondigraph pseudowords. This hypothesis is based on the assumption

that the poor decoders include students who also lack phonemic segmentation ability, and that these latter students, who are still in the
stage of recognizing words as arbitrary sequences of letters, will resort
to a 'grapheme' strategy when responding to familiar real words, tapping once for each letter in a given word, but will be unable to apply
this strategy to unfamiliar pseudowords. Word type should therefore
interact with decoding ability.

METHOD

Subjects

Sixty-three first grade children participated in the study. They were
obtained from six classes, two in each of three Primary Schools
located within the same school region of Perth, Western Australia.
The testing occurred during the third term of the school year.

Tests

The students were administered tests of verbal intelligence, phonemic
segmentation ability, and reading achievement. Form A of the Peabody Picture Vocabulary Test was used to provide an estimate of each
child's verbal intelligence. Standard scoring procedures were used.

The phonemic segmentation test was similar to the one devised by
Tunmer and Nesdale (1982). However, a different set of test items was
generated in an effort to determine the generalisability of the pattern of
results observed in the earlier study. Scoring was based on the
number of items tapped correctly.

The students were also individually administered three subtests of
the Interactive Reading Assessment System (Calfee & Calfee, 1981).
These were real word decoding, pseudoword decoding, and reading
comprehension. The scoring procedures used are described in Hoover
(1983).

Upon completion of the testing, the six classroom teachers were
individually administered a structured interview to obtain information
about their reading programmes. The interviews, which were supplemented by informal classroom observations, focused on instructional strategy but also sought information about classroom organisation, instructional style, feedback pattern, and response pattern. While
there were little or no differences in the last four factors, there were
striking differences in instructional strategy. Three of the teachers employed the so-called 'psycholinguistic' approach to teaching reading,
providing no incidental or formal instruction in phonological recod-

Table 11.1   Mean number of correct responses as a function of word type and digraph type

	Word Type	
Digraph Type	Real	Pseudo
Nondigraph	4.98	4.52
Digraph	3.54	4.00

ing skills. This approach reflects the view that the amount of knowledge of grapheme-phoneme correspondence rules required by the reader is extremely small. The reading methodologies of the three remaining teachers could best be described as 'eclectic', since each used a combination of different methodologies, including a heavy emphasis on the teaching of decoding skills.

RESULTS AND DISCUSSION

The mean numbers of correct responses to the four types of word included in the phonemic segmentation test are presented in Table 11.1.

A Word Type × Digraph Type analysis of variance revealed a significant main effect for Digraph Type, $F(1,62) = 30.03$, $p < .001$, and a significant Word Type × Digraph Type interaction, $F(1,62) = 23.22$, $p < .001$. This pattern of results is consistent with the suggestions that, first, some children who have begun to master the grapheme-phoneme correspondence rules may resort to a spelling strategy, which would lead to overshoot errors on both types of digraph words, while, second, other children who lack phonemic segmentation ability but read words by sight may employ a grapheme strategy, which would result in differences in performance between the two types of familiar real words but not the pseudowords.

In support of the first suggestion was the finding that of the total number of errors made on digraph words, 58.4% were overshoot errors, as compared to 31.2% on nondigraph words. In support of the second suggestion was the finding that when the students were divided into poor and good decoders according to their scores on the pseudoword decoding test, the poor decoders performed better on the nondigraph real words than on nondigraph pseudowords, while the good decoders were able to segment both types of word (see Table 11.2). A Decoding Ability × Word Type analysis of variance revealed significant main effects for Word Type, $F(1,43) = 22.72$, $p < .01$, and

Table 11.2   Mean numbers of correct responses as a function of decoding ability and word type

Decoding Ability	Word Type	
	Real nondigraph	Pseudo Nondigraph
Poor	4.14	3.43
Good	5.82	5.76

Decoding Ability, $F(1,43) = 7.42$, $p < .01$, and a significant Decoding Ability × Word Type interaction, $F(1,43) = 5.33$, $p < .05$.

Table 11.3 displays the intercorrelations, means, and standard deviations of all of the tests administered to the students, as well as age of student and method of reading instruction used by the teacher (i.e., decoding emphasis vs. nondecoding emphasis). As predicted, nondigraph word segmentation was more strongly correlated with each of the subtests of reading achievement than segmentation of digraph words, the latter correlations not even reaching significance. This suggests that phonemic segmentation tests that include digraph words may provide inaccurate estimates of phonological awareness. It is important to note that, while the correlation between nondigraph word segmentation and pseudoword decoding was highly significant, the magnitude of the correlation may have considerably underestimated the strength of the relationship, since the distributions of the two sets of scores were skewed in the opposite directions (nondigraph word segmentation skewness = −1.28, pseudoword decoding skewness = 1.55).

A scatterplot showing the relationship between nondigraph word segmentation and pseudoword decoding revealed the expected non-linear pattern. Using cut-off scores of 15 for the decoding test and 12 for the phonemic segmentation test, a contingency analysis of the data revealed that of the 22 students who passed the decoding test, all passed the segmentation test, whereas, of the 24 students who failed the segmentation test, none passed the decoding test. This suggests that phonological awareness is a necessary, but not sufficient condition for decoding, since there were no students who performed poorly on phonemic segmentation but well on decoding. For those students who scored well on phonemic segmentation, but poorly on decoding, it appears that their difficulty was in not having fully mastered the grapheme-phoneme correspondence rules.

To investigate further the pattern of correlations among the vari-

Table 11.3 Intercorrelations, means, and standard deviations of all variables

Variables	1	2	3	4	5	6	7	8
1. PPVT		-.06	-.07	.11	.27*	.25*	.28*	.26*
2. Age			-.08	.17	.19	.10	.12	.09
3. Digraph Word Segmentation				.55**	.07	-.08	.03	.01
4. Nondigraph Word Segmentation					.61**	.49**	.48**	.21
5. Real Word Decoding						.88**	.89**	.47**
6. Pseudoword Decoding							.83**	.41**
7. Reading Comprehension								.45**
8. Method of Instruction								—
Mean	101.4	74.5	8.5	11.3	25.9	18.8	1.16	—
Standard Deviation	10.7	3.5	3.3	3.2	22.3	24.7	1.14	—

* $p < .05$
** $p < .01$

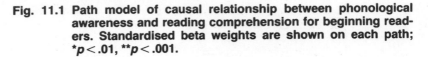

Fig. 11.1 Path model of causal relationship between phonological awareness and reading comprehension for beginning readers. Standardised beta weights are shown on each path; *p < .01, **p < .001.

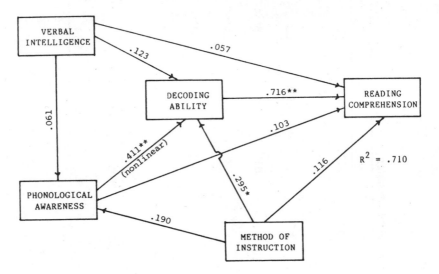

ables, a path analysis was conducted with verbal intelligence, non-digraph word segmentation, and teaching method considered as exogenous variables, and pseudoword decoding and reading comprehension as endogenous variables. Figure 11.1 presents the model with standardised beta weights shown on each path. As predicted, phonological awareness influences reading comprehension indirectly through its influence on decoding. This appears to be true for teaching method as well. Methods of instruction that emphasise decoding skills are more effective in promoting the development of comprehension ability during the early stages of reading acquisition than those that do not. Consistent with this finding is research by Bradley and Bryant (1983) which showed that of four training groups of prereaders matched for age, verbal intelligence, and phonological awareness, the group that received training in both phonological awareness *and* decoding skills showed the greatest gains in reading achievement.

A finding of particular significance is that, while all correlations between the various measures of reading achievement and method of instruction were highly significant, the correlation between method of instruction and phonemic segmentation ability did not reach signifi-

Table 11.4   Tests of significance of differences between means of all variables by method of instruction

Variables	Decoding Emphasis Group Mean (N=38)	Nondecoding Emphasis Group Mean (N=25)	t(df=61)	p
PPVT	103.7	98.0	2.13	$<.05$
Age	74.3	74.9	.72	n.s.
Real Word Decoding	34.3	13.1	4.11	$<.01$
Pseudoword Decoding	27.0	6.4	3.54	$<.01$
Reading Comprehension	1.6	.5	3.91	$<.01$
Phonemic Segmentation	11.8	10.5	1.65	n.s.

cance. Table 11.4 presents tests of significant differences between the means of all relevant variables for the two instructional approaches. The results seem to indicate that reading instruction does not greatly influence the development of phonological awareness *per se*. Given the importance that phonological awareness has for success in learning to read, this finding suggests the need for instruction that is specifically designed to increase the phonemic segmentation ability of those students who are developmentally delayed in this ability.

In summary, there were four major findings from the study. These were (1) that the relationship between phonological awareness and decoding skills is nonlinear; that is, phonological awareness is a necessary but not sufficient condition for the acquisition of phonological recoding ability; (2) that phonemic segmentation tests that include digraph words may provide inaccurate estimates of phonological awareness; (3) that phonological awareness affects comprehension proficiency indirectly through phonological recoding; and (4) that phonological awareness is not greatly affected by reading instruction.

References

Bradley, L. & Bryant, P. E. (1983). Categorizing sounds and learning to read—a causal connection. *Nature, 301*, 419–21.

Calfee, R. C. & Calfee, K. H. (1981). *Interactive reading assessment system (IRAS).* Unpublished manuscript, Stanford University.

Gough, P. B. & Hillinger, M. L. (1980). Learning to read: An unnatural act. *Bulletin of the Orton Society, 30,* 179–96.

Gough, P. B., Juel, J. & Roper-Schneider, D. (1983). Code and cipher: A two-stage conception of initial reading acquisition. In J. A. Niles & L. A. Harris (Eds), *Searches for meaning in reading/language processing and interaction.* (32nd yearbook of the National Reading Conference.) Rochester, N. Y.: N. R. C.

Hoover, W. A. (1983). *Language and literacy learning in bilingual education* (Final report submitted to the National Institute of Education, U.S. Department of Education under Contract No. 400-80-0043). Austin, TX: Southwest Educational Development Laboratory.

Liberman, I. Y., Shankweiler, D., Fischer, F. W. & Carter, B. (1974). Explicit syllable and phoneme segmentation in the young child. *Journal of Experimental Child Psychology, 18,* 201–12.

Nesdale, A. R., Herriman, M. L. & Tunmer, W. E. (1984). Phonological awareness in children. In W. Tunmer, C. Pratt, & M. Herriman (Eds), *Metalinguistic awareness in children: Theory, research, and implications.* Berlin: Springer-Verlag.

Perfetti, C. & Hogaboam, T. (1975). The relationship between single word decoding and reading comprehension skill. *Journal of Educational Psychology, 67,* 461–69.

Tunmer, W. & Nesdale, A. R. (1982). The effects of digraphs and pseudowords on phonemic segmentation in young children. *Applied Psycholinguistics, 3,* 299–311.

Acknowledgements

This work was supported by a grant from the Educational Research and Development Council, and a General Development Grant to the University of Western Australian.

12

Syntactic Processing in Children Varying in Reading Skill Profile

Judith A. Bowey
Victoria College

It is now well documented that, even with verbal intelligence differences controlled, poor readers show delayed syntatic development relative to good readers (e.g., Vogel, 1975). There is, however, little research investigating the nature of the relationship between syntactic development and reading proficiency.

There are several ways in which this association might be explained. For instance, it is possible that syntactic delay and reading problems are both manifestations of general linguistic immaturity (cf. Vellutino & Scanlon, 1982). More specific accounts of the relationship between syntactic delay and reading proficiency may be derived from the literature relating particular linguistic skills to reading achievement. For instance, a metalinguistic variant of the general linguistic immaturity hypothesis would propose that syntactic delay is only indirectly associated with reading impairment, through concomitant metalinguistic delay. This view would agree with the linguistic immaturity hypothesis in viewing syntactic delay as one aspect of general linguistic immaturity. However, it would suggest that it is a concomitant delay in the development of metalinguistic skills that is directly associated with reading difficulties.

The metalinguistic immaturity hypothesis gains support from the considerable body of research relating metalinguistic development to reading ability (see Tunmer & Bowey, 1984), and from studies finding that, even with verbal ability effects controlled, good readers perform better than poor readers on tests of syntactic awareness (Bowey, 1983a, 1983b). More importantly, there is evidence that the role of metalinguistic skill in reading development may be direct—both phonemic awareness training (Bradley & Bryant, 1983) and syntactic awareness training (Weaver, 1979) have been shown to increase reading skill. Furthermore, various aspects of metalinguistic skill appear to be both intercorrelated (Hakes, Evans, & Tunmer, 1980; Smith & Tager-Flusberg, 1982) and, at least in young children, correlated with syntactic proficiency, even with general verbal ability effects controlled (Smith & Tager-Flusberg, 1982).

The linguistic immaturity hypothesis and the metalinguistic variant both predict that syntactic delay would be associated with deficiencies in both decoding and comprehension skills. In this respect, they may be distinguished from Cromer's (1970) *difference* model, which focuses on the direct effects of syntactic processing deficits on comprehension performance. According to this view, syntactic delay is associated with a deficit in comprehension skill relative to decoding skill. According to Cromer, *difference* poor readers possess adequate decoding skills, but experience difficulty in integrating the text as it is read, thus impairing comprehension performance. Since these difference poor readers do not experience decoding difficulties, it follows that their hypothesised problems with online text integration reflect a basic difficulty in syntactic integration. Available evidence relating to the difference model in relation to syntactic processing is indirect, with research to date having simply contrasted good and poor readers, rather than comparing groups differing in reading skill profile.

Two published studies have examined the use of syntactic structure in aural sentence memory as a function of reading ability, and they have produced inconsistent results. Weinstein and Rabinovitch (1971) reported that, with intelligence effects covaried, good fourth-grade readers showed greater use of syntactic structure in learning lists of nonsense words, relative to poor readers. In contrast, Guthrie and Tyler (1976) reported no difference between good and poor readers (reading at fourth-grade level) in the use of syntactic structure in sentence recall. However, by controlling reading level and PPVT *IQ*, Guthrie and Tyler confounded reading ability and mental age, rendering their nonsignificant findings uninterpretable. Further work is required to clarify the relationship between the aural syntactic recall advantage and reading achievement.

The present experiment was designed to provide a preliminary evaluation of the three accounts outlined above. Four groups of fourth-grade children were selected on the basis of performance on initial screening tests. These groups were similar in both chronological and PPVT-R vocabulary age, but varied in reading skill profile. Using

Cromer's (1970) terminology, a *deficit* group was low on both decoding and comprehension skills, and a *difference* group was average in decoding skill, but low in comprehension skill. An *average* group had moderate levels of both decoding and comprehension skills. To complete the design, a *reverse difference* group was selected, having moderate comprehension skill, but low decoding skill. Thus, the deficit and average groups both had balanced reading skill profiles, differing in terms of the level of skill development. They served as controls for the difference and reverse difference groups, which had imbalances in their reading skill profiles.

This design allowed direct tests between the hypothesis that syntactic delay is associated with deficits in both decoding and comprehension skills, and the hypothesis that syntactic delay directly impairs comprehension skill. Rather than examine general syntactic proficiency, it was decided to investigate more specific aspects of syntactic processing within two oral language tasks: the use of syntactic structure in aural memory, and syntactic awareness.

According to the linguistic immaturity hypothesis, poor readers should show delays in all aspects of syntactic processing relative to good readers. Thus, since both the syntactic recall advantage and syntactic awareness are known to be age-related (Bowey, 1983b), it would be expected that groups differing in the level, rather than the balance, of reading skill development would show differences in both the syntactic recall advantage and syntactic awareness. According to the metalinguistic variant of this hypothesis, it is metalinguistic skill that affects reading performance. Thus, although syntactic awareness is correlated with the syntactic recall advantage (Bowey, 1983b), groups differing in level of reading skill development would differ in syntactic awareness, but not necessarily in terms of the syntactic recall advantage. The difference model predicts that both the syntactic recall advantage and syntactic awareness would be directly related to the relative balance between comprehension and decoding skills.

Method

Subjects
From five state schools located in predominantly middle class suburbs of Melbourne, 179 monolingual fourth-graders were administered the following tests: the PPVT-R (Dunn & Dunn, 1981), as a measure of general verbal ability; the St Lucia Graded Word Reading Test (Andrews, 1969), a test of word decoding skill; and the Progressive

Achievement Test (A.C.E.R., 1974), a test of silent reading comprehension. From this larger sample, four reading skill profile groups were selected such that they were similar in chronological and vocabulary ages, but differed in the level of, and the relative balance between, decoding and comprehension skills. There were 12 children in each group. Sample characteristics are provided in Table 12.1.

Materials

Sentence memory materials. Two parallel sets of 12 sentences were constructed. Sentence length varied from 5 to 15 words, with two-word increments, such that in each sentence set there were two sentences of each of six lengths. These two sets comprised the *normal* sentence sets. *Random* sentences were created by randomising word order. In Form A, the random sentences were derived from the normal sentences of Form B, and vice versa. *Anomalous* sentences were created by substituting lexical items from both sets of normal sentences into the normal sentence frames, such that semantic cohesion was minimised (e.g., *The old children flew back.*). Test forms were arranged in blocks of normal, anomalous, and random sentences.

Syntactic awareness task materials. Two parallel sets of 30 grammatically deviant sentences were constructed. These sentences ranged in length from 3 to 10 words, with the average length being 5.7 words. Most of the grammatical errors were natural in that they have been observed in the speech of young children. The range of vocabulary items and syntactic structures employed is generally comprehended by children of the age studied.

Procedure

Both tasks were individually administered (and scored) by an experimenter who was unaware of subject–group assignment.

Sentence memory task. In the initial orientation instructions, children were asked to repeat whatever the experimenter said, and told that some of the items would make sense, while some would not. They were then given three practice items, one example of each of the three item types (*cat and dog, milk and chalk, knife and fork*). Feedback was provided, and the items were repeated, if necessary, until they were correctly recalled. All items were spoken clearly, with normal intonation. Sentence block order and test form were counterbalanced within experimental groups. Items were required to be recalled verbatim in order to be scored as correct. Testing continued within each block until two successive items were failed.

Table 12.1 Mean group performance on screening and experimental measures

Group	Chronological age	Vocabulary age	(Decoding) reading age	Silent reading comprehension (raw score)	Syntactic recall advantage (%)	Syntactic awareness (%)	Random string recall (%)	Anomalous sentence recall (%)
Deficit	118.42[a]	112.92[a]	104.58[a]	13.92[a]	18.75[a]	74.72[a]	17.36[a]	36.11[a]
Reverse Difference	117.00[a]	114.50[a]	105.83[a]	21.33[b]	31.25[a]	80.28[ab]	18.06[a]	49.31[b]
Difference	116.83[a]	109.75[a]	127.58[b]	14.42[a]	28.47[a]	84.72[b]	21.53[ab]	50.00[b]
Average	117.17[a]	117.58[a]	127.92[b]	21.92[b]	31.25[a]	85.83[b]	30.56[b]	61.81[c]

[a] Alphabetical superscripts refer to homogeneous sample subsets as defined by Duncan's multiple range tests ($\alpha = .05$).

*A two-way, group × string, analysis of variance revealed significant effects of group, $F(3,44) = 8.02$, $p < .001$, and string, $F(1,44) = 179.25$, $p < .001$. The group × string interaction was nonsignificant, $F(3,44) = 2.10$, $p > .05$.

Syntactic awareness task. Two syntactic awareness tasks were administered in a separate session, always after the sentence memory task. This enabled the procedure to build upon children's experience. They were already familiar with both the imitation task and the possibility of deviant sentences. For this reason the error imitation subtask was administered first. In both tasks, children were told that all of the sentences they would hear contained a 'mistake', so that they sounded 'wrong'. Children were asked in the error imitation task to repeat each sentence as they heard it, 'to say the sentence exactly the same way, leaving the mistake in'. Following a brief break, the elicited correction task was given. In this task they were to correct the mistake, to 'fix the sentence up, so that it sounds right'. Both tasks were introduced using practice examples, incorporating corrective feedback and repeated testing of difficult items, where necessary.

Results and Discussion

It was originally intended to investigate the use of both syntactic structure and semantic cohesion to facilitate sentence memory. However, preliminary inspection of the data revealed ceiling effects in the recall of normal sentences in 37.5% of the sample. It was thus decided to examine only the syntactic recall advantage, the difference between the number of anomalous and random strings recalled verbatim. Syntactic awareness scores were computed from performance on the error imitation and correction subtasks, with syntactic awareness operationalised as the difference between the number of corrections obtained on the correction and imitation subtasks.

Of central interest are the comparisons between the four reading groups on the two direct measures of syntactic processing. One-way analyses of variance indicated nonsignificant group effects for both the syntactic recall advantage, $F(3,44) = 2.10$, $p > .05$, and syntactic awareness scores, $F(3,44) = 2.41$, $p > .05$. Further analysis, using Duncan's multiple range tests ($\alpha = .05$), revealed no significant group contrasts in the case of the syntactic recall advantage scores. However, Duncan's multiple range tests indicated that the Deficit group obtained lower syntactic awareness scores than both the Difference and the Average groups, ($\alpha = .05$, see Table 12.1).

These results show no support for the hypothesis that syntactic processing difficulties are directly associated with low comprehension skill. Readers showing a relative comprehension deficit obtained the same syntactic recall advantage and syntactic awareness scores as controls equated for both decoding skill and vocabulary age. On the other hand, the difference in the overall level of skill development between average and deficit groups was associated with a significant difference in syntactic awareness although not with the syntactic recall advantage. This pattern of results conforms most closely to that predicted by the metalinguistic immaturity hypothesis, according to which the association between reading ability and syntactic delay is indirect, with syntactic delay associated with slower development of the metalinguistic skills required for reading development.

It is, however, arguable that the use of the syntactic recall advantage measure as an index of syntactic maturity rendered the present experiment a conservative test of the general linguistic immaturity hypothesis, particularly given that the deficit group was not severely impaired in reading achievement. The finding of a significant difference between the average and deficit groups in random string recall performance (see Table 12.1) suggests that the average readers may have used some form of verbal mediation to facilitate their recall of random word strings, thereby reducing their syntactic recall advantage.

It is quite likely that the average readers used a phonetic coding strategy in recalling the random word strings. Consistent with this suggestion is the finding that, when recalling random content word strings, good readers use a phonetic coding strategy, whereas poor readers do not. good readers' memory for random content word strings is superior to that of poor readers only when the words are phonetically dissimilar (Mann, Liberman, & Shankweiler, 1980). It is also possible that in the present study average readers used a syntactic chunking strategy even in their recall of random word strings (which included function words). It has been found that good adult readers dealing with fourth-order approximations to English 'struggled to impose an intonation pattern on the material, segmenting it into phrase-like units. Poor readers read in a monotone as if it were a word list' (Cohen & Freeman, 1978, p. 417). These good adult readers also recalled a substantial part of the fourth-order approximation test. It should perhaps be noted that good readers are also more likely than poor readers to use semantic (taxonomic) structure as an aid to verbal recall (Vellutino & Scanlon, 1982) in tasks where this is an effective mediational strategy.

These findings suggest that good readers have available a range of verbal mediation strategies to facilitate verbal performance, and that they are flexible in their use of such strategies. This conclusion is consistent both with suggestions that developmental increases in memory largely reflect increases in the availability and use of appropriate mediational strategies (Flavell, 1985) and, more specifically, with Vellutino's hypothesis that the most likely source of specific reading difficulty is a linguistic coding deficiency (Vellutino & Scanlon, 1982).

With respect to the present results, the possibility that good readers may have used verbal mediation strategies in their recall of random word strings suggests that the syntactic recall advantage score may underestimate the use of syntactic structure to facilitate sentence recall, at least in the average readers. It is thus not appropriate to draw any firm conclusions from the nonsignificant group differences observed for that measure.

It may instead be more appropriate simply to examine anomalous sentence recall as an index of the use of syntactic structure to facilitate verbal memory. The analysis of anomalous sentence recall revealed several significant differences among the four reading groups (see Table 12.1). Of particular interest are the significant differences between the average and difference groups, and between the reverse difference and deficit groups. These results indicated that groups matched for decoding skill but differing in comprehension skill also showed differences in aural memory for anomalous sentences. However, the finding of superior anomalous sentence recall for both the difference and the average groups relative to the deficit group indicated that this recall difference was not directly associated with the relative balance between comprehension and decoding skills. Rather, it probably reflected the level of general reading skill attainment.

The overall pattern of results obtained in the present experiment indicates that syntactic proficiency, as reflected in performance on both aural memory and syntactic awareness tasks, is associated with the level, rather than the relative balance, of decoding and comprehension skills. They also suggest that the syntactic delay widely observed in poor readers most probably reflects a general verbal deficit. Rather than directly contributing to reading comprehension problems, syntactic delay is probably associated with reading difficulty through concomitant delays in the development of higher-order verbal mediation skills. Metalinguistic tasks, requiring the child to manipulate structural aspects of language, may measure a sensitivity to the features of language that may serve as the basis for verbal mediation (cf. Byrne, 1981).

References

Andrews, R. J. (1969). *St. Lucia Graded Word Reading Test.* Brisbane, Australia: Teaching and Testing Resources.

Australian Council for Educational Research. (1973). *Progressive Achievement Tests.* Melbourne: A.C.E.R.

Bowey, J. A. (1983a, September). *Syntactic control in relation to children's oral reading performance.* Paper presented at the Eighteenth Annual Australian Psychological Society Conference, Sydney.

Bowey, J. A. (1983b, November). *The development of executive syntactic control from preschool to fifth-grade.* Paper presented at the Fourth Australian Language and Speech Conference, Melbourne.

Bradley, L., & Bryant, P. E. (1983). Categorizing sounds and learning to read—A causal connection. *Nature, 301,* 419–21.

Byrne, B. (1981). Reading disability, linguistic access and short-term memory: Comments prompted by Jorm's review of developmental dyslexia. *Australian Journal of Psychology, 33,* 83–96.

Cohen, G., & Freeman, R. (1978). Individual differences in reading strategies in relation to cerebral asymmetry. In J. Requin (Ed.), *Attention and performance VII* (pp. 411–26). Hillsdale, N.J.: Erlbaum.

Cromer, W. (1970). The difference model: A new explanation for some reading difficulties. *Journal of Educational Psychology, 61,* 471–83.

Dunn, L. M., & Dunn, L. M. (1981). *Peabody Picture Vocabulary Test.* (3rd ed.). Circle Pines, Minn.: American Guidance Service.

Flavell, J. H. (1985). *Cognitive development.* (2nd ed.). Englewood-Cliffs, N J.: Prentice-Hall.

Guthrie, J. T., & Tyler, S. J. (1976). Psycholinguistic processing in reading and listening among good and poor readers. *Journal of Reading Behavior, 8,* 415–26.

Hakes, D. T., Evans, J. S., & Tunmer, W. E. (1980). *The development of metalinguistic abilities in children.* New York: Springer-Verlag.

Mann, V. A., Liberman, I. Y. & Shankweiler, D. (1980). Children's memory for sentences and word strings in relation to reading ability. *Memory and Cognition, 8,* 329–35.

Smith, C. L., & Tager-Flusberg, H. (1982). Metalinguistic awareness and language development. *Journal of Experimental Child Psychology, 34,* 449–68.

Tunmer, W. E., & Bowey, J. A. (1984). Metalinguistic awareness and reading acquisition. In W. E. Tunmer, C. Pratt, & M. L. Herriman (Eds), *Metalinguistic awareness in children: Theory, research and implications* (pp. 144–68). New York: Springer-Verlag.

Vellutino, F. R., & Scanlon, D. M. (1982). Verbal processing in poor and normal readers. In C. J. Brainerd, & M. Pressley (Eds), *Verbal processes in children: Progress in cognitive development research.* (pp. 189–264). New York: Springer-Verlag.

Vogel, S. A. (1975). *Syntactic abilities in normal and dyslexic children.* Baltimore, Md.: University Park Press.

Weaver, P. A. (1979). Improving reading comprehension: Effects of sentence organization instruction. *Reading Research Quarterly, 15,* 129–46.

Weinstein, R., & Rabinovitch, M. S. (1971). Sentence structure and retention in good and poor readers. *Journal of Educational Psychology, 62,* 25–30.

Acknowledgements

This research was carried out at the University of Melbourne, and was supported by a University of Melbourne Research Development Grant. I would like to thank Kathryn Brewer, Heather Gibb, Jo Jenkinson, and Jackie Smith for their assistance in data collection.

13

Do Twins and Singletons Have Similar Language and Reading Problems?

David A. Hay, Sally M. Collett, Carol J. Johnston,
Pauline J. O'Brien and Margot Prior.
La Trobe University.

The high incidence of biological stresses accompanying a multiple birth has been well documented (Bryan, 1983). On average twins are four weeks premature and 1000g lighter in birthweight than singletons. These variables are associated with much higher stillbirth and neonatal mortality rates, with greater demand on neonatal intensive care facilities and a greater risk of sudden infant death syndrome (Australian Multiple Birth Association & Hay, 1984).

Much less is known about the behavioural difficulties which may result from a multiple birth. However, a number of studies have indicated delay in both the acquisition and subsequent development of speech and language in twins as compared to singletons (Day, 1932; Koch, 1966; Savić, 1980; Watts & Lytton, 1981). Overall such research indicates post-natal rather than prenatal or perinatal factors as the major contributors to language delay in twins.

These postnatal factors are seen in the family environment and comprise:

1 the reduced quantity and quality of verbal stimulation and interaction with adult language models resulting from the greater demands for care-giving placed upon parents of twins (Lytton, 1980).

2 the intensive interaction between the twins which may reduce the need for developing adequate communication skills and enhance their chances of developing cryptophasia or 'secret language' (Zazzo, 1978).

3　competition between the twins for adult attention, for which their short, loud utterances are ideally suited (Savić, 1980).

While delays in language acquisition and articulation have been related to subsequent reading disability in the singleton population (Rutter, 1978), very little attention has been paid to the possibility that reading disability is more common in twins. In a sample of 9 to 13-year-old male twins from the La Trobe Twin Study, Johnston, Prior and Hay (1984) found 72% were below average on reading accuracy on the Neale Test and 59% on reading comprehension, despite above average WISC-R Performance IQ's. The best single predictor of reading disability in these boys was earlier parental reports of a history of language problems in the preschool years.

As additional evidence, Johnston, Prior and Hay (1984) examined the Australian Council for Educational Research's national survey of literacy and numeracy—the Australian Study in School Performance (ASSP). This survey in 1975 involved a total of 12,875 10- and 14-year olds, 297 of whom were twins. The most striking twin result was that by age 14 only 41% of twin boys had achieved mastery of literacy compared with 71% for singleton males. The respective female figures were 68% and 73%. In a more detailed analysis of the ASSP Hay, O'Brien, Johnston and Prior (1984) found that:

1　many more of the twin boys failed to achieve mastery of numeracy as well as literacy. The verbal nature of many of the numeracy items may have meant mastery of numeracy in twins boys was partly dependent on mastery of literacy.
2　particularly in the 14-year-old group, twin boys had roughly twice as many difficulties with spelling and with reading reversals.
3　on the Work Knowledge Test, a measure of verbal ability, twins differed from singletons in different ways at the two ages: at age 10 they attempted fewer items but were wrong on the same number, at age 14 they attempted almost as many but were wrong on more items.

The change with age introduces the possibility of non-cognitive explanations for the twins' poorer performance. Hay and O'Brien (1983, 1984) report that identical twin boys are easily distracted and 'less interested, less eager, found the testing less enjoyable and did not try their best', and had more difficulty with fluency and articulation. However these data do not indicate if the poorer motivation is a cause or a consequence of the poorer reading skills.

Table 13.1   The numbers and the percentages of children failing to achieve mastery of literacy on the ASSP

	Age 10		Age 14	
	Twin	Singleton	Twin	Singleton
Male	65 (64%)	1625 (52%)	39 (59%)	882 (29%)
Female	35 (51%)	1309 (41%)	20 (32%)	823 (27%)

The present paper examines these issues further by concentrating *only* on those children in the ASSP who failed to achieve mastery of literacy. The basic question is whether twins without mastery are characterised by a different pattern of cognitive or non-cognitive problems than singleborn children.

METHOD

The ASSP developed criterion–reference tests of basic numeracy and literacy skills for a stratified random sample of 10– and 14–year old school children. The test items are detailed in Bourke and Lewis (1976) and the ASSP is summarised in Hay et al. (1984). For the present analysis, all those children achieving mastery of literacy were omitted and the performance of the remaining twins and singletons compared on all reading and numeracy items as well as the Word Knowledge Test. The numbers in each category are shown in Table 13.1 and apply to all subsequent statistics. Also compared were the teachers' reports. These concerned social behaviour in the school setting, as well as their subjective assessment of speech and hearing problems and such specific features as spelling, reading reversals and the ability to understand instructions.

The means of twins and singletons on all items were compared for the four age × sex combinations. The sexes were analysed separately because of the extensive sex differences in twin–singleton comparisons (Hay et al., 1984). The SPSS discriminant function analysis routine was also used to select those variables which best distinguished twins and singletons. However, its results should be interpreted with caution since comparison of the covariance matrices by Box's M indicated that the twins and singletons could not be considered as belonging to the same population. Hay et al., (1984) made the same point during factor analyses of the entire ASSP sample. Many more twins failed all difficult items and hence their factors tended to reflect variation on the easier items. Most singletons passed most easy items and their factors reflected variation on the difficult items. Furthermore, as so many of

Table 13.2   The eight variables on the discriminant function analysis which best distinguished twins and singletons who failed to achieve mastery of literacy in the ASSP

ACER item	Standardised canonical discriminant function coefficients	χ^2 between twins and singletons
Age 10		
MALES		
Money addition	0.54	
Demands attention	0.46	
Subtraction—2 digit	0.40	
Money calculations—addition and division	0.33	
News comprehension (inferential)	0.32	
Volume comparisons	0.32	
Multiplication—1 digit	0.30	
Unco-operative with peers	0.29	
		$\chi^2_{34} = 94.2^{***}$
FEMALES		
Reading paragraph—literal comprehension	0.44	
Family size	0.40	
Newspaper comprehension	0.36	
Subtraction—1 digit	0.35	
Counting, concrete items	0.32	
Reading reversals	0.31	
Linguistic comprehension—syntax and sentence construction	0.31	
Hearing problems	0.30	
		$\chi^2_{19} = 38.8^{**}$;
Age 14		
MALES		
Speech problems	0.50	
Instrument reading	0.49	
Length estimation	0.48	
Adding and subtraction of concrete items	0.43	
Linguistic comprehension—syntax and sentence construction	0.42	
Money calculations	0.40	

Hearing problems	0.34
Reading paragraph—literal comprehension	0.33

$$\chi^2_{27} = 72.1^{***}$$

FEMALES

Word knowledge test—number wrong	0.96
Work knowledge test—total correct ·	0.77
Word knowledge test—total attempted	0.75
Comprehension—syntax and sentence construction	0.58
News information—directory skills. Item 5	0.52
News information—directory skills. Item 4	0.45
Demands attention	0.43
Multiply, concrete items	0.34

$$\chi^2_{27} = 99.0^{***}$$

$^{**}p < .01, \, ^{***}p < .001$

the items, for numeracy as well as literacy, involve much reading, they may covary for this reason alone, complicating any attempt to extract discriminant functions.

RESULTS

Table 13.2 summarises the results of the discriminant function analysis. A the χ^2s show, in all cases the twins can be distinguished from the singletons. For each group the eight items with the largest standardised canonical coefficients are listed.

In the 10-year-old boys the main discriminators were numerical items, generally the more difficult ones and also money calculations. Only one literacy item was included in the top eight and this was a complex item, involving the inferential meaning of a newspaper paragraph. *On all these items* the twins did not do as well as the singletons. In general 10–15% fewer twins than singletons got the item correct but in the case of two digit subtraction, only 45.9% of male twins were correct, compared with 64.4% of male singletons ($\chi^2_1 = 7.93$, $p < .01$). One item of interest not featuring in the discriminant function was the 51.6% of twins compared with only 36.9% of singletons ($\chi^2_1 = 5.00$, $p < .05$) perceived by teachers as having spelling problems.

The questions, *demanding attention* and *unco-operative with peers* from teachers' perceptions of the social behaviour are interesting for two reasons. Firstly, it parallels the La Trobe Twin Study results of Hay and O'Brien (1984) where the teacher completed the Bristol Social Adjustment Guide. Secondly, while maladaptive social behaviour characterises many learning disabled children, in this case it distinguishes the less able twins from the less able singletons.

Except for a similar poorer 2 digit subtraction by the twin girls ($\chi^2_1 = 5.20$, $p < 0.5$) both the analysis of the means and the discriminant function showed a different pattern for the 10-year-old girls where literacy items feature much more prominently in the twin-singleton differences. The important items centred on deriving the meaning of a short passage and the meaning of an unknown word from its context—these two items were answered correctly by 74.6% and 23.55% respectively, of twin girls, compared with 89.4% and 41.6% of singletons ($\chi^2_1 = 11.87$, $p < .001$ and $\chi^2_1 = 3.72$, $p = .05$). Less attention should be paid to the family size variable since an excess of twin girls was shown only in family size 6, suggesting a chance effect.

For the 14-year-old boys the main discriminators were numeracy items such as length estimation and instrument reading as well as related items not featuring prominently in the function e.g., lottery number which involved finding the largest number in a series. Thus numerical scanning skills are much worse in the twins, especially when combined with other tasks (e.g., only 16.2% of twins compared with 37.8% of singletons ($\chi^2_1 = 11.82$, $p < .001$) got correct an item where the fraction closest in size to 3/16 had to be found in a list).

The role of speech problems as the main discriminator is quite different from that in the 10-year-old boys. There are five categories (normal, slurred, nervous, lisps and unintelligible) and the χ^2_4 for 10-year-olds was only 0.93 compared with 11.92 ($p < .02$) for the 14-year-olds where more twins were perceived as slurring their speech or being unintelligible.

For the 14-year-old girls the main discriminator is the number of items wrong on the Word Knowledge Test. The breakdown of the scores on the Word Knowledge Test is given in Table 13.3 with the male data for comparison. (Because of corrections for guessing, the three components of the test are not additive). Female twins are trying almost as many but are getting many more wrong.

Apart from the literacy items concerning syntax and sentence construction and the two adjacent items involving directory skills, the other distinguishing feature is that more twin girls demand attention. Teachers see this as being a 'slight handicap' in 10% of twin girls compared with 3.3% of singletons. Similarly being unco-operative

Table 13.3   Performance of 14-year-old twins and singletons on the Word Knowledge Test of the ASSP

Item	Female		Male	
	Twin	Singleton	Twin	Singleton
Total number attempted	19.5	20.6	18.9	19.5
Total number wrong	16.9	11.7**	13.5	12.05
Total correct	7.5	9.5	6.4	7.9

Significant twin-singleton difference* $p < .05$, *$p < .01$.

with peers is a 'slight handicap' in 10.5% of twins and 4.19% of singletons. Such social disadvantage is not uncommon in adolescent twin girls. It has been most fully documented by Koch (1966) who called it the 'prima donna' effect.

Only one numeracy item, using multiplication in a concrete rather than an abstract context, appears in the discriminant function but this hides a whole group of related numeracy items (subtracting times, subtracting decimals, reading the time and calculating interest) where at least 20% fewer twins than singletons get the items correct.

DISCUSSION

The ASSP results show that specific differences exist between those twins and singletons who lack adequate literacy skills. In all four groups except the 10-year-old boys, syntax and sentence construction was a major discriminator. Potentially a 'spoken' language item, this is the most likely link with the sort of language problems seen in younger twins mentioned earlier. It is unfortunate that the ASSP contains no historical data on the children which could be used to check whether the twins without mastery of literacy are those who experienced extensive language delay in the earlier years.

The causes of the twin–singleton difference may lie also in the problems of motivation and distraction discussed by Hay and O'Brien (1983, 1984). Further, Johnston et al. (1984) make a similar point concerning the much greater deficit of twins on reading accuracy than comprehension. It is not difficult to see how distraction and the inability to concentrate for long periods could be a major issue with twins who are always together. They therefore never have the opportunity to develop habits of unbroken periods of concentration on a task without someone else disturbing them. The question of motivation is more complex. One could postulate either that young twins attract so much attention that they need not develop means of gaining approval through their own efforts or that there is some effect of the constant comparisons between them by peers, teachers and especially parents (Hay & O'Brien, 1984).

In contrast, the importance of the Word Knowledge Test with the 14-year-old girls suggests that it may be lower verbal intelligence which leads to poorer literacy in the twin girls compared with the singletons. However the girls may also have a concentration and accuracy problem—otherwise it is difficult to see why only 52.6% of the twin girls could read the time from a watchface, compared with 79.2% of singletons.

There may be a danger in simply comparing twins and singeltons. Apart from the sex difference, there may be differences between MZ and DZ twins (Hay & O'Brien, 1983), and even within MZ twins. Hay and Howie (1980) found that large birthweight differences in MZ twins were associated with differences in handedness, raising the question of 'mirror-image' twins. This may be common in the 2/3 rds of MZ twins who are monochorionic, splitting on the fourth or later day after conception. Springer and Searleman (1978) found that intrapair differences in lateralisation as assessed by dichotic listening were larger in MZ than in DZ twins, suggesting that the MZ–DZ distinction may have general and central consequences.

Slightly more of the ASSP twin boys are consistently left-handed (13.9%) compared with 8.1% in the singletons (comparable female figures are 10% and 6%). Although not quite significant ($\chi^2_1 = 3.24$, $p = .07$), there is a trend for more twin boys (27%) to show reading reversals than singletons (14.7%). The comparable female data are 0% for twins and 5.4% for singletons, suggesting that a very different situation may apply.

The ASSP data are no help in answering these questions about what may underlie twin–singleton differences—their role is in providing limited data on a large and representative sample of Australian children. However the necessary medical data on zygosity and placental type are available for many of the subjects in the La Trobe Twin Study and a program has commenced of combining these data with the test records and extensive measures of lateralisation at the behavioural, physical and hemispheric level.

The significance of these results cannot be ignored. One Australian child in 46 is a twin, and there are many indications that twins may be underrepresented in the higher levels of education. Hay et al. (1984) point out 23% of U.S. white singletons sit the National Merit Schol-

Table 13.4   14-year-old boys and the perceptions of the teacher regarding remedial reading and numeracy in the ASSP

Percentage of boys	Reading		Numeracy	
	Twin	Singleton	Twin	Singleton
Needing and receiving remediation	18.9	25.4	11.1	11.9
Needing but not receiving	35.1	21.2	27.8	12.8
Not needing	45.9	53.4	61.1	75.3

arship Qualifying Test compared with 12% of female twins and 8% of male twins. With twin-singleton differences of this magnitude, more needs to be done to identify and correct the factors which disadvantage twins.

Table 13.4 emphasises just how easy it is for people to overlook the problems facing twins. As in the complete ASSP sample (Hay et al., 1984), teachers note that more twins need remedial reading and numeracy but there is a substantial proportion of boys in this category not getting such help.

References

Australian Multiple Birth Association & Hay, D. A. (1984). The dilemma of families with very low birthweight twins. In Kuhse, H. & de Garis L. (Eds), *The tiniest newborns: Survival—what price*, (pp. 47–59), Melbourne: Monash University Centre for Human Bioethics.

Bourke, S. E. & Lewis, R. (1976). *Australian studies in school performance* Vol II. Literacy and numeracy in Australian schools: item report. Canberra: Australian Government Publishing Service.

Bryan, E. M. (1983). *The nature and nurture of twins*. London: Bailliere Tindall.

Day, E. J. (1932). The development of language in twins. I. A comparison of twins and single children. *Child Development, 3*, 179–99.

Hay, D. A. & Howie, P. M. (1980). Handedness and differences in birthweight of twins. *Perceptual and Motor Skills, 51*, 666.

Hay, D. A. & O'Brien, P. J. (1983). The La Trobe Twin Study: a genetic approach to the structure and development of cognition in twin children. *Child Development, 54*, 317–30.

Hay, D. A. & O'Brien, P. J. (1984). The role of parental attitudes in the development of temperament in twins at home, school and in test situations. *Acta Genetica Medica et Gemellologica, 33*, 191–204.

Hay, D. A., O'Brien, P. J., Johnston, C. J. & Prior, M. (1984). The high incidence of reading disability in twin boys and its implications for genetic analysis. *Acta Genetica Medica et Gemellologica, 33*, 223–36.

Johnston, C. J., Prior, M., & Hay, D. A. (1984). Prediction of reading disability in twin boys. *Developmental Medicine and Child Neurology, 26,* 588–95.

Koch, H. L. (1966). *Twins and twin relations.* Chicago: University of Chicago Press.

Lytton, H. (1980). *Parent-child interaction: The socialization process observed in twin and singleton families.* New York: Plenum.

Rutter, M. (1978). Prevalence and types of dyslexia. In Benton, A. L. & Pearl, D. (Eds), *Dyslexia: An appraisal of current knowledge* (pp. 3–28). New York: Oxford U.P.

Savić, S. (1980). *How Twins Learn to Talk: A study of the speech development of twins from 1 to 3.* New York: Academic Press.

Springer, S. P. & Searleman, A. (1978). Hemispheric asymmetry of function in twins. In W. E. Nance, G. Allen, & P. Parisi, (Eds), *Twin Research 2*: Part A. Psychology and Methodology (pp. 57–62). New York: Alan R. Liss.

Watts, D. and Lytton, H. (1980). Twinship as handicap: fact or fiction? In L. Gedda, P. Parisi, & W. E. Nance, (Eds), *Twin Research 3*: Part B. Intelligence, Personality and Development (pp. 283–6). New York: Alan R. Liss.

Zazzo, R. (1978). Genesis and peculiarities of the personality of twins. In W. E. Nance, G. Allen, & P. Parisi, (Eds), *Twin Research 2*: Part A. Psychology and Methodology (pp. 1–11). New York: Alan R. Liss.

Acknowledgements

This work is supported by NH&MRC, the Buckland Foundation, the Felton Bequest, the Percy Baxter Charitable Trust and the William Paxton Charitable Fund. The co-operation of Dr S. Bourke of the Australian Council for Education Research in providing the computer tapes of the Australian Study in School Performance is gratefully acknowledged. The views in this paper are not necessarily those of ACER.

SECTION 3
PERCEPTUAL MOTOR
DEVELOPMENT

Most of the literature concerned with perceptual motor development in children has focussed on developmental milestones or norms, by documenting the age at which the average child can perform certain skills. This literature has been concerned with the development of gross motor skills including crawling, walking and skipping, and fine motor skills including drawing, maze tracing and writing.

Although the perceptual motor skills that are required for the successful completion of such tasks are clearly viewed as important, there has been little research into the processes involved in their development. Further, even though we may be able to classify a child as being delayed with respect to the development of perceptual motor skills, very little is understood about the reasons for such a delay or the possible consequences of it.

In the three chapters in this section, perceptual motor development is discussed with special emphasis on process-oriented task analysis and causal diagnosis in learning disorders. That is, rather than only discussing *when* a child can first perform skills, the development is considered with respect to *why* the child attains these skills. This process-oriented approach forms the basis of causal diagnosis and leads to the identification of specific problems that can be alleviated through therapy programmes.

In the chapter by Laszlo, the Perceptual Motor Abilities Test (PMAT) is described along with its uses in the identification of children requiring assistance. The test includes a range of tasks designed to examine the development of a range of perceptual and motor abilities in children. Laszlo also describes the successful outcome of a therapy programme, based on a diagnosis using the PMAT, with two children who were experiencing difficulties in school.

Broderick in her chapter considers the difficulties children experience when copying geometric figures. In a series of carefully designed tasks, she ensured that performance was not impaired by task demands that were not related to the skills being investigated. This provided a clear assessment of the specific perceptual-motor factors that are important in drawing skills.

Finally, Stanley, Grimwood, Rutherford and Hopkins consider the relationship between neurological deficits and learning disabilities with an emphasis on the vestibular-postural and oculomotor systems. In their study which involved a group of learning disabled children and a matched control group, they found that the children with learning disabilities showed clear signs of vestibular-postural and oculomotor dysfunction. Although the authors acknowledge this did not necessarily imply that the dysfunction plays a direct causal role in learning disability, their study, along with the work of Laszlo and Broderick, emphasises the importance of further research in the area of perceptual motor skills.

CHRIS PRATT

14

Development of Perceptual Motor Abilities in Children from 5 years to Adults

Judith I. Laszlo
Unversity of Western Australia

INTRODUCTION

Motor development is often described in terms of developmental milestones, that is the age at which the 'average' child is expected to perform such skills as walking, skipping, drawing or tying shoe laces with a double bow. This descriptive approach is helpful in defining *when* we can expect children to reach certain levels of motor development, but does not consider the underlying reasons *why* or *how* the child achieves proficiency in the tasks

Based on the closed-loop model of perceptual motor behaviour, Laszlo & Bairstow (1983) constructed the Perceptual Motor Abilities Test, PMAT, for children aged 5–12 years of age with the aim of establishing the developmental trends of the various perceptual and motor processes which contribute to motor behaviour.

Firstly we designed tasks to test sensory function. As vision and hearing tests are well developed, we concentrated on kinaesthetic perception. Kinaesthesis is the modality which signals information relevant to the state of muscles and joints. It is generated continuously whether we are moving about or staying still. It gives information about muscle tension, position of body parts and about the extent, direction and velocity of movements. Kinaesthesis allows for error detection during the performance of a task, and furthermore memory traces of movements are stored in kinaesthetic terms. It is obvious that kinaesthesis plays a crucial role in the acquisition and performance of skilled movements. Yet an adequate test of kinaesthetic function has not been available. The clinical test of kinaesthesis, pointing fingers with eyes closed, or the Ayres test of kinaesthesis where the child is required to draw a line, do not measure sensory or perceptual function alone, but include motor output factors as well. Thus on the basis of these tests it is not possible to separate sensory from motor involvement. An athetoid child would not be able to perform either task due to uncontrollable involuntary movements and thus fail the test, yet he might be fully aware of where his hands are. That is his kinaesthetic perceptual ability could be adequate.

METHOD

Subjects
491 primary school children and 20 adults participated in the study. The children, who were in the 5–12 age range, were drawn from six metropolitan primary schools. The adults were students of the University of Western Australia.

Tasks
The PMAT battery was administered to all subjects. Only a brief description of the tasks are included here. Full details of the tasks, scoring procedures and rationale are reported in Laszlo and Bairstow (1985). The tasks were selected to measure both perceptual and motor abilities. In the following description tasks are grouped according to the abilities they were designed to measure.

Perceptual abilities
Four aspects of *kinaesthetic function* were included in the PMAT battery: acuity, perception and memory, gross static kinaesthesis and velocity discrimination.

1   Kinaesthetic acuity was measured by comparing the position of the two hands in the absence of visual guidance. The subject's hands were moved passively by the tester (Bairstow & Laszlo, 1981; Laszlo & Bairstow, 1982).
2   Kinaesthetic perception and memory was tested by a pattern reorientation task. Here again the subject's hand, holding a stylus was passively guided around the patterns (Bairstow & Laszlo, 1981).
3   Testing the level of gross static kinaesthesis was achieved by asking the subject, who was lying on the floor, to assume the posture held by the 'Pink Panther' which was shown to him.
4   In velocity discrimination two pencil torches were mounted on rails. The torches could be moved along the rails by two separate motors at various velocities. A translucent screen shielded the apparatus from the subject's view. In the kinaesthetic condition the

subject was holding the torches (lights were switched off), in the visual condition, the pin point torch lights were viewed on the translucent screen, while in the cross modal condition one torch light was on, and the other off. The subject held the 'off' torch, and his arm was moved passively. In this task the subject was required to indicate as soon as he made his judgment whether arm or light were moved the faster.

Motor abilities
While it is possible to test isolated sensory functions, the output or motor variables are interconnected. The interdependence of planning and programming variables necessitate some compromise solutions: rather than attempting to find tasks measuring single factors one must be content to choose tasks in which processes have differential importance. The test tasks are grouped according to the processes on which they depend. The following motor abilities were measured: movement planning, spatio-temporal and spatial programming. Balance was also tested.

1   *Planning and spatio-temporal programming*
    (a)   *Ward game.* The subject was to roll 20 billiard balls, one at a time at a moving target which was mounted on a modified billiard table.

2   *Spatio-temporal programming*
    (a)   *Video-game.* The subject attempted to cross over moving targets with a light pen. The targets were presented on a TV screen. Target size, velocity and trajectory were systematically varied over 90 trials.
    (b)   *Ball roll.* Four balls, graduated in size, were rolled down a chute, one at a time. The chute was set at five different angles. The subject's task was to run forward from behind a starting line when the ball was released and catch the ball before it hit the ground.

3   *Planning and spatial programming*
    (a)   *Ball handling.* The subject had to place 24 balls of various sizes from one small bucket into another as fast as possible. Ball sizes ranged from cricket ball to small marble.
    (b)   *Drawing.* Line drawings of a square, diamond and horseshoe were presented to the subject. He was to copy each shape as accurately as possible both in size and shape, at his own pace.

4 *Spatial programming*
   (a) *Tracing.* The same shapes as in the drawing task were used. The subject had to trace over the outlines without deviating from them. Accuracy was stressed in the instructions.
   (b) *Dotting.* Eleven dots were to be touched with a coloured pen, in set order, with accuracy.

5 *Balance*
   (a) Heel-to-toe stand with eyes open or closed.
   (b) Standing on one foot with eyes open or closed.

RESULTS

The developmental trends are summarised in Figure 14.1. Stepwise rather than even developmental trends were found in all tasks. Comparison of age groups across tasks confirmed the graphically presented trends. Primary school children were shown, in terms of perceptual–motor abilities, to form four statistically significantly different groups, Year 1, Year 2, Years 3 & 4, and Years 5, 6 & 7. The adults formed a fifth distinct group.

Factor analyses (Varimax rotated factor matrix after Kaiser normalisation) showed that children develop efficient spatio-temporal programming ability by Year 3, but effective planning and error corrective programming is not evident prior to Year 5.

Evidence for a general motor factor 'Motor G' was not found. This means that perceptual–motor ability does not depend on a single, global motor process. Individual differences in the rate of development of motor behaviour, and the attained level of skills must depend on the development of specific perceptual or motor abilities.

There were no differences found between boys and girls in any task other than balance. The Year 2, 3 and 4 girls performed both heel-to-toe and one foot stand tasks better than boys. Significant differences between right- and left-handed children were not found in any of the PMAT tasks. These findings argue strongly against innate motor ability differences between boys and girls, or left and right handed children.

Overall the findings can be summarised in the following way. Children in Years 1 and 2 perform perceptual and motor tasks at a low level of efficiency. They seem to rely on trial and error methods rather than on planned task strategies. Kinaesthetic information processing is poor at this age. In Years 3 & 4 children can be characterised by their stereotyped response style. Movements are often repeated without

Fig. 14.1 Developmental trends of the PMAT tasks.

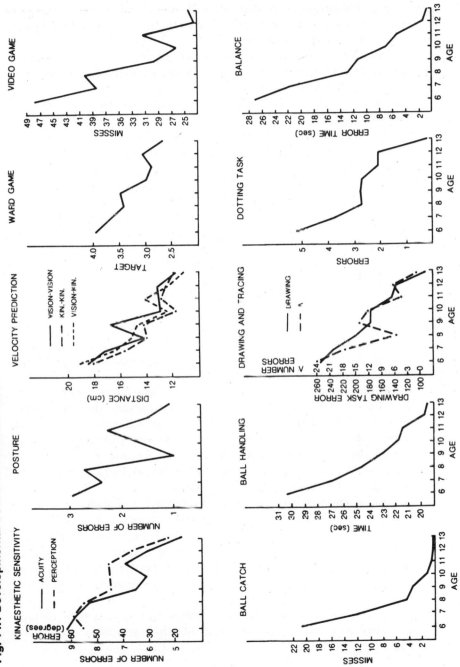

change in the response pattern. Performance at different tasks seems to be determined by processes involved in the spatio-temporal or spatial programming of movement.

From Year 5 and onward, two additional factors develop: planning and error corrective programming. Response style becomes flexible, indicating that task strategies are well planned, and that the movement parameters are generated in accordance with planned task strategies. Improvement in error corrective programming is made possible by the development of kinaesthetic sensitivity, which is necessary in error detection, and by improved motor programming ability.

DISCUSSION AND CONCLUSIONS

What are the possible implications of these findings? In the theoretical field they enable us to describe perceptual motor development in terms of component processes. The results allow the mapping of developmental trends of abilities contributing to overall motor behaviour. As an example kinaesthetic sensitivity could be mentioned. It is the first time that kinaesthetic perceptual ability has been adequately measured and consequently the developmental progression charted. It was shown that kinaesthetic sensitivity develops at a slower rate than visual information processing. Indeed in Years 1 and 2, 33% of children show only a rudimentary level of kinaesthetic processing ability. Overall this fine grained analysis allows better insight into the capabilities of children of different ages and provides a guideline to realistic demands. Tasks dependent on fine error detection and correction or high level planning would be difficult in Years 1 and 2 for the many children who lack kinaesthetic sensitivity and effective spatio temporal programming ability necessary in, for instance, fine paper-pencil skills. Are we starting training in such skills too early for the 'average' child? (Laszlo & Bairstow, 1985).

Finally, children suffering from perceptual motor disabilities can now be diagnosed in terms of causative factors rather than being restricted to observation of symptoms. With the aid of the PMAT a perceptual motor profile can be drawn up, comparing the child's performance on each test task with the expected level for his age. Specific training procedures can then be designed to alleviate the diagnosed difficulties.

As an example of this diagnostic method leading to specific therapy the work with two clumsy children, Matthew and Mike, can be de-

Fig. 14.2 Kinaesthetic training and its effect on copying geometric figures.

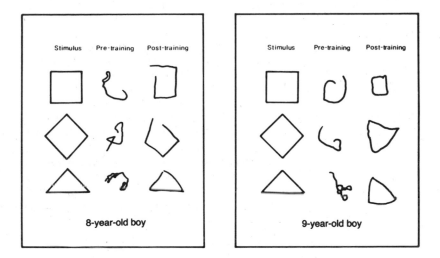

scribed (see Laszlo & Bairstow, 1983, for full details). In general it was found that 74% of clumsy children suffer from dyskinaesthesia, i.e., they have only rudimentary kinaesthetic sensitivity.

Matthew is an 8-year-old who was repeating Year 2 because he could not learn to print. He was diagnosed as suffering from Minimal Brain Dysfunction and was given extensive remedial teaching in paper–pencil skills over two years. When tested he was found to perform the kinaesthetic tasks randomly. We trained him in six 15 minute sessions to improve kinaesthetic processing ability. At retest his kinaesthetic scores were at the 12-year-old level. He improved his printing skill and five months later at the end of the school year he became the printing champion of his class.

Mike, aged 9, had to be moved from his school to a 'special' school as a result of his inability to cope with printing. He scored at the 5-year-old level on the kinaesthetic tasks, before he was trained in kinaesthetic awareness in seven 20 minute sessions. He reached kinaesthetic scores at his own age level on retest, and showed improved facility at printing. Figure 14.2 demonstrates pre- and post-training drawings of these two boys.

Thus, with the aid of the PMAT, specific perceptual and/or motor disabilities can be diagnosed. This causal diagnosis leads to focal therapy, where training programmes can be designed to alleviate specific dysfunctions. Consequent to successful training, the child's total perceptual–motor performance level would improve.

References

Bairstow, P. J., & Laszlo, J. I. (1981). Kinaesthetic sensitivity to passive movements in children and adults, and its relationship to motor development and motor control. *Developmental Medicine and Child Neurology, 23*, 606–16.

Laszlo, J. I., & Bairstow, P. J. (1982). Tests of kinaesthetic sensitivity: Kinaesthesis in normal development and physical disability. In D. Garlick (Ed.), *Proprioception, posture and emotion.* Sydney: Committee of Postgraduate Medical Education.

Laszlo, J. I. & Bairstow, P. J. (1983). Kinaesthesis: Its measurement, training and relationship to motor control. *Quarterly Journal of Experimental Psychology, 35A*, 411–21.

Laszlo, J. I., & Bairstow, P. J. (1985). *Perceptual-motor behaviour: developmental assessment and therapy.* London, Holt Saunders.

15

Perceptual Motor Development in Children's Drawing Skill

Pia Broderick
University of Western Australia

Children are encouraged to trace, copy and draw various forms freely from an early age in our educational system, in preparation for the learning of printing and writing skills. Any fine manipulative skill presents difficulties for the young child but, with increasing age, these difficulties decrease gradually until reaching a normal adult level. However, throughout development, and even into adulthood a noticeable difference appears to exist between the copying performance of squares and diamonds. The task of copying a geometric figure from a visual model involves adequate perceptual and cognitive abilities. Both visual and kinaesthetic information is required to reconcile the copy drawn with the model, and to correct errors evident in the copy. As well, fine motor abilities are essential in planning, programming, execution and possible correction of errors in the movements. All these factors must come together to produce a copy of the geometric model, and these abilities develop in children at different rates. The efficiency of performance in the copying task depends on adequate development of all these abilities.

It has been shown that children as young as 1–2 years can recognise and discriminate between various geometric forms (Bee & Walker 1968; Maccoby & Bee 1965). However, there is then a considerable delay before the child can draw a recognisable copy of these figures (Arnheim, 1954; Cratty, 1970; Piaget & Inhelder, 1956). Well before being able to copy the figures, children can match figures with models. It has been shown that figure matching is successful when matching models within a like frame, that is a square model within a square frame and a diamond model within a diamond frame (Freeman, 1980;

Naeli & Harris, 1976). In a drawing situation, typically the child would be required to draw on square or rectangular paper. The edges of the paper may provide a parallel frame for the square but not for the diamond, so the paper may aid the drawing of the square only. Studies have shown that children between four and ten years of age can competently use these external visual reference points when drawing (Bayrakter in Freeman, 1980).

Various studies have investigated the influence of surrounding cues or picture frame cues on the discrimination, construction, placement and drawing of squares and diamonds. For example, in drawing or matching of the square and diamond figures 4- to 5-year-olds were found to be influenced by picture frame cues (Naeli & Harris, 1976). In a square frame the square was both better matched and drawn than the diamond, while the converse was true for the diamond frame. In circular frames squares were more accurately placed or drawn than diamonds. In the studies mentioned above, performance was measured in terms of orientation alone. Accuracy of the drawn figure was not considered.

The results of the Perceptual Motor Abilities Test (Laszlo & Broderick, 1985) showed that 5- to 6-year-old children could often not draw diamonds at all although their squares were quite recognisable. While these children could not copy the diamond freehand, all could trace the lines of the figure adequately, establishing that the necessary movements could be made. The study to be reported was designed to establish some of the reasons for the differential difficulty children experience when drawing squares and diamonds. The specific aims of the study are to establish the individual developmental trends for copying squares and diamonds; to analyse the component processes of the drawing skill and attempt to pinpoint the reasons for the differential difficulty of the two figures; and to obtain a measure of drawing accuracy, in addition to orientation measures.

METHOD

Subjects
Four age groups, each of 20 children were chosen for this study to cover the primary school years. The age groups used were 5.5–6 years; 7.5–8 years; 9.5–10 years; 11.5–12 years. A fifth group of 20 adults (age 18–29) were students of the University of Western Australia.

Procedure

A square and a diamond were the only two figures used in the study. The diamond was the square rotated through 45°. All subjects were required to draw both the square and the diamond under five different drawing conditions. The order of task completion was randomly assigned to each subject and half the subjects in each age group began each task with the square while the other half began each task with the diamond. The conditions or tasks were chosen according to the emphasis each placed on the different components of drawing skill.

Tasks

Task 1 required the subject to copy from models a square and a diamond onto separate sheets of rectangular A4 paper. Copying involves formulation of the plan of the movement, generation of a motor unit activation pattern, i.e., motor programming, perception of the feedback information generated by the ongoing movement and possible modification of the motor unit activation pattern. This task gives a base performance level for the drawing of squares and diamonds for all subjects, although the importance of individual processes and even groups of processes cannot be isolated here.

In Task 2, a model 3 times the size of that used in Task 1 was shown to the subject and he was required to copy it, again onto A4 paper. It was thought that the large figures would present more scope for the detection of errors and subsequent corrective error programming, as larger movements generate more easily discernable kinaesthetic feedback than smaller ones.

Task 3 was used to investigate the theory of the influence of picture frame cues. The standard size models were presented on circular paper and the subject was required to copy them onto circular paper. This was designed to remove the picture frame cues and was expected to result in a deterioration in drawing accuracy for both squares and diamonds (Naeli & Harris, 1976).

Task 4 was designed to remove some visual information from the drawing situation. The subject was given a pointed wooden stylus shaped like a pencil and was asked to copy the two models which were of standard size. Two sheets of A4 paper with a carbon paper insert allowed a trace to be made for scoring and comparison purposes.

Task 5 involved drawing the two figures without any visual information available concerning the resulting trace. A masking box was used to shield the hand, paper and pencil from the subject's sight.

The models of the square and diamond were always in front of the subject. Without visual information the detection of movement errors had to be based on kinaesthetic information alone.

Scoring

Two scores, orientation error and angular variability were recorded for every drawing for every subject. Orientation error is the measure of position accuracy of the drawing in relation to the paper. This score was determined by reference lines drawn on the drawing sheet corresponding to the orientation of one side of the model figure. Two lines were drawn through the opposing angles of the copied figure, intersecting the orientation reference line. The two angles enclosed by the orientation reference line and the lines drawn through the copied figure were measured and the mean of the absolute deviations from $45°$ was taken as the orientation error score.

Angular variability is a measure of the average difference between adjacent angles in a polygon (Attneave, 1957). This measure reflects the degree of conformity of the drawn figure to the model. For each drawn figure, all angles were measured and the difference calculated between each pair of adjacent angles. The absolute angle differences were summed and the mean calculated to obtain the angular variability score. A perfect copied figure (regardless of orientation) would consist of four $90°$ angles resulting in an angular variability score of zero indicating a perfectly regular figure. As the irregularity of the shape increases, the angular variability score increases accordingly.

RESULTS AND DISCUSSION

Orientation

A three way analysis of variance (5 ages × 5 tasks × 2 figures with repeated measures on the last two factors (Winer, 1962) yielded significant main effects on all three factors: age, $F(4,95) = 15.89$, $p < 0.01$, task, $F(4,380) = 22.05$, $p < 0.01$, and figure, $F(1,95) = 63.15$, $p < 0.01$. Two first order interactions were also significant: age × task, $F(4,380) = 9.05$, $p < 0.01$, and age × figure, $F(4,95) = 5.53$, $p < 0.01$.

The orientation error results are presented graphically in Figure 15.1. Post hoc Newman-Keuls tests support, in the main, the trends shown in Figure 15.1 and the results obtained from the overall analysis of the data. That is, overall age differences were more pronounced for diamond orientation than for the square. Year 1 children differed significantly from all other age groups, while adults orientated the di-

Fig. 15.1   Orientation error scores for the square and diamond for each task, at each age group. Task 1: copying 40 mm figures; Task 2: 120 mm figures; Task 3: 40 mm figures on round paper; Task 4: partial visual information reduction; Task 5: total visual information reduction.

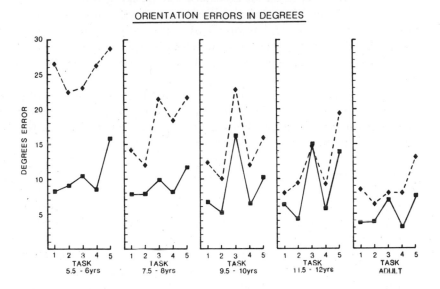

ORIENTATION ERRORS IN DEGREES

amond significantly more accurately than Year 3 and Year 5 children. For square orientation, only two consistent trends were supported; both Year 1 and Year 3 children orientated the square less accurately than adults.

Within age, within task comparisons between square and diamond orientation yielded significant differences for all five tasks in the three youngest age groups. In Year 7, the two figures differed in Task 2, 4 and 5, for Adults in Tasks 1, 4 and 5. These are the differences which could be responsible for the significant age × figure interaction.

The major findings which emerge from these results is that the orientation accuracy of the diamond develops at a slower rate than that of the square. Additionally, the difference between the orientation error of the figures in Tasks 4 and 5 from age 12 years onwards indicates that reduction of visual information is more detrimental for the orientation of the diamond than the square. That is, kinaesthetic feedback can be more effectively used in the easier figure, but kinaesthesis must be supplemented by vision to achieve similar accuracy in orientation of the diamond.

While task differences over all ages did yield significant differences (see F value) the Newman-Keul's comparisons within age between tasks and between figures yielded a less than clear cut picture. The only consistent difference occurred for Task 5. For the square, Task 5 was shown to differ from all other tasks at all age groups with the exceptions that in Years 3 and 7 Tasks 3 and 5 did not differ significantly. Again for the diamond Task 5 proved to be significantly more difficult than the other tasks (exceptions: Year 1, Tasks 1 and 4; Year 3 Task 3; and Adults Task 1 to Task 5 did not yield significant differences).

Thus it becomes obvious that task manipulations do not have a systematic effect on orientation accuracy except that Task 5, where visual information is eliminated, is performed less accurately than the other tasks, in most cases for both figures.

Angular variability

A three way analysis of variance (5 ages × 5 tasks × 2 figures) was performed (Winer, 1962). All three main effects were significant: Age, $F(4,95) = 15.05$, $p < 0.01$; tasks, $F(4,380) = 17.02$, $p < 0.01$ and figures, $F(1,95) = 90.59$, $p < 0.01$. Significant age × figure, $F(4,95) = 6.04$, $p < 0.01$ and age × task, $F(4,380) = 3.29$, $p < 0.05$ interactions were also established. The results are summarised in Figure 15.2.

Post hoc Newman-Keul's tests between age groups, within tasks and figures, showed that for the square Year 1 angular variability differed from all other ages in all tasks (exceptions: Years 1 and 3 in Tasks 2 and 3), while year 3 differed from adults on all five tasks. Other consistent age effects were not found. Stronger developmental trends were shown for the diamond (see Figure 15.2) than the square. All ages differed from each other in all tasks with one exception (Year 3 versus Year 5 in Task 5). However, as shown in Figure 15.2, a reversal in the developmental trend can be seen, i.e. the diamonds were copied with less accuracy by the Year 3 children than by Year 1 children.

Thus, while gradual developmental trends were established in accuracy of the shape of the diamond, from Year 3 onwards overall improvement in shape accuracy for the square could not be found. The Year 3 children copied the square as well as Year 7 children, though they did not reach adult performance level. The unexpected high error score of the Year 3 group for the diamond could be due to the fact that most of the children at that age group diverged from the model and drew elongated 'stereotyped' diamonds.

Fig. 15.2   Angular variability error scores for the square and diamond for each task, at each age group. Task 1: copying 40 mm figures; Task 2: 120 mm figures; Task 3: 40 mm figures on round paper; Task 4: partial visual information reduction; Task 5: total visual information reduction.

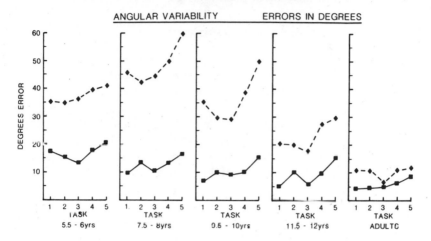

Within age group and within task angular variability was always shown to be higher for the diamond than the square with the exception of Task 3 for adults. Thus at all ages tested, copying a regular shape when copying the square proved less difficult than when copying the diamond.

Within age groups and within figures task differences were compared also. For the square only one consistent trend did emerge: Task 5 differed from all other tasks at all age levels with only few exceptions (differences were not found between Tasks 3 and 5 in adults; and Tasks 4 and 5 in Year 3 and adults). For the diamond both Tasks 4 and 5 differed from Task 3 at all age levels. Furthermore, Task 1 differed from Task 5 at all but adult level, while Task 1 and 4 differences were found for Years 1, 5 and 7. Task 1 versus 3 differences did emerge in Years 5, 7 and adults. An inspection of Figure 15.2 shows that in these cases Task 1 performance was superior to that in Task 3.

Clearly the regularity of the copied square is less influenced by task manipulations than that of the diamond. Indeed the regularity of the square was influenced only by total loss of visual feedback, showing that vision and kinaesthesis together result in better drawing of the square than can be achieved with kinaesthesis alone. Reliance on visual information is even more pronounced when drawing the diamond as can be seen from performance deterioration even at partial loss of vision as in Task 4. Neutral picture frame cues did not affect regularity of the square but did increase the error scores for the diamond in the three older age groups, i.e., at age levels where environmental cues are incorporated into movement planning.

Overview

The relationship between the two error scores, orientation and angular variability, needs to be examined. In previous studies only orientation scores were recorded, and these were accepted as comprehensive indices of manipulative and drawing proficiency of squares and diamonds. However, orientation is, in the main, a measure of perceptual ability, and does not reflect motor abilities directly. In the present experiment angular variability scores were also included, along with orientation scores. Angular variability is dependent on the regularity of the drawn shape, thus it relates to motor abilities, primarily to movement planning and motor programming.

A comparison of the two scores relevant to developmental trends in the copying tasks of squares and diamonds yield somewhat different results. At all ages the diamond was less accurately drawn than the square as measured by angular variability. This was in contrast to the accuracy of orientation, where differences between the two figures could not be found at age 12 years and adults. It could be hypothesised that the difference between diamonds and squares is twofold. Oblique lines demand more complex motor programmes than horizontals and verticals. Therefore combining these obliques to form a diamond requires a higher level of planning ability than is required for drawing the square. The reason for the greater difference between the two figures in the youngest age group compared to older subjects could be explained by the rudimentary development of both spatial programming and planning ability.

The two performance measures are affected differently by task manipulations. Orientation of both figures was adversely affected only by the total loss of visual information. In contrast, both partial and total visual feedback loss diminished shape accuracy in the diamond, but only total visual feedback loss affected accuracy in the square. The introduction of neutral picture frame cues had, in general, a greater influence on orientation performance than on shape accuracy.

Thus it is apparent that the two scores reflect different aspects of performance. Both perceptual and motor factors should be investigated to arrive at an explanation for the greater difficulty of drawing figures comprised of oblique lines versus horizontal-vertical lines.

Finally although Task 2, the copying of figures three times larger than those in Task 1, was included in the study to optimise conditions for error detection and correction, no systematic difference was found between Tasks 1 and 2 in either figure, with either performance measure. There could be two reasons for the failure of finding performance enhancement with large figures. Either the enlargement of the figures in Task 2 was not sufficient to facilitate error detection and error correction, or error detection is not an important factor in figure drawing. It is the former of these reasons which is considered to be the decisive factor.

References

Arnheim, R. (1954). *Art and visual perception*. Berkeley: University of California Press.

Attneave, F. (1957). Physical determinants of the judged complexity of shapes. *Journal of Experimental Psychology, 53*, 221–7.

Bee, II. L., & Walker, R. S.(1968). Experimental modification of the lag between perceiving and performing. *Psychonomic Science, 11*, 127–8.

Cratty, B. J. (Ed) (1970). *Perceptual and motor development in infants and young children*. New York: Macmillan

Freeman, N. H. (1980). *Strategies of representation in young children*. London: Academic Press Inc.

Laszlo, J. I. & Broderick, P. A. (1985). The perceptual-motor skill of drawing. In N. Freeman (Ed.), *The representation of visual order*. Cambridge University Press.

Maccoby, E. E., & Bee, H. L. (1965). Some speculation concerning the lag between perceiving and performing. *Child Development, 36*, 367–77.

Naeli, H., & Harris, P. L. (1976). Orientation of the diamond and square. *Perception, 5*, 73–7.

Piaget, J., & Inhelder, B. (1956). *The child's conception of space*. London: Routledge & Kegan Paul.

16

Vestibular-Postural and Oculomotor Control Problems in Learning Disabled Children

Gordon Stanley, Lorraine Grimwood, Elizabeth
Rutherford and Ian Hopkins
University of Melbourne

The involvement of neurological deficits in the vestibular-postural and oculomotor systems of learning disabled children is controversial at two levels. Firstly the theoretical accounts put forward by such writers as Ayres (1972), Delacato (1966) and Levinson (1980) are either inconsistent with current neurological and neuropsychological theory or too speculative to be acceptable. Secondly there is some debate as to the incidence of such disorders if they are to play any causative role.

Establishing a causal role for any relationship between neurological deficit and learning disability is not easy and the present paper does not address this issue directly. Our relatively modest aim was to investigate a number of measures of vestibular–postural and oculomotor functions in a group of learning disabled children and to see in what ways they differed from average learning controls.

THE SAMPLE

The problem of sample selection when investigating learning disability is not a trivial one (Stanley, Smith & Powys, 1982). Often studies use samples with above average IQ in line with many earlier clinical reports suggesting that certain syndromes of specific learning disorder occur in above average children. In the present study we selected children presenting at a learning disability clinic or in remedial classes in the western suburbs of Melbourne. They were aged between 8 and 11 years, had a reading deficit greater than 17 months below chronological age, were not disadvantaged in language due to ethnic back-

154

Table 16.1 Means and standard deviations for the learning disabled and control children. Asterisk indicates significant difference by *t*-test at *p* < .01 level.

n	Learning disabled 22 (18M 4F)	Control 22 (19M 3F)
Age	9.69 (1.04)	9.62 (1.02)
PPVT IQ	102.32 (8.78)	102.54 (10.44)
Mazes	11.04 (3.17)	12.14 (2.70)
Coding	6.82 (2.30)	9.82 (3.30)*
Digit span	7.54 (2.30)	10.54 (3.58)*
St Lucia RDG	5.98 (.90)	10.40 (1.67)*
Wrat arithmetic	14.64 (14.32)	50.00 (20.09)*
Motor proficiency	19.95 (26.09)	60.41 (25.34)*

ground, were free from any primary emotional or social problem, were within the normal range of IQ and did not have any previously diagnosed neurological disorder. Controls were selected from the same socio-economic background and the same schools to have the same age and Peabody Picture Vocabulary (PPVT). Characteristics of the two groups and differences are presented in Table 16.1.

It should be noted that the children in this sample were impaired significantly in both reading and arithmetic relative to controls. Poor performance on coding and digit span is reported often for dyslexic children (Stanley, 1978) but the present sample was also impaired markedly on the Bruininks-Oseretsky test of motor efficiency, though this was not a criterion test for its selection.

THE VARIABLES

Neuroanatomical and neurophysiological reviews emphasise the close association of vestibular, proprioceptive oculomotor and cerebellar mechanisms (e.g., Kornhuber, 1974 a, b). Considerable attention has been paid to visual-vestibular connections and vestibular influence on eye movement control; on vestibular-proprioceptive interaction, particularly neck proprioceptors in control of posture; on vestibular, proprioceptive and oculomotor interaction in control of posture; on vestibular-spinal responses and cerebellar involvement in all such mechanisms (Pompeiano, 1974). Involvement in all these systems is seen in the classic example of precise co-ordination of eyes, head/neck movements, trunk and limb movements, in maintaining posture and

Table 16.2   Listing of variables studied.

Vestibular-Postural Control Variables

● Vestibular	– post-rotary nystagmus.
● Unconscious proprio-ception/muscle tone	– cocontraction.
● Primitive postural reflexes	– assymmetrical tonic neck reflex.
● Righting and equilibrium	– neck righting; – labyrinthine righting; – standing balance; eyes closed; – reactions to displacement in standing, sitting and long sitting; and – Heath Railwalking Test.

Oculomotor Variables

● Oculomotor	– pursuits; – accommodation/convergence system including vergence reserves; – fixation stability and phoria screening.
● Visual Screening	– visual acuity; – hypermetropia screening; – stereopsis.

equilibrium, and steady gaze necessary for the performance of any goal–directed activity.

Vestibular–postural and oculomotor variables were selected as outlined in Table 16.2. Variables selected were those amenable to standardised clinical assessment. Given the fact that clinical assessment procedures are not blind the two testers (LG and ER) interchanged roles. For a selection of the sample video recordings were made to enable a check on the reliability of assessment. Of 43 sets of observations there was only difference on one for two testers. The performance of 10 undergraduate occupational therapy students unconnected with the study was less impressive in their agreement on ratings. Nevertheless an average of 77 per cent agreement occurred and instances of disagreement tended to involve relative position on subjective scales rather than presence or absence of an effect.

RESULTS

There were 15 variables tested to measure the integrity of the vestibular-postural system. The test results of 12 of these variables were treated as scaled data and subjected to chi-square (χ^2) analysis.

Table 16.3   Results of significance tests between mean scores for learning disabled and control children on vestibular-postural variables.

Variable	Significance Test t-test or χ^2 Test
Post rotary nystagmus-duration	t (42) = 1.80; $p < .05$
Post rotary nystagmus-quality	χ^2 (1) = 12.12; $p < .001$
Post rotary nystagmus-reaction	χ^2 (2) = 14.67; $p < .001$
Heath rail walking	t (42) = −1.82; N.S.*
Muscle cocontraction-elbow	χ^2 (2) = 20.94; $p < .001$
Muscle cocontraction-neck	χ^2 (2) = 18.28; $p < .001$
Standing balance-eyes closed	t (42) = −0.49; N.S.*
Equilibrium standing	χ^2 (2) = 16.50; $p < .001$
Equilibrium sitting	χ^2 (1) = 8.94; $p < .01$
Equilibrium long leg sitting	χ^2 (2) = 15.13; $p < .001$
Primitive postural reflex-tonic neck reflex	χ^2 (1) = 11.38; $p < .001$
Primitive postural reflex inhibit	χ^2 (2) = 9.17; $p < .01$
Tonic labyrinthine reflex-prone	χ^2 (2) = 14.79; $p < .001$
Tonic labyrinthine reflex-supine	χ^2 (2) = 21.58; $p < .001$
Primitive postural reflex-rolling	χ^2 (2) = 14.31; $p < .001$

* Not significant at the .05 level

Results of the other three variables were analysed by t-tests. Thirteen of the vestibular–postural variables indicated differences between the groups as shown in Table 16.3. The oculomotor control variables indicated a similar trend with eight out of ten differentiating between the learning disabled and the control children.

Discussion

The present results support the small body of literature implicating brain stem–cerebellar dysfunction in certain groups of underachieving children (Ayres, 1978; de Quiros, 1976). Vestibular-postural dysfunction was noted in our study across a range of measures. Signs of vestibular-postural dysfunction, reported in younger age groups (Grimwood and Rutherford, 1980) were still apparent in this study's older age group (8–11 years).

The results also suggest that an indepth assessment of a number of

Table 16.4   Results of significance tests between mean scores for learning disabled and control children on oculomotor control variables.

Variable	Significance Test t-test or χ^2 Test
General Visual Pursuit	χ^2 (2) = 15.30; $p < .001$
Pursuit across midline	χ^2 (2) = 21.33; $p < .001$
Convergence Sufficiency	χ^2 (1) = 3.61; N.S.*
Accommodation facility	t (42) = 2.34; $p < .05$
Vergence reserves-convergence	t (42) = 3.06; $p < .01$
Vergence reserves-divergence	t (42) = −4.36; $p < .001$
Fixation stability-uncovered	χ^2 (1) = 13.86; $p < .001$
Fixation stability-covered	χ^2 (1) = 15.72; $p < .001$
Esophoria	χ^2 (1) = 5.64; $p < .02$
Exophoria	χ^2 (1) = 2.03; N.S.*

* Not significant at the .05 level

oculomotor and related functions reveals a pattern of dysfunction in underachieving children. Mechanisms implicated by writers such as Hoffman (1980) were also noted as dysfunctioned in the learning disabled group in this study.

Poor motor performance, as determined by psychometric assessment or clinically determined as neurological soft signs has been regarded as a predominant feature of minimal brain dysfunction. In the present study poor motor performance was seen in association with vestibular–postural and oculomotor dysfunction.

It would appear that postural control is needed in order to develop skilled motor control such as control in prime movers (large muscle groups) and postural fixation for fine skilled finger movements. Kornhuber (1974 b) has stressed the importance of the vestibular system to the general motor system. The oculomotor system is part of the general motor system, and it would seem that signs of motor awkwardness in pursuits and visual–motor co-ordination may have considerable relevance for a range of classroom activities.

Difficulty in postural and oculomotor items, and poor motor performance, was seen in the same experimental group. This suggests that brain stem–cerebellar dysfunction, as reported in this study, may well affect higher integrative function such as skilled motor performance.

Motor performance has been linked to attention (Dykman et al.,

1971). Motor unco-ordination and short attention span are seen in younger children, and in older underachieving children. While no specific measures of attention were undertaken in this study, significant differences occurred between the groups on the motor performance variable and the short term memory variables of Coding and Digit Span which are known indicators of attention.

While the present study has provided surprisingly clear results, the identification of a syndrome of neurological impairment in a group of learning disabled children does not necessarily imply that the impairment plays a direct causal role in the learning disability.

References

Ayres, A. J. (1972). *Sensory integration and learning disorders*, Los Angeles: Western Psychological Services.

Ayres, A. J. (1978). Learning disabilities and the vestibular system, *Journal of Learning Disabilities, 11*(1), 30–41.

Delacato, C. II. (1966). *The treatment and prevention of reading problems*, Springfield, Ill.: C. C. Thomas.

de Quiros, J. B. (1976). Diagnosis of vestibular disorders in the learning disabled, *Journal of Learning Disabilities, 9*(1), 40–58.

Dykman, R. A., Ackerman, P. T., Clements, S. D., & Peters, J. E. (1971). Specific learning disabilities: an attentional deficit syndrome. In H. R. Myklebust (Ed.), *Progress in learning disability*, Vol. 2, New York: Grune and Stratton.

Grimwood, L. M., & Rutherford, E. M. (1980). Sensory integrative therapy as an intervention procedure with Grade One 'At risk' readers—a three year study, *The Exceptional Child, 27*(1), 52–61.

Hoffman, L. G. (1980). Incidence of vision difficulties in children with learning disabilities, *Journal of the American Optometic Association, 51*(5), 447–51.

Kornhuber, H. H. (Ed.) (1974a). *Vestibular System Part 1: Basic Mechanisms*. Berlin: Springer-Verlag.

Kornhuber, H. H. (Ed.) (1974b). *Vestibular System Part 2: Psychophysics, Applied Aspects and General Interpretations*. Berlin: Springer-Verlag.

Levinson, H. J. (1980). *Dyslexia: A solution to the riddle*. New York: Springer-Verlag.

Pompeiano, O. (1974). Cerebello-Vestibular Interrelations. In H. H. Kornhuber (Ed.), *Vestibular system part 1: Basic mechanisms*. Berlin: Springer-Verlag.

Stanley, G. (1978). Developmental Dyslexia. In G. V. Stanley & K. W. Walsh (Eds), *Brain impairment: Proceedings of the 1976 Brain Impairment Workshop*. Melbourne: University of Melbourne.

Stanley, G., Smith, G., & Powys, A. (1982). Selecting intelligence tests for studies of dyslexic children. *Psychological Reports*. 50, 787–92.

SECTION 4
SOCIAL ASPECTS OF
DEVELOPMENT

Research on social aspects of development has broadened considerably in the past decade or so. While interest in the range of social behaviours displayed by children at different ages in different situations has continued, more attention has been directed to social development across the life span. In addition, an increasing interest has been shown in assessing the extent to which these behaviours are mediated by social cognitive processes. And, as part of this concern, there has been a more recent focus on the perceptions and attitudes, as well as the behaviour, of people (e.g., siblings, parents) considered to be influential components of the social environment. The six chapters concerned with social aspects of development in this volume, reflect this breadth of interest.

Siegal presents two studies which showed that the extent of social experience in a day care setting influenced the ability of 4-year-old children to discriminate between social and moral rules. While these findings question Piaget's account of moral development and attest to the importance of daycare experience in this development, they also raise important issues concerning the basis of the daycare effect.

The chapter by Yates and Yates is concerned with the relationship between two aspects of impulse control in 5- to 8-year-old children: reflection–impulsivity and delay of gratification. Although it is intuitively plausible that these two aspects of impulse control should be related, previous research has generally failed to confirm this expectation. However, Yates and Yates found in three studies that individual differences in impulsivity are predictive of delay of gratification, but only under particular circumstances.

The next four chapters are concerned with the perceptions and attitudes of several different groups including parents, siblings, adolescents, the middle aged and elderly. In the first chapter, Toussaint reports findings from a much needed study of the attitudes of mothers to part-tine and full-time care of 4- and 5-year-old children. As might be expected, it was found that mothers using no form of childcare (i.e., playgroups, kindergartens, daycare) were opposed to both part- and full-time care, although they were more opposed to the latter. Among users, the results suggest that part-time care has become more socially acceptable with the mothers recognising benefits for both themselves and their children. In contrast, disadvantages were seen for both parent and child in full-time care, even among user parents.

Knight, in her chapter, examines the proposition that parents are 'constructivists' in terms of their beliefs about their children's competence and personality. That is, parents construct and modify their beliefs on the basis of common but individual experiences. Mothers and fathers of children of different ages were questioned concerning their satisfaction with the progress of their child on several dimensions and the stability of behaviour on these dimensions. Consistent with a constructivist position, the results suggested that parents operate as developmental optimists—they believe that good aspects of their children will remain stable while the bad things will improve.

The chapter by Kirkman is probably unique in its focussing on the effects on a child's development of being raised with a disabled sibling. Analysis of the non-disabled siblings responses to questions concerning the times that were easy and difficult with a disabled sibling, and the reasons for these experiences, revealed that pleasant times were considerably exceeded by difficulties. The latter occurred most frequently in adolescence and stemmed from several different sources.

In examining the attitudes toward and perceptions of adolescents, the middle-aged and elderly by these same groups, Luszcz and Fitzgerald, in the final chapter, consider the possibility that adolescents and the elderly can be construed as generation gap allies relative to middle aged adults. The results indicated that the cohorts were valued differentially and that the differences in the perceptions of cohorts were most pronounced in the perceptions that adolescents and elderly adults have of each other.

ANDREW R. NESDALE

17

Daycare, Rules, and the Heteronomy Construct

Michael Siegal
University of Queensland

According to Piaget (1932), young children's social development is characterised by a heteronomous morality. Children are egocentric and lack the ability to coordinate the perspectives of others with their own. Since they have a unilateral respect for all the rules of those in authority, the distinction between moral rules and those that apply to social conventions occurs out of a global fusion of all social concepts.

By contrast, Turiel (1983b) has proposed that young children discriminate between rules that are defined to be within social and moral domains. For Turiel, social rules are arbitrary conventions defined with reference to a particular social setting. Rule transgressions are evaluated as wrong depending upon whether they occur within this setting. Outside the relevant context, such acts are no longer evaluated as naughty. By contrast, moral rules are not arbitrary and are not tied to social contexts. Moral rule transgressions are intrinsically wrong regardless of whether a social rule exists.

In support of Turiel's analysis, Smetana (1981, 1985) found that preschool children aged 2½ to 4½ years discriminate between rules in the two domains. These results are interpreted to cast doubt upon the heteronomy construct. However, the degree to which subjects were previously exposed to social experience was not examined and there is evidence to suggest that young children who may have had limited peer interaction do respect the sacredness of adult rules (Siegal, 1982, pp. 121–151).

Recently, we have completed two studies that were aimed at examining the effects of social experience in a daycare context (Siegal & Storey, 1985). It was predicted that daycare veterans, having had extensive social interaction, would be more likely than their newly enrolled counterparts to discriminate between social and moral rules.

The daycare studies

Each child participated in one study only. The subjects in both studies consisted of two groups of 10 boys and 10 girls each attending pre-school programs in Brisbane. One group had attended the same child-care centre for 18 months or more from 9 am to 5 pm at least three full days a week. The mean age of these daycare 'veterans' in the first study was 4.4 years and in the second 4.1 years. The children had been in care for a mean of 2 years, 6 months (range = 1.6 to 3.6). The second group had been newly enrolled for the past three months in the same centre attended by the veterans. The mean age in the first study was 4.3 and in the second 4.2. No child in the group had had previous daycare or preschool experience.

The parents of the children were engaged in professional occupations, mainly as physicians, lawyers, computer scientists, and university lecturers. Both mothers and fathers had a college education. It can be assumed that the two groups of children did not have parents who differed in their attitudes toward daycare. Parents of newly enrolled children previously had had their children on a waiting list for daycare for between 10 and 24 months. They were unable earlier to meet the enrolment quotas imposed by the centres because the family had recently moved into the area and/or did not have access to information about the demands for daycare services.

In the first study the children were given the moral and social rules items used by Smetana (1981) closely following the same procedure. Wording was changed slightly to conform with Australian usage, and one social conventional item, 'a child not saying grace before meals', was changed to 'a child eating ice-cream with a fork' to ensure familiarity. The other social transgressions consisted of not participating in show and tell, not sitting in a designated place during story time, putting a toy away in an incorrect place and not placing belongings in a designated place. The moral stimuli consisted of hitting, not sharing a toy, shoving, throwing water at another child and taking another child's apple.

Pilot testing indicated the desirability of reducing the number of responses required by the children owing to time pressures within the children's program of activities. Thus only two of the four questions used by Smetana were employed in the initial study.

Each subject was seen individually and shown ink drawings of the ten transgressions. For each stimulus item, the subjects were asked to point to a scale of four faces in order to indicate the naughtiness of the transgression. As in the Smetana study, a series of four faces was depicted with progressively larger and more exaggerated frowns and verbally labelled to indicate that the transgressor was 'OK' (happy face), 'a little bit bad', 'very bad', or 'very, very bad' (big scowl). Before using the scale, all the subjects demonstrated that they could correctly identify each scale point by pointing to the appropriate face. Responses were recorded on a 4-point scale from (1) OK to (4) very, very bad. Subjects were then asked, 'Do you think the child should get into trouble?' and if so, 'A little or a lot?' Responses were coded on a 3-point scale which ranged from (0) 'no' to (2) 'a lot'.

Only the veterans' responses were comparable to those found in the Smetana study. While veteran and newly enrolled children rated moral transgressions similarly, the veterans were significantly less likely than the newly enrolled to perceive social transgressions as naughty, $t(38) = 4.09$, $p < .001$. As predicted, the veterans prescribed more punishment for perpetrators of moral transgressions than for those of social transgressions, $t(19) = 6.90$, $p < .001$; the difference was insignificant in the newly enrolled group. Again, while the two groups rated moral transgressions similarly, the veterans were significantly less likely to perceive social transgressions as deserving of punishment, $t(38) = 3.71$, $p < .01$.

We undertook a second study in an attempt to replicate the initial findings and to examine the children's conceptions of moral and social rules as contingent upon a particular setting. The children in the study were given three moral and three social transgressions. In addition to questions concerning the naughtiness of the transgressions, they were asked whether a transgression would be worthy of adult intervention or anger and wrong even if teachers didn't mind or wouldn't get cross. The responses to the questions were analysed in 2 (groups) × 2 (domains: moral vs social) analyses of variance. Several Group × Domain interaction effects were significant. For example, compared to the newly enrolled, veterans again differentiated moral from social transgressions as naughtier, $F(1,38) = 53.51$, $p < .01$. They judged moral transgressions as wrong even if teachers didn't mind, $F(1,38) = 22.19$, $p < .01$ and as worthier of adult intervention, $F(1,38) = 8.82$, $p < .01$.

The results of the two studies indicate that across a range of situations, moral transgressions are regarded as equally serious by veterans and newly enrolled alike while the distinction between morality and convention is unclear for the newly enrolled.

Veterans preferred adults to be discriminating in their interventions. They had more highly developed expectations of the use of adult authority than did the newly enrolled, and preferred that it be exercised in moral rather than social situations. The finding of Rubenstein, Howes and Boyle (1981) that daycare children are more independent in their compliance with adult directives can be interpreted in this light. If social transgressions are regarded by veterans as acceptable, conflict may ensue which is not present in the parent-child interactions of newly enrolled children who had had a more limited social experience.

Validity of the heteronomy construct

Daycare is a highly relevant context for examining the proposition that children's early social concepts are global and undifferentiated. But despite its theoretical and practical importance, disturbingly little is known about the effects of daycare on development (Belsky, Steinberg & Walker, 1982), and the extent to which daycare workers or peers exert a disproportionate effect on children's conceptions of rules is a matter requiring further study. Nevertheless, some informed speculations can be offered on the source of children's ability to discriminate between rule domains.

While Piaget contended that mature conceptions of rules in both domains are constructed from peer-oriented social interactions, Turiel (1983b) has proposed that this distinction arises from qualitatively different aspects of the individual's social interactions. For example, adults have been shown to respond differently to social conventional and moral transgressions. Though both adults and peers respond to moral transgressions, adults rather than peers initiate responses to transgressions against social rules (Nucci & Nucci, 1982; Nucci & Turiel, 1978; Smetana, 1985).

The basis for children's understanding, however, remains unclear (Shweder, 1982). In this connection, the data which Piaget used to support his claims came from children living in the poorer parts of Swiss cities who were unlikely to have been exposed to intensive peer group influence at the age of 5 years and under. Such intensive exposure, for example, is given to children who attend daycare centres on a full-time basis. That these children distinguish between social and moral rules can be interpreted as consistent with Piaget's heteronomy concept. Indeed, for Piaget (1932, p. 266), these was 'no question of clear cut stages in moral psychology'. His cognitive account of moral judgement allowed for the promotion of the child's moral development through spontaneous peer group activities. Development involves a structural reorganisation in thought where children relinquish an egocentric orientation and come to coordinate the perspectives of peers with their own. Daycare children are exposed to extensive peer group influence, though Piaget directed his remarks at school-aged children who were posited to have the cognitive skills to benefit from social interaction.

Alternatively, should daycare children differ from others in judging social rule violations less severely and in distinguishing between social and moral transgressions, it may be because they are exposed to permissive adult caretakers who practice less authoritative childcare practices than do parents at home (Hess, Price, Dickson & Conroy, 1981). But such an interpretation is rather unlikely. Despite wide variations in childrearing methods, there are few differences in judgements of transgressions among abused, neglected, and nonmaltreated children (Smetana, Kelly & Twentyman, 1984). Moreover, whether or not caregiving is firm and authoritative, the child's understanding of rules may reflect perceptions of control and a willingness to obey rather than the exercise of control per se (Lewis, 1981; Siegal & Barclay, 1985; Siegal & Cowen, 1984). Adults' verbal reactions to preschoolers' social and moral transgressions may differ but they are interventions all the same. These may set the stage for differences in the quality of social interaction which are imperceptible when compared to the behaviour of peers who rarely respond to social transgressions at all and may in fact condone such actions. An extension of a hypothesis proposed by Berndt (1983) is that children who seldom interact with their peers are less likely to be popular. Thus they may be unlikely to distinguish between the moral rules endorsed by both adults and peers and the adult-endorsed social conventions which peers tend to disregard.

The relation between children's orientations to rules and their social interaction with peers is liable to be extremely complex (see Hymel, 1983, for a review of the intricate uses of sociometric measures in studies of peer group popularity). Coie, Dodge and Coppotelli (1982), for example, distinguish among unpopular school children who are rejected, neglected or controversial. Rejected children may participate in more negative social interactions than do the neglected or controversial. Yet it is unclear whether they have different rule conceptions. Furman and Masters (1980) observed that unpopular children are more likely to violate rules that are endorsed either by peers or adults. Since unpopular preschoolers may be poorly accepted in general by others, they may place a low priority on the inviolability of social conventions. Harter and Pike (1984) have devised the Pictorial Scale of Perceived Competence and Social Acceptance for Young Children that includes subscales focusing on peer and maternal acceptance. Whether children's abilities to distinguish between the social and moral domains are associated with social acceptance on the Harter and Pike scale remains to be determined.

More research is needed before these issues can be addressed definitely. At the moment, the validity of the construct of heteronomy cannot be ruled out. Contrary to Piaget, there is a lack of support for the 'proposition that development progresses from egocentrism to perspectivism through structural reorganisations' (Turiel, 1983a, p. 73). Some redefinition of Piaget's approach, however, may still provide a more accurate characterisation of social–cognitive development. Without influencing perspective-taking ability, peer group interaction may affect the child's respect for authority through the ability to discriminate between moral and social rules.

References

Belsky, J., Steinberg, L. D., & Walker, A. (1982). The ecology of daycare. In M. E. Lamb (Ed.), *Nontraditional families: Parenting and child development* (pp. 71–116). Hillsdale, NJ: L. Erlbaum.

Berndt, T. J. (1983). Correlates and causes of sociometric status in childhood: A commentary on six current studies of popular, rejected and neglected children. *Merrill-Palmer Quarterly, 29*, 439–48.

Coie, J. D., Dodge, K. A., & Coppotelli, H. (1982). Dimensions and types of social status: A cross-age perspective. *Developmental Psychology, 18*, 557–70.

Davidson, P., Turiel, E., & Black, A. (1983). The effects of stimulus familiarity on the use of criteria and justifications in children's social reasoning. *British Journal of Developmental Psychology, 1*, 49–65.

Furman, W., & Masters, C. (1980). Peer interactions, sociometric status, and resistance to deviation in young children. *Developmental Psychology, 16*, 229–36.

Harter, S., & Pike, R. (1984). The Pictorial Scale of Perceived Competence and Social Acceptance for Young Children. *Child Development, 55*, 1969–82.

Hess, R. D., Price, G. C., Dickson, W. P., & Conroy, M. (1981). Different roles for mothers and teachers: Contrasting styles of child care. *Advances in Early Education and Day Care, 2*, 1–28.

Hymel, S. (1983). Preschool children's peer relations: Issues in sociometric assessment. *Merrill-Palmer Quarterly, 29,* 237–60.

Nucci, L. P., & Nucci, M. S. (1982). Children's social interactions in the context of moral and conventional transgressions. *Child Development, 53,* 403–12.

Nucci, L., & Turiel, E. (1978). Social interactions and the development of social concepts in preschool children. *Child Development, 53,* 403–12.

Piaget, J. (1932). *The moral judgment of the child.* London: Routledge & Kegan Paul.

Rubenstein, J. L., Howes, C., & Boyle, P. (1981). A two-year follow-up of infants in community-based daycare. *Journal of Child Psychology and Psychiatry, 22,* 209–18.

Shweder, R. A. (1982). Beyond self-constructed knowledge: The study of culture and morality. *Merrill-Palmer Quarterly, 28,* 41–69.

Siegal, M. (1982). *Fairness in children: A social-cognitive approach to the study of moral development.* London: Academic Press.

Siegal, M., & Barclay, M. S. (1985). Children's evaluations of fathers' socialisation behavior. *Developmental Psychology, 21,* 1090–6.

Siegal, M., & Cowen, J. (1984). Appraisals of intervention: The mother's versus the culprit's behavior as determinants of children's evaluations of discipline techniques. *Child Development, 55,* 1760–6.

Siegal, M., & Storey, R. M. (in press). Daycare and children's conceptions of moral and social rules. *Child Development, 56,* 1001–8.

Smetana, J. G. (1981). Preschool children's conceptions of moral and social rules. *Child Development, 52,* 1333–6.

Smetana, J. G. (1985). Preschool children's conceptions of transgressions: The effects of varying moral and conventional domain-related attributes. *Developmental Psychology, 21,* 18–29.

Smetana, J. G., Kelly, M., & Twentyman, C. T. (1984). Abused, neglected, and nonmaltreated children's conceptions of moral and social-conventional transgressions. *Child Development, 55,* 277–87.

Turiel, E. (1983a). Domains and categories in social-cognitive development. In W. F. Overton (Ed.), *The relationship between social and cognitive development* (pp. 53–89). Hillsdale, NJ: L. Erlbaum Associates.

Turiel, E. (1983b). *The development of social knowledge: Morality and convention.* New York: Cambridge University Press.

18

Reflection-Impulsivity and Delay of Gratification Choice

S. M. Yates and G. C. R. Yates
South Australian College of Advanced Education

This paper is concerned with two aspects of impulse control in children between 5 and 8 years: reflection-impulsivity as assessed by the
Matching Familiar Figures Test (MFT: Kagan, Rosman, Day, Albert,
& Phillips, 1964), and delay of gratification as assessed by the choice
dilemma test (Mischel, 1974). We have found evidence for a significant relationship between these two important aspects of development in three separate experimental studies although the results from
our third experiment indicate that this relationship is to be anticipated
only under certain conditions.

Although it is intuitively attractive to postulate that different aspects
of impulse control ought to be significantly inter-related, the typical
research finding has been that diverse measures of inhibition, impulsiveness, self-control, and delay capability fail to intercorrelate significantly, or intercorrelate at a significant, but, perhaps disappointingly,
low level. This basic finding has been reported in samples at the preschool level (Flynn, 1974; Paulsen & Johnson, 1980; Toner, Holstein,
& Hetherington, 1977), at the primary school level (Kendall & Wilcox, 1979; Kendall, Zupan, & Braswell, 1981), at the college level
(Glow, Lange, Glow, & Barnett, 1983; Macbeth, 1974), and in young
adult offenders (Wormith & Hasenpusch, 1979). These studies clearly indicate that the various measures of inhibitory control used in
research (e.g., self-report, teacher ratings, choice tests, delay maintenance tests, persistence measures, and impulsivity measures) simply
do not relate to each other in any direct or facile manner.

Several studies have specifically reported the relationship between delay of gratification choice behaviour and MFFT data. Ward (1973, cited in Messer, 1976), in a study of disadvantaged preschool children, found no differences in delay choice between impulsive and reflective children. Inouye and Sato (1977) used a 10-item delay choice measure in a study with 5- and 6-year-old Japanese children. Traditional median split procedures were used on MFFT scores to define the four quadrant groups (i.e., fast-accurates, impulsives, reflectives and slow-inaccurates). Similar levels of delay choice were evident across MFFT groups in the case of the 5-year-old children. However, within the sample of 6-year-old children, the slow-inaccurate group delayed more than the other three groups who evidenced similar levels of delay choice.

Mann (1973) compared impulsive and reflective 6- and 8-year-olds on a series of decision-making tasks including two delay of gratification dilemmas. As a group, the impulsives chose to delay on 31% of the available occasions, whereas the reflectives delayed on 52% of these occasions. However, on each of the two tests, the difference between impulsives and reflectives achieved only marginal significance (.05 < p < .10). In a study into the construct validity of a rating measure of self-control with school age children, Kendall and Wilcox (1979) reported that a single item delay choice test correlated at a low but significant level with MFFT errors, whereas the correlation of delay choice with MFFT latency was not significant.

Two studies with preschool children are also relevant. Paulsen and Johnson (1980) reported non-significant correlations between a delay choice measure and MFFT latency and errors. Toner et al. (1977) did find a significant correlation between delay choice and MFFT errors in a sample of preschool boys, but the correlation between MFFT latency and delay choice was not significant, and MFFT with delay choice correlations were not significant in separate analyses conducted on the girls in this study.

Although existing published studies point to the relative independence of delay choice and impulsivity, other findings taken from a wider perspective do suggest that cognitive impulsivity could influence important aspects of children's decisional self-control. The finding that impulsive and reflective children respond differently on a wide range of cognitive tasks has been consistently documented (Messer, 1976). Reflectives, relative to impulsives, have been found to respond more maturely on moral reasoning tasks (Schleifer & Douglas, 1973), to exhibit a more active problem solving approach in describing appropriate responses towards social conflict (Peters & Bernfeld, 1983), and to be more responsive to their own private self-instructional speech (Meichenbaum & Goodman, 1969). Eysenck (1981) reported a strong relationship between questionnaire measures of impulsiveness and antisocial conduct in 13- and 14-year-olds. Messer and Brodzinsky (1979) reported that impulsive children exhibited higher levels of covert aggressive thinking and overt aggressive behaviour than reflective children. Recently, Genshaft (1983) reported that, within the control group of a study into self-control training with 7-year-olds, reflective children were able to resist temptation for longer than impulsive children. Such data can be regarded as consistent with the view that reflection-impulsivity has implications for thinking, evaluating, and decision-making in problematic situations relevant to impulse control.

One interesting aspect of the existing research into children's delay choice is the considerable diversity of assessment procedures employed. A delay test may consist of one, or perhaps a series of dilemmas, and the nature of the rewards, their relative attractiveness and time-related contingencies, vary considerably from study to study. Furthermore, it appears that (a) in the majority of the studies the choice test is administered in an essentially verbal manner so that the subject does not actually see the pair of rewards he or she has to choose between, and (b) in many studies even the so-called immediate reward involves some element of delay. For example, in the procedure of Paulsen and Johnson (1980), children chose between a smaller reward available later in the day, and a larger reward available the next day. In such contexts the choice test, although justifiably referred to as delay of gratification, actually involves a decision between two delayed alternatives. It is entirely conceivable that variations in delay test procedures have had a considerable effect upon the nature of the relationships reported within previous experiments.

We initiated the first experiment in the present series in the attempt to provide a more rigorous investigation into the relationship between delay choice and cognitive impulsivity. We postulated that a significant relationship may emerge if the delay test specifically involved a salient immediate reward within the child's perceptual field (i.e., literally within his or her grasp). In such a context the delay option could become a relatively difficult choice and thus differences between impulsive and reflective children in pattern of choice behaviour may emerge.

Experiment 1

Twenty-four boys and 23 girls (aged 5.2 to 7.1 years, median 6.1 years) participated as subjects. They were selected from a pool of approximately 100 children in a junior primary school in metropolitan Adelaide, on the basis of their parents having responded positively to a written research request. The children were tested individually in an unoccupied classroom. The MFFT (Elementary school version, 6 alternatives per plate over 12 plates) was administered in the normal manner with assessment of mean latency of first response per plate, and total frequency of errors. Once this was completed each subject was informed that he or she had earned a prize from 'the lucky dip box'. A genuine lucky dip box, which had been previously hidden, was then presented, and through the opening of this box the subject could clearly see a number of reward prizes (various trinkets) wrapped in tissue paper. The experimenter then delivered the following statement: 'If you want you can take your prize now. But ... if you would like, instead of taking one now, you can come back tomorrow and have two prizes ... Which would you like? ... Would you prefer to take one prize now or wait until tomorrow and have two?

Analyses revealed no significant differences in the data from boys and girls. Median split procedures on MFFT latency and errors enabled 19 impulsive (10 boys, 9 girls) and 20 reflective (9 boys, 11 girls) children to be defined. In the delay test only 1 of the 19 impulsives choose to defer gratification, whereas 11 of the 20 reflectives did so: This difference achieved significance (corrected X^2 (1, $N = 39$) = 9.1, $p < .01$). Of the remaining 9 children who were tested but could not be classified as either impulsive or reflective, 4 elected to delay.

Experiment 2

The magnitude of the effect found in the first experiment was surprising particularly in view of the known literature concerning personality correlates of children's delay behaviour (see Mischel, 1974). Thus, it was decided to replicate the procedure using a different version of the delay test. For the second experiment we devised a measure enabling possible delay scores to range from 0 to 10, enabling analyses to proceed using conventional parametic statistics.

Twenty-two boys and 23 girls (aged 6.2 to 7.7 years, median 6.10 years) were tested individually in an unoccupied classroom at a junior primary school. Following the administration of the MFFT, each subject completed a short questionnaire unconnected with this study and was informed that he or she earned some coins. The experimenter then opened a drawer in the table and took out a stack of 10 2-cent coins saying, 'See! These are your coins. They are yours because you have earned them for helping me today.' The coins were lined up directly in front of the subject, i.e., closer to the subject than the experimenter, and the above statements were repeated.

The experimenter then took another stack of 10 2-cent coins from the drawer and said, 'See here! These are mine. You have 10, and I have 10. If you want you can take all the coins with you when you go back to class. But if you want to ... you can leave some of your coins with me. If you would like to leave some of your coins I will come back to school on the same day next week, that is (day of week), and give you your coins back and, as well, the same number of my own coins ... That's hard to work out, isn't it?' A more elaborated script using several structured probes in order to check on the subject's understanding was then administered before the child's decision was elicited. The number of coins left behind constituted each individual's delay score.

From the full sample of 45 subjects it was possible to define 19 impulsive (8 boys, 11 girls) and 16 reflective (7 boys, 9 girls) children through median split procedures on MFFT data. On the delay choice measure the reflective children obtained a mean score of 4.13 whereas the impulsive children obtained a mean score of 2.32. A 2 × 2 ANOVA on delay scores with impulsivity status and sex as independent variables indicated a significant effect for impulsivity status ($F(1,31) = 5.26$, $p < .05$). No additional effects were significant.

Experiment 3

Despite the fact that remarkably different delay testing procedures were used, Experiments 1 and 2 yielded similar findings. It can be concluded that reflection–impulsivity meaningfully relates to delay of gratification choice in at least *some* contexts. But the research cited earlier indicates that MFFT cannot be relied upon to predict delay choice under all circumstances. Thus, Experiment 3 was undertaken in the effort to investigate possible moderating influences i.e., to help to isolate conditions under which the impulsivity characteristic might predict delay choice.

We postulated that the MFFT–delay choice relationship found in the first two experiments could hinge upon the fact that the children were asked to make realistic choices concerning rewards that were physically salient within immediate perception. Within Experiment 3 we devised a delay test format in which each child was asked to respond to seven *hypothetical* choice dilemmas on the basis of the experimenter requesting: 'I want to find out what sort of things children like ... Do you think it would be better to have two super balls now, or wait until the same day next week and have three super balls?' (i.e., the first of the seven items). Following on from the seven hypothetical preferences, the child was offered a *realistic* choice through being asked to decide which one of the previous choices he or she would actually take.

The subjects were randomly allocated to either *high* or *low reward exposure* treatment. High reward exposure children were specifically informed that they would be receiving a prize for participating in the study, and further, they made their 8 choices (7 hypothetical, 1 realistic) in response to the actual reward objects. In contrast, low reward exposure subjects responded to photographs of the rewards, and were not informed that participating in the study was prize-worthy. This treatment manipulation was based on the assumption that, compared to seeing photographs, exposure to real reward objects would be relatively frustrating to the child's efforts at self-control (see Miller & Karniol, 1976) and that impulsive children would be less able to resist this source of frustration, relative to reflective children.

Fifty-eight boys and 41 girls (age range 6.5 to 7.9, mean of 7.0 years) participated as subjects. All were tested individually in a quiet office in a junior primary school. The MFFT was administered, followed by the reward preference test. Initial analyses indicated no significant effects due to sex on any of the MFFT or delay choice measures. Median split procedures on MFFT data allowed 40 impulsives, 37 reflectives, 9 fast-accurates, and 13 slow-inaccurates, to be identified. Chi-square tests indicated that these four groups evidenced similar levels of delay choice on each of the 7 delay preference items, but on the final choice item the impulsives evidenced significantly fewer delay choices relative to the other three groups who evidenced similar delay levels (χ^2 (3, $N = 99$) = 9.9, $p < .05$) (see Table 18.1).

It was found that subjects in the two reward exposure treatments exhibited similar levels of delay choice on each of the 8 choice items. The possibility of an interaction between the reward exposure manipulation and impulsivity status was tested through (a) conducting separate chi-square analyses for the two treatment groups on the delay

Table 18.1   Experiment 3: Percentage of delay preferences in hypothetical and realistic choice contexts

| MFFT Group | n | Percentage of delay choices | |
		Hypothetical Choice	Real Choice
Reflectives	37	67	54
Slow-inaccurates	13	70	54
Fast-accurates	9	78	56
Impulsives	40	67	22

levels of the MFFT groups, and (b) conducting separate analyses within each MFFT grouping assessing for differences in delay level between the two treatments. The only significant result to emerge from these analyses parallelled the earlier finding: i.e., that relative to the other 3 groups, the impulsive subjects evidenced less delay on the final choice item. Within the low reward exposure treatment 21% of the impulsives delayed on this item, compared to 53% of the reflectives. Within the other treatment 24% of the impulsives, and 55% of the reflectives, opted to delay gratification.

General discussion

The data from the three experiments suggest the following conclusion: the MFFT can be predictive of individual differences in children's delay of gratification in choice contexts which involve a genuine conflict between one reward alternative displaced in time and another alternative immediately within the child's grasp. In such contexts reflective children are more likely to forsake immediate gratification than are impulsive children. On the other hand, reflective and impulsive children may exhibit similar delay propensities when the delay dilemma involves a hypothetical preference merely to be stated.

A consistent pattern of results is evident across the three experiments. On *three* occasions subjects were asked to respond to realistic choice dilemmas, and on *seven* occasions subjects were asked to respond to choice dilemmas couched in the form 'would it be better to choose X now or X + Y in the future'. Significant differences between the responses of impulsive and reflective subjects were found only in the case of the three realistic dilemmas. Contrary to our initial theorising, the relationship between the impulsivity characteristic and delay choice seems not to be moderated by the arousal of the child's generalised anticipation or expectancy of actually obtaining some form of reward, since an experimental treatment in which subjects were given the delay preference test knowing they had come into the experimental room to collect a reward, and being deliberately exposed to possible reward objects, had little bearing upon the responses of either the impulsive or reflective children. Only when directly informed that their next choice was in fact to be honoured did the impulsives and reflectives diverge in delay choice, and this effect was found in both treatment conditions in Experiment 3, i.e., it made no difference whether the real choice was presented with actual objects or with photographs of those objects.

The actual difference in the frequency of delay choice in the impulsive and reflective children, found in the first experiment, is worthy of note: of the 19 impulsives one chose to delay, compared to 11 of the 20 reflectives. In this experiment a delay of gratification dilemma was presented at the very moment each child was to collect a well-earned prize. An offer was then made for the child to have two prizes the next day instead of taking one immediate one. Perhaps this type of situation involves such a severe test that the impulsive child is relatively unable to re-orient attention away from the promise of immediate gratification and onto the value of postponing pleasure. If this is the case then the impulsive child could be responding in a similar manner to the preschoolers in Mischel's (1974) delay tolerance studies who were relatively unable to wait for preferred reward when attending toward actual reward objects.

However, other interpretations of the present findings are also possible. For example, it has been established that, relative to reflectives, impulsive children tend to respond more quickly on decision tasks (Mann, 1973), especially when problems become increasingly difficult (Lawry, Welch, & Jeffrey, 1983). Impulsives may give insufficient consideration to available alternatives (Mitchell & Ault, 1979), or they may be more willing to accept a lower level of reward through following a course of action that involves less effort (Glow et al., 1983).

The present study draws attention to the fact that delay of gratification choice tests can take different forms which may considerably influence the nature of the results they elicit. The present results help to specify conditions under which children's cognitive impulsivity predicts their delay disposition. Rather than seeking overall relationships between a psychological characteristic, such as impulsivity, and a behavioural outcome, such as delay of gratification, it is more profitable to closely examine the attributes of contexts within which individual characteristics might play an important role. While such ideas are not new, there are few examples of their application within the field of research concerned with children's impulse control.

References

Eysenck, S. B. (1981). Impulsiveness and antisocial behaviour in children. *Current Psychological Research, 1*, 31–7.

Flynn, T. M. (1974). The personality characteristics of school readiness in disadvantaged preschool children. *Journal of Instructional Psychology, 1*, 45–52.

Genshaft, J. (1983). A comparison of techniques to increase children's resistance to temptation. *Personality and Individual Differences, 4*, 339–41.

Glow, R. A., Lange, P. H., Glow, P. H., & Barnett, J. A. (1983). Cognitive and self-reported impulsiveness: Comparison of Kagan's MFFT and Eysenck's EPQ impulsiveness measures. *Personality and Individual Differences, 4*, 170–87.

Inouye, A., & Sato, S. (1977). Delayed preference behavior in relation to cognitive styles in preschool children. *Japanese Psychological Research, 19*, 193–8.

Kagan, J., Rosman, B. C., Day, D., Albert, J., & Phillips, W. (1964). Information processing in the child: Significance of analytic and reflective attitudes. *Psychological Monographs, 78*, (1, Whole No. 578).

Kendall, P. C., & Wilcox, L. E. (1979). Self-control in children: Development of a rating scale. *Journal of Consulting and Clinical Psychology, 47*, 1020–9.

Kendall, P. C., Zupan, B. A., & Braswell, L. (1981). Self-control in children: Further analyses of the Self-control Rating Scale. *Behaviour Therapy, 12*, 667–81.

Lawry, J. A., Welsh, M. C., & Jeffrey, W. E. (1983). Cognitive tempo and complex problem solving. *Child Development, 54*, 912–20.

Macbeth, L. (1974). The ability to delay gratification: A trait or not a trait? *Multivariate Behavioral Research, 9*, 3–19.

Mann, L. (1973). Differences between reflective and impulsive children in tempo and quality of decision making. *Child Development, 44*, 274–9.

Meichenbaum, D. H., & Goodman, J. (1969). Reflection impulsivity and verbal control of motor behavior. *Child Development, 40*, 785–97.

Messer, S. B. (1976). Reflection-impulsivity: A Review. *Psychological Bulletin, 83*, 1026–52.

Messer, S. B., & Brodzinsky, D. M. (1979). The relation of conceptual tempo to aggression and its control. *Child Development, 50*, 1043–9.

Miller, D. T., & Karniol, R. (1976). The role of rewards in external and self-imposed delay of gratification. *Journal of Personality and Social Psychology, 33*, 594–600.

Mischel, W. (1974). Processes in delay of gratification. In L. Berkowitz (Ed.) *Advances in experimental social psychology*, vol. 7, New York: Academic Press.

Mitchell, C., & Ault, R. L. (1979). Reflection-impulsivity and the evaluation process. *Child Development, 50*, 1043–49.

Paulsen, K., & Johnson, M. (1980). Impulsivity: A multidimensional concept with developmental aspects. *Journal of Abnormal Child Psychology, 8*, 269–77.

Peters, R. D., & Bernfeld, G. A. (1983). Reflection-impulsivity and social reasoning. *Developmental Psychology, 19*, 78–81.

Schleifer, M., & Douglas, V. I. (1973). Moral judgments, behaviour, and cognitive style in young children. *Canadian Journal of Behavioural Science, 5*, 133–44.

Toner, I. J., Holstein, R. B., & Hetherington, E. M. (1977). Reflection-impulsivity and self-control in preschool children. *Child Development, 48*, 239–45.

Wormith, J. S., & Hasenpusch, B. (1979). Multidimensional measurement of delayed gratification preference with incarcerated offenders. *Journal of Clinical Psychology, 35*, 218–25.

Acknowledgement

This article was completed while both authors were visiting the Department of Educational Psychology, University of Calgary, Calgary, Alberta, and the assistance of this department is gratefully acknowledged. Experiment 3 was conducted by the senior author in partial fulfilment of the requirements for the degree of Master of Education at the University of Adelaide, Australia.

19

Parental Attitudes to Early Childhood Care

Dorothy Toussaint
Murdoch University

Recently in Australia there has been a steady call for increased Government provision of care and educational facilities for all children under 5. Changes in government have led to a firmer commitment and a major rise in such provision now seems a real likelihood.

A great deal of research has been carried out on the possible effects of daycare. Such research has concentrated mainly on the child's social and intellectual development, and possible changes in the emotional bond between parent and child (e.g., Belsky & Steinberg, 1978). However, how a mother perceives her 'role' in society, and what she believes will be the effect of using child care, must greatly influence her utilisation of such services as they become available. Parental perceptions may also influence the effects of care in the same way that maternal attitudes toward employment have been shown to be important mediating variables on the effects of employment on parent–child interaction (Farrel, 1980; Yarrow, Scott, de Leeuw & Heinig, 1974).

Sibbison (1972) carried out a study in America to examine the relationship between maternal attitudes to child care; the usage of childcare services; and how variables such as socio–economic status, educational level and residency were related to such attitudes. It was found that a mother's perception of her role and responsibilities was significantly associated with usage, and this transcended socio–economic and demographic variables. However, this study did not explore maternal attitudes in any depth, other than whether they were orientated to the mother or the child, or the reasons for such attitudes. Contemporary Australian women may have quite different views. Some Australian studies have been carried out (e.g., Burns, 1978) but these have tended to be surveys to locate areas of need for children's services rather than attempts to look closely at parental attitudes.

The present study was part of a wider project examining various aspects relating to the care and education of children under 5 years of age. The particular aspects examined here are maternal attitudes to care in general; and possible differences in attitude towards part-time or full-time care. Respondents were sought from four specific groups of Anglo-Australian families who were using the different types of care and education facilities available for children in their fourth year in Western Australia. As none of these user groups is more 'acceptable' than any other for 4-year-olds in Western Australia, it was hypothesised that parental choice was the result of underlying differences between the groups and investigation of these differences was part of the total research project.

METHOD

Subjects
Eighty-nine mothers were interviewed. All had a child born in 1978, and were interviewed in the child's fourth or fifth year. Mothers were of four types—non-users or the Home group (16), Playgroup (20), Kindergarten (32) and Daycare (21). Of the last, seven children were part-time (15 hours a week or less) and 14 were full-time (more than 15 hours a week). Subjects were mainly contacted personally at the various facilities attended by their children. Home mothers were contacted via other subjects or through a survey conducted at some preschools to determine the type of facilities used prior to preschool.

Procedure
This paper reports the results from three open-ended questions based on those used by Sibbison (1972):
1. Can you think of any possible reasons why children under 5 may need to be taken care of by someone other than their father or mother during the day?
2. In general, do you think part-time care (15 hours a week or less) for children under 5 is a good idea or a bad idea?
3. In general, do you think full-time care (more than 15 hours a week) for children under 5 is a good idea or a bad idea?
The responses to each question were grouped according to whether they were positive or negative toward the concept being examined, and within this, whether they were orientated exclusively toward the

Table 19.1   Category responses to Question 1

Response Categories	Group Percentages				Total
	H	P	K	D	%
(n)	(16)	(20)	(32)	(21)	(89)
Only if difficult circumstances e.g. illness, appointments	56	55	56	57	56
Financial—mother has to work	69	75	73	90	77
Single parent	6	25	27	10	19
Allows mother career or free time	50	70	54	76	63
For child's social/ psychological growth	44	40	30	43	38
For child's educational growth	0	5	9	5	6
Provides stimulation, enjoyment and a break for the child	6	10	9	5	12

Key: H = Home mothers, P = Playgroup mothers, K = Kindergarten mothers, D = Daycare
    mothers

child, exclusively toward the adult or toward the child and adult both. For example, one mother replied that she thought full-time care would not be good because she would miss out on too much of her child's valuable growing-up time. This was classified negative, adult orientated. Another mother responded by saying that children in full-time care would feel unloved and rejected by the parent. This was classified negative, child orientated. On the other hand, one mother replied that full-time care enabled her to switch off and concentrate on her job, and her child was able to socialise and become independent. This was classified positive, adult and child orientated. Categorisation of responses in this way made it possible to examine whether attitudes to child care were based on concern for the developing child, concern for the mother herself, her role and responsibilities; or a combination of both.

RESULTS AND DISCUSSION

Table 19.1 presents the reasons given why children may need to be cared for by someone other than their parents during the day.

The need for extra-familial care for children was overwhelmingly accepted, with all groups similar in the reasons given. The reason mentioned most often was the facilitation of maternal employment for

Table 19.2   Category responses to care of children under 5

Advantages

Child	social benefits
	stimulation and enjoyment
	independence and confidence
	school readiness skills, discipline, routine.
Adult	free time for self, employment or otherwise

Disadvantages

Child	misses out, feels rejected, unloved, insecure
	subjected to varying standards, confused.
	tired and stressed
	unable to develop individuality
	not cared for so well physically, perhaps abused
	home and mother best for child at this stage
Adult	misses out on child growing up
	unable to build up relationship with child
	unable to teach child family ways, values, etc.
	duty and/or tradition.
	physically exhausted, stressed, rushed.
	other e.g. feeling of guilt, etc

financial reasons. Although Australian society in general has not tended to condone women with young children being in the work force, financial hardship is the most socially acceptable reason. However, it was interesting to note that, although 90% of the Daycare group cited this as a reason for child care, 76% of them also mentioned care as allowing a mother time to spend away from her family to pursue her own interests. This was similar to results from other studies of employed women. For example, New Zealand research on working mothers of young children found that, although 81% cited the provision of extra income as a major satisfaction of their employment, 61% also cited the satisfaction of getting away from home (Fergusson, Beautrais, Horwood & Shannon, 1982).

It is interesting to compare these results with Sibbison's (1972) study. Mostly the respondents in that study mentioned the same reasons with similar distribution to the present group except that 7% rejected the use of care in any circumstances and less mentioned allowing the mother free time (10%) or the need for paid employment (60%) as a reason for using early child care. This seems to indicate a change in maternal attitudes towards the use of care for young children.

However, although many respondents gave reasons for the use of care, they did not necessarily always approve of these reasons, espe-

Table 19.3   Orientation of responses to part-time care (expressed as group percentages)

Group	Positive response benefits for				Negative response disadvantages for			
	adult	both	child	Total	adult	both	child	Total
Home	0	12	50	62	25	0	12	38
Playgroup	0	45	15	60	15	20	5	40
Kindergarten	9	28	47	84	3	9	3	16
Daycare	0	67	33	100	0	0	0	0
Total	3	38	37		9	8	4	
		(79)				(21)		

cially if they were not using any form of care themselves. In view of this, the next two questions explored whether mothers saw child care as advantageous or disadvantageous, both to themselves and to their children. However, the care of children under 5 is an all-embracing term and parents tend to put qualifications on its use, such as hours of care, type, and age of child. Many of these elements were investigated as part of the wider study. The only qualification reported here was hours of care, either part-time or full-time, and generally the mothers' comments did not refer to children under about 3 years of age.

The category responses for perceived advantages and disadvantages of care can be seen in Table 19.2.

Table 19.3 shows the orientation of the groups to part-time care. Child care on a part-time basis received a generally positive response with 79% of the mothers endorsing its use. These respondents tended to mention social benefits for the child most often (76%), while 54% spoke of its value in giving free time to the parent. Others mentioned that it helped to give a child independence and confidence (46%); and provided the child with stimulation and enjoyment (45%). Only 5% of the respondents mentioned the gaining of school-related skills. There were no significant differences between the four groups.

Mothers who were currently using what could be called 'care', that is the Daycare and Kindergarten mothers, had a more positive attitude towards part-time care in that they gave positive responses more frequently than the other two groups, $\chi^2(1) = 11.08$, $p < .001$. The consensus of opinion seemed to be that this would benefit either the child, or the child and adult about equally. This is in contrast to the responses given by mothers in both the Burns (1978) and Sibbison (1972) studies where greater advantages were perceived for the child

Table 19.4   Orientation of responses to full-time care (expressed as group percentages)

Group	Positive response benefits for				Negative response* disadvantages for			
	adult	both	child	Total	adult	both	child	Total
Home	0	0	0	0	31	56	12	100
Playgroup	0	5	0	5	30	55	10	95
Kindergarten	3	16	0	19	16	53	12	81
Daycare	0	19	14	33	33	28	5	67
Total	1	11	3		26	48	10	
		(16)				(84)		

*includes the responses of 2 subjects ambivalent about the use of full-time care but rejecting it for themselves

alone (57% and 67%, respectively). Perhaps the reason for this could be the recent nature of the present study. Women may now feel more open about acknowledging the need for a break from their children.

There was no difference between the groups on the child/adult orientation dimension, except a tendency for Daycare mothers to more readily acknowledge benefits for both mother and child. They were also unanimously positive about the use of part-time care. It seems women already using care have found the break an enjoyable one for them and their children.

With full-time care, the responses were mainly negative with 84% of the group against its use. Table 19.4 presents the reaction of the various groups. Again the mothers using Daycare and Kindergarten responded less negatively than the Home and Playgroup mothers, $\chi^2(1) = 7.65$, $p < .01$. It may be surprising to see such a negative response (67%) from the Daycare group. However, of this group, only two-thirds were using full-time care, and half of these responded negatively. With the part-time group, all voted against the use of full-time care. Sibbison (1972) also found that full-time care was not popular with her respondents.

Table 19.5 shows the percentage distribution of the various disadvantages given by the four groups. With the child orientated reasons, the main concern expressed was that the child would be deprived of the benefits of a close mother-child relationship and home environment, perhaps leading to feelings of insecurity. Many adult orientated reasons were given, with the emphasis on the adult missing out on much of the child's growing-up time and less opportunity for a close relationship to develop between mother and child. Some respon-

Table 19.5   Comparison between groups on perceived disadvantages to full-time care (Subjects giving negative responses only)

Disadvantages	% responses				
	H	P	K	D	Total
(n)	(16)	(19)	(26)	(15)	(76)
Child					
Misses out	56	32	61	40	46
Subjected to different values	12	5	15	7	10
Too much for him, tiring	6	26	8	7	12
Unable to develop individuality	0	16	4	0	5
Quality of care physically less	0	16	4	0	5
Adult					
Misses out	69	63	35	40	50
Relationship with child disturbed	50	16	46	53	41
Unable to pass on family ways	25	37	19	7	22
Duty and/or tradition	31	26	42	7	29
Physically exhausted, stressed	25	16	4	27	16
Other	6	0	0	7	3

Key: H = Home mothers, P = Playgroup mothers, K = Kindergarten mothers, D = Daycare mothers

dents took this further and predicted dire consequences for the parent-child relationship during the adolescent period in particular.

Others who themselves had been left in care when young spoke of how they had hated it and were determined to avoid this with their own children. On the other hand, a woman whose mother had sacrificed her career to stay home with her young family, felt this had been a mistake and made her mother very bitter. Although some women may reject outside care for the sake of their children, it seems it will not be appreciated if there is at all an element of sacrifice involved.

Although there was a tendency for the Daycare group to place less emphasis than the other groups on traditional reasons against full-time care, such as parental duty and the teaching of family values, no significant group differences emerged.

It appears from this study, therefore, that use of part-time child care seems to have become more socially acceptable to mothers of young children who acknowledge there are benefits for themselves and their children. Full-time care was not popular, even with half the mothers already using it, and disadvantages were seen for both parent and child. Pattern of usage made some difference to responses. Mothers using no form of early care or education, or a playgroup, were almost totally against the use of full-time care and more inclined to react negatively towards part-time care as well, whereas those whose children already attended a kindergarten or daycare were not so disapproving.

References

Belsky, J. & Steinberg, L. D. (1978). The effects of day care, a critical review. *Child Development, 49*, 929–49.

Burns, A. (1978). Australian attitudes to child care. In Graycar, A. (Ed.), *Perspectives in Australian social policy*. Melbourne: Macmillan, 256–65.

Farrel, A. M. (1980). Effects of preferred maternal roles, maternal employment and sociodemographic status on school adjustment and competence. *Child Development, 51*, 1179–86.

Fergusson, D. M., Beautrais, A. L., Horwood, L. J. & Shannon, F. T. (1982). Working mothers and day care. *New Zealand Journal of Educational Studies, 16*, 168–76.

Sibbison, V. H. (1972). The influence of maternal role perception on attitudes toward, and utilisation of early child-care services. Pennsylvania Day Care Study Report, Technical Report #10.

Yarrow, M. R., Scott, P., de Leeuw, L. & Heinig, C. (1974). Child rearing in families of working and non-working mothers. In Bee, H. (Ed.), *Social issues in developmental psychology* (pp. 112–29). New York: Harper and Row.

20

Parents' Satisfaction With Progress and Beliefs About Stability of Traits

Rosemary A. Knight
Australian Capital Territory Health Authority, Canberra

'Scott is forward, bright for his age', 'Joanne is good at puzzles. She catches on very quickly. You only have to show her once or twice', 'Sophie is a very happy child—she'll go to anyone and is good at being liked', 'I like the way Natalie always tries her best'. Everyday comments such as these suggest that all parents both form beliefs and make emotional judgments about their children's competence and personality. Given the ubiquity of such statements, it is startling to realise that empirical work on the processes and content of parental reasoning, cognitions and satisfactions has been minimal until the last decade, a point made strongly by Holden, Whittenbrake, McCleary and West (1981).

In a recent burst of interest, research has begun to focus on both the content and variability in parents' beliefs and the reasons or background variables which may account for them. The present paper addresses the latter issue while documenting some features of parents' beliefs.

The basis of parents' beliefs remains surprisingly obscure. One appealing but not widely tested hypothesis is that parents act as 'constructivists' (McGillicuddy-DeLisi, 1982). It is argued that parents construct and modify their beliefs on the basis of common but individual experiences. Flavell (1970) pointed to the enormous potential for change which may occur as parents interact with their children and are exposed to the role demands of parenting. Similarly, McGillicuddy-DeLisi et al. (1979) maintained that parents' beliefs may change 'possibly as a result of experience with increased numbers of children or with changes in the child due to development' (p. 93). Such claims

188

are consistent with Stolz' (1967) proposal that, although several factors may influence parents' beliefs, nonetheless, 'the experience of rearing a child is the reality testing and may result in a re-organisation of values' (p. 282).

According to this perspective, parents play an active and individualised role in the formation and maintenance of beliefs about child development, essentially developing their own 'personal constructs' (Kelly, 1955). It is conceivable that, if the experience of parenthood itself is sufficient to alter parents' beliefs, then more specific features of this role are likely to be important. Potentially, experience–induced changes in beliefs may occur in at least two ways: either as a function of the parents' role (such as being a mother or a father) or from characteristics of the child (such as age and sex). The present study examined the constructivist model of parents' beliefs, with experience being measured here by parent gender, age and sex of eldest child.

In addition to variations according to experience, there is some evidence to suggest that parents' beliefs may be interrelated (see Knight, 1981). From attribution theory, Langer (1975) has claimed that the most highly valued skills are the ones over which we have most control. Goodnow, Cashmore, Cotton & Knight (1985) found that both Lebanese and Australian born mothers expected 'desirable' behaviours to be stable over time, and 'undesirable' behaviours to change. Finally, Hess (in press) has suggested that parents' degree of satisfaction may play an important role in shaping beliefs. A further aim of the present study was therefore to test whether parents' beliefs about the stability of traits and satisfaction with progress were correlated with one another.

Method

Subjects

A sample of 120 parents (60 mothers and 60 fathers married to each other) was interviewed. Each couple had an eldest child of 4, 7 or 10 years old. At each age level, half of the eldest children were boys, and half were girls.

The sample consisted mainly of traditional or 'typical' families. In summary, they were nuclear families with a mode of 2 children. The parents were mostly 'Anglo–Australians' from middle–class suburbs with an upward bias in educational and occupational level. All fathers were in paid employment, with most mothers engaged in home duties and in charge of child care.

Materials

Parents completed several questionnaires as part of a larger study (see Knight, 1983). For the data reported here, mothers and fathers independently rated the same set of 15 items with reference to their eldest child, in answer to the following questions:

1   For each of the following characteristics, how satisfied are you with your child's current performance? (The rating scale was: 1—room for improvement; 2—quite happy, OK; 3—very happy and satisfied.)

2   How likely do you think it is that these characteristics will remain stable or change over time? (The rating scale was: 1—expect the behaviour to change; 2—expect the behaviour to last.)

The set of 15 items was selected from Russell's (1979) list of those characteristics which parents most valued and believed they could most influence. Items were chosen from three domains: socio-emotional (e.g., 'expresses love and affection', 'is well mannered and well-behaved'); cognitive (e.g., 'is able to work things out, to think, reason and solve problems', 'understands easily or catches on quickly'); and style (e.g., 'tries hard at things', is not easily distractable and holds interests in tasks').

Procedure

Parents were recruited through schools and kindergartens in Sydney from three different geographical areas, similar in socio-economic status. Mothers and fathers were interviewed separately in their own homes at a date and time covenient to them. The data were, however, all collected in the one session so that parents could not discuss the questions or their answers with each other until afterwards.

RESULTS

Method of Analysis

The data were analysed in two ways. Using multivariate analysis techniques, parents' responses on the two rating scales (the dependent variables) were first separately examined in relation to experience, indicated here by age and sex of eldest child and parent gender (the independent variables). Second, the data were examined for interrelationships among parents' beliefs: the multivariate technique of analysis (see Bock, 1974) canonical correlation was used as a unique way of analysing the *overall* relationship between two sets of ratings, each comprising 15 items, rather than relying on a 15 × 15 correlation matrix.

Fig. 20.1 Mean ratings for satisfaction with progress

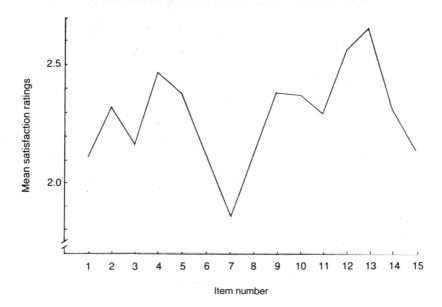

Mothers' and fathers' responses were treated as repeated measures data since although parents were interviewed separately, they were not selected independently. A significance level of $p < .01$ was adopted for all analyses.

Parents' Satisfaction Ratings and Beliefs About Stability
Figures 20.1 and 20.2 show the mean ratings by parents (i.e., average ratings of mothers and fathers on Questions 1 and 2) for their satisfaction with the current progress of their eldest child and their beliefs about the stability of these behaviours on the same set of 15 characteristics.

The data in Figure 20.1 for *satisfaction with progress* show that parents were mostly happy with their eldest child's behaviour. For all except one item (item 7—'is not easily distractable') the means were between 1 and 2. Parents were either reluctant to admit there is 'room for improvement' (rating 1) or were genuinely satisfied with their child's progress.

Fig. 20.2 Mean ratings for perceived stability of behaviour

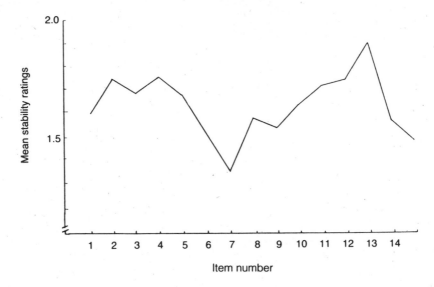

Figure 20.2 also shows that for *stability of behaviour*, parents believed more behaviours to be stable over time than likely to change. The modal response was 2 on all except two items (item 7—'is not easily distractable' and item 15—'is not shy with strangers'). Despite a preference for negative wording on items 7 and 15 found in a pilot test, the grouping of these two items here suggests that the negative wording might have been somewhat confusing for parents.

The behaviours seen as most and least stable were also those with which parents were most and least happy in terms of their child's current progress. That is, parents were most happy with their child's behaviour on items 13, 12 and 4 ('is curious and interested in how and why things happen', 'expresses love and affection' and 'has a sense of humour?). These same behaviours were rated as most likely to remain stable. Similarly, items 7 and 15 ('is not easily distractable' and 'is not shy with strangers') were rated as most likely to change, and parents were least happy with their child's progress in the areas.

Although Figures 20.1 and 20.2 show that some items behave in similar ways on the two sets of ratings data, there is no obvious

Table 20.1   Perceived stability of behaviour and satisfaction with progress: summary of results for canonical correlations

A. Summary results for multivariate F tests

	Perceived stability of behaviour	
	Mothers	Fathers
	F (225, 331)	F (225, 331)
Satisfaction	1.43 **	1.64 **

B.   Canonical correlations with perceived stability of behaviour: Bartlett's X^2 values

Ratings	Parent	Roots	X^2	df	R^2
Satisfaction	Mothers	1 to 15	300.52 ***	225	.81
		2 to 15	232.41 *	196	.70
Satisfaction	Fathers	1 to 15	331.27 ***	225	.79
		2 to 15	265.68 ***	196	.73
		3 to 15	211.63 **	169	.63
		4 to 15	170.21	144	.61

*** $p < .001$;   ** $p < .01$;   * $p < .05$

pattern. That is, these items showed no obvious clustering according to domain (e.g., cognitive behaviours, socio-emotional behaviours, and features of style). When the data were analysed for the effects of experience without regard to domain, no significant differences were found as a function of parent gender, age or sex of eldest child.

The apparent diffuse relationship between parents' satisfaction with progress and their beliefs about the stability of behaviour (cf. Figures 20.1 and 20.2) was confirmed by the results from the canonical correlation analysis. As shown in Table 20.1, there was a significant relationship for both mothers' data ($R^2 = .81$) and fathers' data ($R^2 = .79$)

Given the strong relationship between parents' beliefs about stability and their satisfaction with current progress, it is probable that, where parents are happy with their eldest child's behaviour, they expect it to remain stable. Conversely, when parents believe that a particular behaviour is not up to standard, they expect (or hope) it will change. A reverse direction of effect seems unlikely.

Discussion

The parents' beliefs which were measured here did not vary as a function of parent gender or age and sex of eldest child. Instead, the significant findings concerned the relationship between parents' beliefs about stability and degree of satisfaction with progress. In explanation, it is posited that the constructivist account may yet be relevant, but that the mediating process involved is probably a *functional* one. The suggestion is that parents construct and adhere to some beliefs for self-protection to make life with their children more bearable, or more rewarding. It is argued, therefore, that parents operate as developmental optimists. Believing that the good things will remain stable or that the bad things will improve, is useful: it makes some sense of the task of parenting and allows one to continue.

The possibility of a functional basis to parents' beliefs within the constructivist model has been largely ignored or under-estimated. Once alerted to this explanation, however, other compatible evidence is not hard to find. Grusec and Dix (1982) investigated parents' attributions of altruism and found that the more positive the behaviour, the more internal and stable were parents' attributions: the more negative the outcome, the more likely were parents to attribute the behaviour to more external, unstable factors.

Pharis and Manosevitz (1980) compared young adults about to become parents with those who had no current intention to be parents. The former judged babies to be less difficult, less disruptive of one's life and competent at an earlier age than did the latter. Hess, Price, Dickson and Conroy (1982) found that mothers and teachers in full-day preschool centres were alike in expecting earlier competence than did teachers in half-day centres. Presumably those caregivers with less need or responsibility can afford to have more relaxed developmental timetables.

Nevertheless, it seems unlikely that need or necessity is the only mechanism operating in the construction and change of parents' beliefs. For instance, ideas about parents may not only be from 'personal constructs' (see Kelly, 1955) but also from schemas handed down by others, such as family of origin, peers, or the mass media and the wider culture. In line with Shweder's (1982) concepts, parents' beliefs may be somewhat 'pre-packaged'. Partial support for this notion comes from the work of Goodnow et al. (1984) in which ethnicity is seen as a strong correlate with parents' beliefs.

Similarly, it may be that parents' beliefs are modified only by certain critical experiences. Sameroff and Feil (in press) suggest that parents reflect upon and modify their beliefs only when forced to by surprising circumstances, such as the birth of a handicapped child. Holden et al. (1981) have also argued that the 'problem-solving' nature of parenting means that it is likely that behaviour which is problematic or difficult to understand will most invite reflection.

In conclusion, (as in attribution studies) a position of responsibility, combined with greater opportunities for observation may alter parents' cognitions about child development and of feasibility. The future task of research on the source of parents' beliefs is really not one of arguing for experience, need or cultural transmission as single factors, but of sorting out the way they interact and the conditions that at times give one a stronger weighting than the other.

References

Bock, R. D. (1975). *Multivariate statistical methods in behavioural research.* New York: McGraw-Hill.

Flavell, J. H. (1970). Cognitive changes in adulthood. In L. R. Goulet & P. B. Baltes (Eds), *Life-span psychology.* New York: Academic Press.

Goodnow, J. J., Cashmore, J., Cotton, S., & Knight, R. (in press). Mothers' developmental timetables in two cultural groups. *International Journal of Psychology, 19,* 193–205.

Grusec, J. & Dix, T. H. (1982). The socialisation of altruism. Paper presented at SRCD study group on Altruism and Aggression, Washington, D. C., April.

Hess, R. (in press). Approaches to the measurement and interpretation of parent-child interaction. In R. W. Henderson (Ed.), *Parent-child interaction: Learning and adjustment in children.* New York: Academic Press.

Hess, R., Price, G. G., Dickson, W., & Conroy, M. (in press). Different roles for mothers and teachers: Contrasting styles of child care. In S. Kilmer (Ed.), *Advances in early education and day care,* Vol. 2. Greenwich, Connecticut: Johnson.

Holden, G. W., Whittenbrake, J. E., McCleary, B. W., & West, M. J. (1981). The parent as naive psychologist. Paper presented at the Sixth Biennial Meeting of ISSBD, Toronto.

Kelly, G. A. (1955). *The psychology of personal constructs,* Vols. I & II. New York: Norton.

Knight, R. A. (1983). *Parents' beliefs about child development.* Unpublished Ph.D. Thesis, Macquarie University.

Knight, R. A. (1981). Parents' beliefs about cognitive development: The role of experience. In A. R. Nesdale, C. Pratt, R. Grieve, J. Field, D. Illingworth, & J. Hogben (Eds), *Advances in child development and research: Theory and research.* Perth: University of Western Australia Press.

Langer, E. J. (1975). The illusion of control. *Journal of Personality and Social Physchology, 32,* 311–28.

McGillicuddy-DeLisi, A. V. (1982). Parental beliefs about developmental processes. *Human Development, 25,* 192–200.

McGillicuddy-DeLisi, A. V., Sigel, I. E., & Johnson, J. E. (1979). The family as a system of mutual influences: Parental beliefs, distancing behaviors, and children's representational thinking. In M. Lewis & L. A. Rosenblum (Eds), *The child and its family.* New York: Plenum.

Pharis, M. E., & Manosevitz, M. (1980). Parental models: A means for evaluating different prenatal contexts. In D. B. Sawin, R. C. Hawkins, L. O. Walker, & P. H. Perticuff (Eds), *Exceptional infant,* Vol. 4. New York: Brunner-Mazel.

Russell, G. (1979). *Comparisons between mothers and fathers. Some problems of method and some preliminary findings.* Paper presented at the Symposium of Some Influences on Changing Family Relationships, Australian Psychological Society Annual Conference, Hobart, August.

Sameroff, A. J. & Feil, L. A. (in press). Parental concepts of development. In I. E. Sigel (Ed.), *Parents' belief systems.* Hillsdale, N. J.: Erlbaum.

Shweder, R. A. (1981). *Anthropology's romantic rebellion against the enlightenment; or there's more to thinking than reason and evidence.* Paper presented at the Social Science Research Council Conference on Conceptions of Culture and its Acquisition, May.

Stolz, L. M. (1967). *Influences on parent behavior.* Stanford, Calif.: Stanford University Press.

21

'Difficult' and 'Easy' Periods For Young Siblings of Disabled People

Maggie Kirkman
University of Melbourne

The special needs of siblings of disabled children have been emphasised by the recent proliferation of groups designed for them (e.g., the Australian Noah's Ark Toy Libraries). Such community awareness has not yet been informed by a comprehensive body of research. This paper reports the results of a preliminary study which investigated, among other things, whether there were particular developmental periods in which siblings felt most or least vulnerable.

The project took the form of a survey of adults who had grown up with a disabled brother or sister. It was conducted to aid in the design of a study of young children. The overwhelming response to the survey and the long, thoughtful replies provided much richer material than had been expected.

Erikson's psychosocial stages have been used as a framework for describing the results (Erikson, 1959a, 1965, 1971). For convenience, the stages have been linked with ages as seems appropriate for the pertinent psychosocial events in our culture. The first three stages are treated as one because no useful distinctions could be made between them in this sample. The last two stages go beyond child development and have therefore been omitted.

METHOD

Subjects
The sample comprised 151 volunteers who returned one of 250 questionnaires. 'People over eighteen who grew up with a handicapped brother or sister' were requested to contact the author, who was

197

Table 21.1   Type of disability represented in the sample

Disability	N	%
Intellectual	63	42
Down's Syndrome	31	21
Physical/?Intellectual (= cerebral palsy, 20; spina bifida, 5)	25	17
Physical (+ post-polio, 4; muscular dystrophy, cystic fibrosis, arthrogryposis, 2 each; osteogenesis imperfecta, kidney disease, heart defect, haemophilia, multiple sclerosis, 1 each)	15	10
Psychiatric (4) /Autistic (6)	10	7
Deaf	7	5
	151	

(The data refer to normal siblings; between them there were 127 disabled siblings)

given publicity in July 1983 by two newspapers and a radio station in Victoria. Responses from people younger than 18, with more than one handicapped sibling, or with a sibling whose handicap did not occur in early childhood were excluded (N = 18).

Although no claim can be made that this is a representative sample, the respondents were heterogeneous on many variables. Their ages ranged from 18 to 76, with a mean of 32. The mean age of their disabled siblings was 26, and ranged from 10 to 89. Most respondents (75%) were female, although their siblings were equally divided between the sexes, and there was an almost even split between same-sex and different sex pairs. Seventy-three percent of respondents were older than the disabled child, whilst 3% were twins. The modal family size was three, with a range of two to 12. The socio-economic status of the fathers covered the full range, although it was weighted towards the professional end of the scale. The disabilities represented in the sample are described in Table 21.1

Procedure
The questionnaire (comprising 26 questions) was distributed and returned by mail. This paper focuses on respondents' answers to two questions. The first is: 'Was there a particular time when you found having a handicapped brother or sister *most difficult*? If yes, please say how old you were then and why it was a difficult time'. The second question is similar, except that it asks about a time which was 'easy or pleasant'.

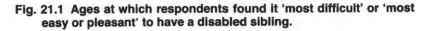

Fig. 21.1 Ages at which respondents found it 'most difficult' or 'most easy or pleasant' to have a disabled sibling.

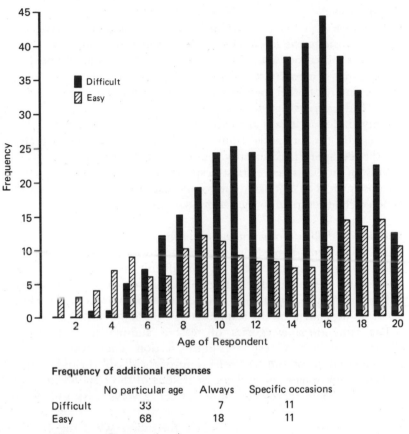

Frequency of additional responses

	No particular age	Always	Specific occasions
Difficult	33	7	11
Easy	68	18	11

(There are 151 respondents)

Results And Discussion

The ages nominated for difficult and easy times were tallied and represented in a frequency histogram (Figure 21.1). Difficulty predominates between the ages of 6 and 19; the most difficult years are between 13 and 18. Towards the end of adolescence there is an increase in the frequency of 'easy and pleasant' times.

Three fundamental types of explanation were given for these particular problems or pleasures. The most frequent concerned aspects of the respondents' development, but the development or behaviour of the disabled child and reasons extrinsic to the children were also cited.

These last two will be discussed briefly before closer attention is paid to the development of the non-disabled sibling.

Extrinsic issues

Issues which made life difficult but, although related to the disability, were extrinsic to the interaction of the siblings were cited by 10 respondents for various ages. Three reasons covered them all: the death or departure of a parent; the institutionalisation of the disabled child; and the failure of other members of the family to cope with disability, which had repercussions for the children.

Only six found it easy at various times for external reasons. Three enjoyed the gifts or special equipment acquired by the disabled child and the rest appreciated improved community attitudes.

Most of the examples relating to specific occasions were for external reasons, such as an enjoyable trip to the beach or sorrow each time the disabled child returned to the residential institution.

The disabled child's development or behaviour

More respondents named the development or behaviour of the disabled sibling as responsible for easy or difficult times. However, there was usually an obvious interaction between the development of both siblings, so these details are recorded in addition to, rather than instead of, issues dependent on the respondent's childhood.

The same three categories of reasons summarise both the 25 'difficult' and 43 'easy' responses in this section. These were:

1   The usual or intermittent behaviour of the disabled child, such as being affectionate, or violent, or jealous of the respondent's normality. These represented most of the 'always' easy or difficult responses.
2   It was difficult for some and easy for others when the disabled child was *younger* (lovable and easy to manage as a baby; requiring too much care when young).
3   It was difficult or easy when the disabled child was *older* (easier when he began to be more independent; harder when he reached puberty and began to make sexual advances).

Explanations in terms of the non-disabled child's development

The bulk of the explanations arose from the developmental experience of the non-disabled child. These are discussed in terms of Erikson's first six psychosocial stages; the first three stages are combined as 'infancy'.

1 *Infancy*

In the years from birth to five, positive memories predominated, although this period received the fewest nominations (possibly because most respondents were older than their siblings). Only seven people found this period the most difficult, usually as a result of anxiety experienced by the parents.

The significance of the family at this age was represented also in the three basic reasons given for it being an easy time. (1) As infants, respondents felt secure and at ease within the family. (2) They found their disabled sibling to be good company and a valuable playmate. (3) Respondents stated that they were happy when they were too young to realise that a problem existed.

2 *Childhood*

The years between infancy and the onset of puberty (6 to 11) are to Erikson the most socially decisive. The school and the neighbourhood define the radius of significant relations. Whilst the reasons for this period being experienced as increasingly difficult reflect this social emphasis, those who remember it with pleasure do so still in the context of the family. Essentially, some children continued to feel at ease in the family and found their disabled sibling (who may still have been very young) to have been a good playmate.

The most noticeable change during childhood for this sample is the steady increase in those who found it difficult, so that difficulty predominates from now on. The positive dynamic at this stage is a sense of industry, a feeling of being able to accomplish useful things. It is socially decisive because industry involves doing things beside and with others. The danger lies in developing a sense of inferiority and inadequacy. Such feelings arise more from outer hindrances than an inner crisis, which Erikson identifies as setting this stage apart from the rest. The explanations given by respondents certainly reflect their awareness of outer hindrances, and relate to the family, the school and the wider public.

It is in childhood that respondents began to feel the lack of parental attention and to resent the priority given to their disabled sibling, for whom more lenient rules could often be seen to operate. One respondent cited the years from seven to 11 as the most difficult, and said that it was: 'A time when I felt most cheated and lonely, not having friends to play, birthday parties, and my parents not being involved with my school' (81: Intellectual disability). It was not uncommon for the non-disabled children to feel that their disabled siblings prevented them from participating fully in a childhood social life.

The school, however, was the focus for developing feelings of inadequacy and inferiority. Many respondents were teased or ignored because of their sibling or endured the anger and humiliation of seeing their disabled brother or sister ridiculed. Erikson wrote that 'when a child begins to feel that it is the colour of his skin, the background of his parents, or the cost of his clothes rather than his wish or his will to learn which decide his social worth, lasting harm may ensue for the *sense of identity*' (Erikson, 1959a; p. 88). Having one's social worth decided by the fitness of one's sibling occupies a similar category. These issues become more explicit during adolescence.

Another issue which also emerges now and develops in adolescence is that of embarrassment. Children were embarrassed for their friends to come home to meet their disabled sibling and frequently embarrassed by his/her odd behaviour and the reaction of the public to that behaviour. These uncomfortable feelings were often exacerbated by the fact that the children loved their siblings and felt guilty about wishing they would disappear. Guilt and shame are recurring themes, with shame arising both from having to confront the world with a disabled sibling and from the sense that such negative feelings are unworthy.

3   Adolescence

The period of adolescence (12 to 18) is central to Erikson's (1971) theory. Although he stresses that identity formation neither begins nor ends here (Erikson, 1959c), it is during adolescence that *identification* ceases to be an appropriate mode of adjustment and a true *self identity* begins to emerge. Rapid body growth and genital maturity cause all continuities once relied on to be questioned. During this normative crisis, adolescents are preoccupied with what they appear to be in the eyes of others in comparison with what they feel they are. According to Erikson, the primary concern of adolescence is the consolidation of social roles. It is consistent with Erikson's theory that in this sample there is a trough in 'easy or pleasant' times and a dramatic increase in difficult times.

(a) *Embarrassment*: Embarrassment could be general, or specific to bringing friends home or to meeting new friends, but it was usually felt in reference to the peer group. One male respondent explained why the hardest time to have a handicapped sister was from about 15 to 17:

I was embarrassed about her and perhaps also ashamed. There was also a time when I was fed up and sick and tired of her. It was mostly due to my attitude; nothing had changed about her. (35: Intellectual disability)

This is also the time when relationships with the other sex take on new meanings and become more central. A great deal of embarrass-ment was felt about the disabled sibling and many anxious moments were planning introductions and explanations:

Bringing boyfriends home, at some stage you always had to explain that you had a handicapped brother, and (it) always seemed hard to find the right time without overdoing it—like 'How do you do—I have a handicapped brother!'. (46: Intellectual disability)

(b) *Identity and identification*: In addition to embarrassment, overt reference was made to problems of identity. Identity is 'both a persistent sameness within onself ... and a persistent sharing of some kind of essential character with others' (Erikson, 1959c; p. 102). Some respondents felt that being the brother or sister of a disabled child (and experiencing the family chaos often entailed) was sufficient to exclude them from sharing the essence of their peer group:

I grew up very shy and reserved, my aim in life being to be as inconspicuous as possible, particularly in my teens. Feelings of inferiority grew worse in my mid-teens. Having a handicapped brother was part of all that. (71: Intellectual disability)

Others feared that their peers would identify them with their disabled sibling and not accept them for the different person they believed (or hoped) they were. In this anxiety can be seen both the importance of social relations in establishing self-identity and the lingering identifications of earlier periods. Part of one's sense of personal worth arises through comparison with siblings, who can be seen as both family and peers (Bank & Kahn, 1982). Feelings of being similar to a brother or sister help to draw siblings together, whereas feelings of difference keep them apart. Disability complicates these processes because siblings may fear being the same as a stigmatised person even though they feel close to him/her. It is possible to identify with valued qualities (affection, a good sense of humour) and many do so in childhood. However, in adolescence, more is seen of the determination *not* to be like a disabled sibling. The phenomenon of feeling different from one's sibling has been termed 'deidentification' (Schachter, Shore, Feldman-Rotman, Marquis & Campbell, 1976). In the adolescent crisis, it can be perceived as part of the shift from identification to identity. A certain amount of deidentification may reside in healthy sibling relationships because this is what allows flexibility and the development of individuality. However, when a sibling is disabled, deidentification may also act as a useful protection against poor self-esteem.

(c) *Intolerance and ideology*: Both embarrassment and identity problems can be exacerbated by adolescent intolerance. Erikson sees intolerance as a necessary defence against the sense of identity diffusion, which is the danger at this stage. Adolescents can be clannish, intolerant and cruel, excluding those who are different—amongst whom can be numbered the disabled and their siblings.

Erikson (1965; p. 254) describes the adolescent mind as an 'ideological mind'. Some respondents were able to withstand intolerance because they had developed a strong ideology of individual worth, including the acceptance of disability. They had gathered around them enough like-minded friends to be able to reject those intolerant of disability and to use this rejection as a means of defining themselves. More often, however, internal battles were fought between the necessity of identification with peers and the desire to protect one's sibling. A few emerged from these battles feeling that the depths of compassion thus forced upon them forever set them ideologically apart:

> It made me feel that I wasn't the same as everyone else. Having known suffering—seeing someone suffer endlessly—socially, physically, mentally for so many years, many things other people say and do seem shallow and self-centred. (73: Intellectual disability)

(d) *The family*: The remaining reasons for adolescence being difficult concern the family relationships between normal and disabled siblings.

Within the family, the common claim was that the normal children were given inadequate parental support and attention (Kirkman, 1983). This often had repercussions on self-concept, as for the 14- to 16-year-old who 'felt unimportant, as if (my disabled sister) was all that mattered' (28: Down's Syndrome). These feelings and earlier ones of not being valued by their parents probably rendered siblings vulnerable to a sense of inferiority among their peers.

Restrictions on social life were also experienced during adolescence (Kirkman, 1984), and some respondents felt more subtle restrictions on their 'escape' from the family because of the demands of a disabled sibling. They faced the problem of how to leave the family without appearing to evade responsibility. Part of the familial hold over the non-disabled children was perceived as the necessity for them to excel as compensation for a non-achieving child. When this requirement to achieve was coupled with the demand not to compete with the disabled child (a paradox mentioned by 14 respondents), the result was puzzlement and confusion.

Adolescents could find themselves in moral turmoil because of these constraints on separation and individuation. They felt resentful and blamed their disabled sibling, but also felt guilty because such feelings were perceived by these fundamentally caring brothers and sisters as wrong. They were obviously aware of the moral issues surrounding both disability and sibship, and were at risk of lowered self-esteem because of failing to live up to their own standards. The resulting distress was likely to increase any difficulties between disabled and normal siblings.

(e) *Sibling relationships*: Four main reasons were given for difficulties based on sibling relationships. The first two concerned (1) crises in the life of the disabled child which coincided with problems or demands in the life of the normal sibling; and (2) continuing resentment of the special treatment given the disabled child.

The other two reasons are related to the growing independence of the adolescent. This was often resented by the disabled child who could demonstrate that resentment in unpleasant ways. With or without overt jealousy, the healthy sibling sometimes experienced what Lifton (1971) has called in another context 'survivor guilt', which seemed to grow with the increasing awareness of personal freedom. Both the jealousy and the guilt are exemplified by the following quotation, where the disabled sibling was described as:

> Very good at emotional blackmail. I used to live her life how she wanted it to be or stayed at home. Tried to punish myself for not being the one who was sick. (132: Physical)

On the other hand, an affectionate relationship between disabled and non-disabled siblings was the central reason for these years providing easy and pleasant times.

In Erikson's scheme, the adolescent crisis of identity is resolved towards the end of the stage. The decrease in difficult times for this sample suggests that, as respondents became more certain of themselves (and perhaps more independent of the family), having a disabled sibling became less of a critical focus.

4   *Early adulthood*

The (diminishing) difficulties in early adulthood for this sample usually involved problems in developing relationships with the other sex or in trying to establish an independent life whilst feeling drawn to the problems at home.

The pleasures (easier times) are seen specifically as arising from growing older and learning to appreciate, or at least adjusting to, the disabled sibling. Adults concurrently became aware of developing what they saw as a special tolerance and compassion for others, a generosity of spirit that they attributed to life with a disabled sibling.

CONCLUSION

It is important to note that only about 33% of the sample declared particular difficulties in any one year (although a maximum of about 10% found it easy or pleasant). However, it was only about 10% who claimed overall that they had no particular time that they found difficult with a disabled sibling. One respondent provided a succinct summary of her attempt to assess the effect of a disabled sibling on her life. She speaks for many others:

> I would say that having a handicapped brother affected me in *all* areas, *all* my life. In one way I would say it has been a wonderful learning experience, and I'm a much better person for living through it. But I wish I hadn't had to experience it. What a way to become a better person!! (76: Intellectual disability)

References

Bank, S. P. & Kahn, M. D. (1982). *The Sibling Bond*. New York: Basic Books.

Erikson, E. (1959a). Identity and life cycle: selected papers. *Psychological Issues, 1*, Monograph 1.

Erikson, E. (1959b). Growth and crises of the healthy personality. *Psychological Issues, 1*, Monograph 1, 50–100.

Erikson, E. (1959c). The problem of ego identity. *Psychological Issues, 1*, Monograph 1, 101–64.

Erikson, E. (1959d). Appendix. *Psychological Issues, 1*, Monograph 1, 165–6.

Erikson, E. (1965). *Childhood and Society*. Middlesex: Penguin.

Erikson, E. (1971). *Identity: Youth and Crisis*. London: Faber & Faber.

Kirkman, M. (1983). Adult siblings of the handicapped: early family relationships. *Proceedings of the Australian Family Research Conference, vol. 5 Support Networks*. Institute of Family Studies, Melbourne.

Kirkman, M. (1984). *The effect of a handicapped child on the schooling, friendships, and social life of the normal sibling.* Paper presented at the 13th Annual Meeting of Australian Social Psychologists, Adelaide, May.

Lifton, R. J. (1971). *Death in Life: The Survivors of Hiroshima.* Middlesex: Penguin.

Schachter, F. F., Shore, E., Feldman-Rotman, S., Marquis, R. E., & Campbell, S. (1976). Sibling deidentification. *Developmental Psychology, 12,* 418–27.

22

Social Distance and Life Goals as Bases for Intergenerational Perceptions

Mary A. Luszcz and Karen M. Fitzgerald
Flinders University of South Australia

Many studies have examined attitudes towards and perceptions of the elderly (see Green, 1981, and Lutsky, 1980), yet few have compared these perceptions to those held about other cohorts. It has been argued (Luszcz, 1983, in press) that perceptions of the aged (or any other cohort) can be more meaningfully interpreted if they are placed in a context of similar judgements made for other age cohorts. Previous research has shown that views of old age vary according to the dimensions being evaluated and the age of the person making the evaluation (Ahammer & Baltes, 1972; Ahammer & Bennett, 1977; Fitzgerald, 1978; Luszcz, in press), but characteristics of cohorts that may account for these results have rarely been examined. In the present study the impact of age-stratification, misinformation about ageing, and differences in the focus of life tasks (Erikson, 1963) were examined as bases of conceptions of ageing held by adolescents, middle-aged and elderly adults.

The selection of cohorts arose from the notion that adolescents and elders can be construed as generation gap allies (Chellam, 1980–81; Kalish, 1969) relative to middle-aged adults. This attribution is based, at a social level, on the dependent status of adolescents and elderly adults relative to more autonomous and productive midlife adults (Chellam, 1980–81) and, on a psychological level, to the possibility that they share common life tasks pertaining to evolving and accepting the self. To the extent that adolescents learn the values and prejudices of their socialisers, i.e., middle-aged adults, it becomes important to know what attitudes the latter exhibit and the extent to which these concur with those of adolescents and older adults.

Thus a multigenerational approach was adopted in the present research to place attitudes toward the elderly into perspective relative to younger age groups, and assess possible effects of age stratification, life goals, and knowledge on attitudes toward the elderly, as well as other age groups. A comparison was made between the views that adolescent, middle-aged and elderly adults had of themselves, other members of their own age cohorts, and the other cohorts.

METHOD

Subjects
Thirty adolescent, middle-aged, and elderly adults were sampled. The mean ages for them were 16, 46, and 68 years, respectively. There were 14 male and 16 female adolescent and elderly subjects and 11 male and 19 female middle-aged subjects. All were volunteers and living actively in the same Adelaide communities.

Procedures, Scales and Instruments
Information was obtained via a series of scales that were administered in the order they are described below. Adolescents completed them at their school and most elderly individuals at their social clubs. A few elderly subjects and all middle-aged ones completed the instruments at home and returned them by post.

The scales included Kidwell and Booth's (1977) Social Distance Scale, a Goals of Life Index adapted from Chellam (1980–81), Miller and Dodder's (1980) revision of Palmore's (1977) Facts on Aging Quiz, and Holtzman, Beck, and Kerber's (1979) version of the Rosencranz and McNevin (1969) ageing semantic differentials.

The Social Distance Scale was used to examine how people feel about relating to members of various age cohorts. Subjects were asked to check the age groups (ranging from 15 through over-60) that they would consider suitable for each interaction. *Low scores* indicate social *proximity* or high intended contact.

The Goals of Life Index was used to compare priorities valued by each cohort. Subjects were asked to rank in order of importance six priorities of peace of mind, satisfaction with my job, understanding myself, finding my place in life and accepting it, serving the community of which I am a part, and giving love and security to others. Ranks were coded 1 through 6 so that *high* scores indicate *high priority*.

The Facts on Aging quiz (Luszcz, 1982; Palmore, 1977) comprises 24 true-false items designed to cover basic physical, mental and social facts as well as common misconceptions about aging. It generates an estimate of factual knowledge about aging and, by examining patterns of errors, a score indicating a net anti-aged or pro-aged bias.

Lastly, subjects used the Holtzman et al. semantic differentials to characterise various target groups. The instrument comprises 28 pairs of bipolar adjectives contributing to one of the following four dimensions. Personal acceptability *vs* unacceptability connotes the extent to which one is considered to be socially at ease and pleasing to others. Instrumentality *vs* ineffectiveness is taken to reflect one's adaptability and vitality or active pursuit of goals. Autonomy *vs* dependency relates to the extent to which one is self-sufficient and more a contributor to than a recipient from a social system. Integrity *vs* nonintegrity implies a sense of personal satisfaction or being at peace with oneself in the Eriksonian sense.

The adjective pairs were rated along a 7-point likert type scale. Lower scores indicate more favourable characterisations. All subjects completed ratings for themselves and for each cohort: adolescent (12 through 19-year-olds), middle-aged adult (40 to 55 years) and elderly adult (60 or older).

RESULTS

Social Distance Scores

A two-way ANOVA compared the social distance scores for the 6 target age categories for each of the 3 age groups. Only the interaction, $F(10,480) = 32.3$, $p < .001$ was significant. The pattern of significant differences showed preference for one's own and immediately older group for adolescents, own ±10 years for middle-aged adults and own −10 years for elderly. Beyond these bounds, social distance was fairly uniform, although there was a trend of increasing social distance as one moved further from one's own cohort.

Goals of Life

A two-way ANOVA comparing the age groups (3) on their life goals (6) indicated a significant effect of life goals, $F(5,435) = 47.7$, $p < .001$ and the interaction of age with life goals, $F(10,435) = 4.9$, $p < .001$. Newman-Keuls post-hoc multiple comparisons of the 18 cell means located the source of the interaction. In general, peace of mind, giving love and security to others, self understanding and acceptance were given higher priority than job satisfaction and community service. Within life goals, the only age differences observed were in the adolescents and middle-aged adults valuing self-understanding more than

Table 22.1   Summary of significant effects of semantic differential analyses

	Semantic Differential Scale			
	Instrumentality	Autonomy	Acceptability	Integrity
Subject's Age by Cohort Target Analysis				
Subject's Age (2,172)[a]	–	–	–	–
Target Cohort Rated (2,172)	102.94[b]	24.60	5.88	12.96
Interaction (4,172)	7.12	3.32	–	–
Subject's Age by Self:Peer Target Analysis				
Subject's Age (2,87)	9.97	3.07*	7.33	–
Self:Peer (1,87)	14.06	7.15	39.71	30.90
Interaction (1,87)	4.38	2.98*	–	–

[a] indicates degrees of freedom
[b] F values, all $p < .01$, except * $p < .05$; dashes (–) indicate nonsignificant effects

the two adult groups did. The concurrence in life goals was substantiated by a significant coefficient of concordance, $W(5) = .84$.

Facts on Aging

A one-way ANOVA comparing percent correct on the Facts on Aging quiz showed a significant effect of age, $F(2,82) = 4.78$, $p < .01$, indicating that adolescents (60% correct) knew less about aging than the elderly (69%). The middle-aged group differed from neither (67%). All groups held negative net biases about aging, although they were not significantly different. The correlation between net bias and knowledge (i.e., correct responding) was positive, $r(85) = .39$, $p < .001$, indicating that the more one knows about aging the more positive are one's views. Kendall's coefficient of concordance, $W(23) = .86$, $p < .001$, on rank order of errors showed a similar ordering of misconceptions across cohorts.

Semantic Differentials

Separate two-way ANOVA's comparing the subject's age group and the target cohort were done on each dimension. There was a significant effect of group rated for each dimension and significant interac-

Fig. 22.1 Interactions of target group by subject age cohort and subject age cohort by self-peer ratings for semantic differential scale of autonomy.

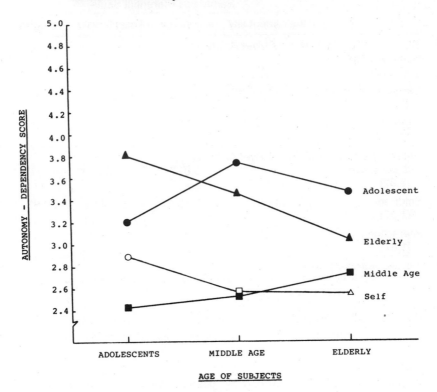

tions on instrumentality and autonomy (see Table 22.1). ANOVA's comparing self *vs* peer ratings for each cohort also showed main effects for acceptability and integrity with interactions on autonomy and instrumentality.

The groups agreed that acceptability (2.67) and integrity (2.65) were more characteristic of middle age. Further, the elderly (3.37) were perceived to be less integrated than adolescents (2.99). All subjects also perceived themselves to be more acceptable (2.23) and integrated (2.25) than their cohort peers (2.88 and 2.89, respectively.)

The views held by the subjects of their peers and the other cohorts diverged for autonomy and instrumentality. All groups agreed that autonomy was most characteristic of middle-age. The source of the interaction rests in the views adolescents and elderly adults had of each

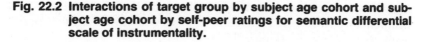

Fig. 22.2 Interactions of target group by subject age cohort and subject age cohort by self-peer ratings for semantic differential scale of instrumentality.

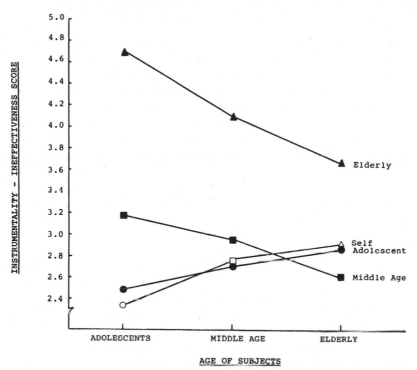

other (see Figure 22.1). Each of these groups viewed their own cohort as more autonomous than the other. The middle-aged subjects perceived no significant difference in the autonomy of the other two groups, although they ascribed significantly less autonomy to both groups than the adolescents and elderly ascribed to themselves.

The instrumentality results (Figure 22.2) show there is consensus that the elderly are least instrumental, but the magnitude of the difference varies significantly with subject's age. Again, the adolescents attribute the least and the elderly the most instrumentality to old people, and the middle-aged an intermediate amount. The adolescents also viewed themselves as significantly more instrumental than middle-aged adults.

Interactions of age and self *vs* peer ratings also occurred for the autonomy and instrumentality dimensions. For autonomy, the self-peer bias is not shared by the middle-aged (Figure 22.1). For instrumentality, it is only the elderly who view themselves more positively than their peers (Figure 22.2).

Correlations

The extent to which elderly targets were characterised as personally acceptable was predicted by social proximity toward the 60+ group and low priority for community service ($R = .38$). Instrumentality in the elderly was predicted by these same factors and increasing age of subjects ($R = .43$). Elderly target's integrity ($R = .36$) and autonomy ($R = .40$) were predicted by high knowledge of the elderly and social proximity. Increased knowledge of aging also was correlated with characterising the elderly as instrumental, $r(85) = -.24$, $p < .03$.

DISCUSSION

In summary, with the exception of the instrumentality results, middle age is viewed most positively overall. The elderly are the most devalued cohort (seen as least integrated and effective) while middle-aged adults occupied the favoured position (most acceptable, autonomous, and integrated). On acceptability, the adolescents as well as the elderly are viewed less favourably than are the middle-aged. Only on the integrity dimension are elderly also viewed more negatively than the adolescents. In fact, this is the only result in the study where all groups concur in a negative perception of the aged. The elderly see their cohort as less autonomous than middle-aged adults and less instrumental than adolescents, but they do not characterise their cohort as a whole as negatively on these dimensions as do adolescents or middle-aged adults.

The discrepancies in characterisations of cohorts are most pronounced in the perceptions adolescents and elderly adults have of each other. One way of accounting for these discrepancies is by recourse to age stratification notions, whereby each group on the one hand exaggerates the differences between themselves and other groups and, on the other hand, sees themselves in a more positive light than do those outside their cohort. Some support for the age stratification view also derives from the intermediate views that middle-aged adults express about the other two groups. They are closer chronologically to each of the extremes and thus may hold more moderate views of them. Furthermore, social proximity toward the 60-plus group and increased knowledge of aging were both predictive of more favourable attitudes toward elders. As knowledge of aging was also positively correlated with proximity toward older people, enhanced social interactions may improve attitudes.

It seems that in making self-ratings subjects of all ages converge upon the level of autonomy or instrumentality believed to characterise the cohort which is viewed most favourably overall on that dimension, i.e., the middle-aged and adolescents, respectively. Considering that the elderly in the study were relatively young and active, their bias is probably warranted and accurate relative to all those over 60. As for the adolescents, their own egocentric personal fable (Elkind, 1967) together with their pursuit of self-understanding (Adams & Jones, 1981) may incline them to consistently overestimate their strengths in terms of autonomy relative to their peers'.

The present findings substantiate trends seen in an earlier study (Luszcz, in press) leading to the conclusion, compatible with Ahammer and Bennett's (1977) findings, that younger members of our society commonly misperceive aging and the aged in a more negative light than the experience of the elderly leads them to consider to be accurate. The self-ratings of the elderly also suggest that perhaps the 'social breakdown syndrome' (Kuypers & Bengston, 1973) itself may be breaking down. According to this model, the elderly are likely to respond to the generally negative labels applied to them in society by believing and accepting them. Although the elderly view their cohort as a whole somewhat negatively, the degree of dependency and ineffectiveness they attribute to older adults is less than that attributed to them by adolescents and middle-aged adults. Furthermore, at a personal level, they see themselves as superior to their peers and on a par with the cohort that as a whole is seen to be most autonomous or instrumental. These data inform contemporary notions of what Fitzgerald (1978) has termed a 'paradox' emerging in the literature concerning what society believes about 'the' elderly and what they themselves believe.

References

Adams, G. R., & Jones, R. M. (1981). Imaginary audience behavior: A validation study. *Journal of Early Adolescence, 1*, 1–10.

Ahammer, I. M., & Baltes, P. B. (1972). Objective *vs* perceived age differences in personality: How do adolescents, adults, and older people view themselves and each other? *Journal of Gerontology, 27*, 46–51.

Ahammer, I. M., & Bennett, K. C. (1977). Viewing 'older people': A comparative method-comparative sample approach. *Australian Journal of Psychology*, *29*, 97–110.

Chellam, G. (1980–81). Intergenerational affinities: Symmetrical life experiences of the young adults and the aging in Canadian society. *International Journal of Aging and Human Development*, *12*, 79–92.

Elkind, D. (1967). Egocentrism in adolescence. *Child Development, 38*, 1025–34.

Erikson, E. (1963). *Childhood and society*. New York: Norton.

Fitzgerald, J. M. (1978). Actual and perceived sex and generational differences in interpersonal style: Structural and quantitative issues. *Journal of Gerontology*, *33*, 394–401.

Green, S. K. (1981). Attitudes and perceptions about the elderly: Current and future perspectives. *International Journal of Aging and Human Development, 13*, 99–119.

Holtzman, J. M., Beck, J. D., & Kerber, P. E. (1979). *Dimensional aspects of attitudes toward the aged*. Presented at the 32nd Annual Scientific Meeting of the Gerontological Society, Washington, D. C.

Kalish, R. A. (1969). The old and the young as generation gap allies. *The Gerontologist, 9*, 83–9.

Kidwell, I. J., & Booth, A. (1977). Social distance and intergenerational relations. *The Gerontologist, 17*, 412–20.

Kuypers, J. A., & Bengston, V. L. (1973). Social breakdown and competence. *Human Development, 16*, 181–201.

Lutsky, N. S. (1980). Attitudes toward old age and elderly persons. In C. Eisdorfer (Ed.), *Annual review of gerontology and geriatrics, Vol: 1*. New York: Springer.

Luszcz, M. A. (1983). An attitudinal assessment of perceived intergenerational affinities linking adolescence and old age. *International Journal of Behavioral Development, 6*, 221–31.

Luszcz, M. A. (in press). Characterising adolescents, middle-aged, and elderly adults: Putting the elderly into perspective. *International Journal of Aging and Human Development*.

Luszcz, M. A. (1982). Facts on aging: An Australian validation. *The Gerontologist, 22*, 369–72.

Miller, R. & Dodder, R. (1980). A revision of Palmore's Facts on Aging quiz. *The Gerontologist, 20*, 673–79.

Palmore, E. (1977). Facts on Aging: A short quiz. *The Gerontologist, 17*, 315–20.

Rosencranz, H. A., & McNevin, T. E. (1969). A factor analysis of attitudes toward the aged. *The Gerontologist, 9*, 55–9.